MARTIN DUBERMAN

Reaching Ninety

MARTIN DUBERMAN

Reaching
Ninety

CHICAGO
REVIEW
PRESS

Published by Chicago Review Press Incorporated
814 North Franklin Street
Chicago, Illinois 60610
ISBN 978-1-64160-880-0

Library of Congress Control Number: 2022950044

Typesetting: Nord Compo

Printed in the United States of America
5 4 3 2 1

For Eli

"I think we are well advised to keep on nodding terms with the people we used to be, whether we find them attractive company or not. Otherwise they turn up unannounced and surprise us, come hammering on the mind's door at 4 AM of a bad night and demand to know who deserted them, who betrayed them, who is going to make amends . . . "

—Joan Didion, *Slouching Towards Bethlehem*

"Consider what immense forces society brings to play on each of us, how that society changes from decade to decade; and also from class to class; well, if we cannot analyze these invisible presences, we know very little of the subject of the memoir; and again how futile life-writing becomes. I see myself as a fish in a stream; deflected; held in place; but cannot describe the stream."

—Virginia Woolf, "Sketch of the Past"

CONTENTS

PART I

1930-1986

I n the all-male high school I attended, the female roles in our theater productions were necessarily played by boys. I myself performed both male and female parts, usually side by side with my closest friend, Bob Sandler. Our repertoire was no minor thing: I managed to inhabit roles as varied as "glamorous stewardess," "rugged seaman," and "murderous old spinster."

Bob and I were notorious for sidesplitting fits of laughter—breaking up rehearsals over some innocuous line, stopping the scene in its tracks. It was a case of high spirits, not bottled-up hysteria, and it didn't take much to set us off. We drove our delicate drama teacher to distraction; once, in an uncontrollable rage, he slapped Bob hard across the face. That *did* subdue us—momentarily. I'd also get into occasional fits of hilarity with another friend, Eddie Bernstein, my costar on our undefeated tennis team. When in route by car to play against another school, we'd be seized by gales of exuberant, rowdy laughter, which drove the coach no less than the drama teacher to distraction. *He* never slapped us, which in retrospect, I suppose, confirms that he was straight ("real men don't lose emotional control"), and delineates the quite different affective boundaries separating sports and theater.

In Sutton Vane's 1923 play *Outward Bound*, I played an alluring, enigmatic stewardess, she who mysteriously fends off the passengers' pestering questions about the ship's destination. They don't realize,

1

you see, that they're dead and that their ocean liner is doomed to circle aimlessly through eternity. Only at the play's end does the stewardess finally reveal—in a thrillingly trashy line that I delivered with melodramatic flair—that "we're bound for heaven, sir. And hell too. They're the same place you see."

Post-performance, wrapped in applause at the triumphant verisimilitude of my leap across genders, I was oblivious to what may have been a dim view among some of the spectators at the apparent ease of my transformation. I myself (who now, I'm told, inhabit a casual masculinity) find my relaxed assumption of the stewardess role hard to credit, yet the memory firmly holds, as does yet another that accompanies it. One night when Bob Sandler and I were crossing the quad along with our dates to the scheduled post-performance dance in the school gym, Bob's girlfriend suddenly realized that *I* was the "actress" who'd played the stewardess. "But you *can't* be," she gasped, "you have such beautiful legs!"

Perhaps the moment remains vivid because it rudely confirmed the dawning awareness that—despite my high standing as a scholar/athlete—I was somehow "different," and not enviably so. Yet I have no recall of how I processed the news (or if I even needed to)—no stations of the cross traversed, no family rows or resolutions, no snide taunts from fellow students. I do recall that with the onset of adolescence my mother suggested "a few sessions" with a psychotherapist. I'd grown quiet around the house—in stark contrast to my ebullience outside it—and she'd apparently become concerned about my withdrawal when at home, possibly connecting it to my deepening voice and sprouting whiskers. My mother's instincts were keen—my father, oppositely, opted for determined disengagement—and she may well have surmised that sexual arousal of the "wrong" kind was imminent.

Certainly, the psychiatrist made that assumption. I have a cloudy recollection of recounting a dream involving another man and me masturbating each other, after which the therapist confidently assured me that treatment could and would redirect my sexual energy to the "appropriate" gender. He was apparently an early acolyte of what would soon become known, and later discredited, as "conversion therapy"—which I'd like to believe was why I actively disliked him, and after a few more sessions refused to continue treatment. I embarked instead on my own conversion: I bought a set of dumbbells and started to work out in my room. Several classmates openly admired my burgeoning muscles.

They suited well my next theatrical role: a seaman in *Bound East for Cardiff*, one of Eugene O'Neill's "sea plays." It too had an indelible one-liner that, if no match for Sutton Vane's campy "heaven or hell," sticks in my mind to this day: "Mon [man] but it's clear outside the nicht—like day." Come to think of it, that may be why the line proved unforgettable: I needed to retain the seaman's sullen butch persona to cancel out the alluring stewardess.

Bob Sandler and I remain in touch—and still able to produce a mutual giggle over the most memorable of our joint appearances: the two elderly spinsters in *Arsenic and Old Lace*, who fill their empty days killing off lonely old men with a bit of arsenic dropped into their home-made elderberry wine. Just recently, commiserating over the phone about hitting ninety, Bob and I managed to summon up yet another howl of laughter over our once-celebrated stardom as the two murderously darling old dames. I should probably add, to satisfy the simpletons, that Bob (and Eddie Bernstein too) was and has always been a Kinsey "O"—exclusively heterosexual. He may have been given, like a stereotypical girl of the time, to fits of the giggles, and *was* beautiful enough to have made an easy transition to drag, but his lust was as firmly concentrated on women as any mythic member of the football team.

As early as high school Bob dreamed of becoming a professional actor, but his stern father laid down the law and he ended up in business school. For a time, I was as smitten as Bob with the idea of becoming an actor. I spent the summer before senior year in high school at a theater camp for adolescents interested in making a career of acting. We were a serious-minded bunch and actually toured Vermont and New Hampshire in Thornton Wilder's *Our Town*. I played the starring role of George, and the staff, which included a number of would-be or has-been professionals, showered me with praise. I have a garbled memory

of Philip Burton—surrogate father to the famed Richard—visiting our
camp, seeing one of our *Our Town* performances, and leaving word
(I later learned) that contrary to his usual practice he urged that my
acting ambition be encouraged, that I was "a natural."

Burton's comment was repeated to my parents when they came up
to Vermont for a visit. Shocked when told about Burton's high compliment, my mother left strict orders that I was not to be encouraged by
even one word more of praise from the camp's staff. But she was too
late in locking the stable doors; on returning home I announced that
I would not be going to college—though I *might* be willing to attend
Carnegie Tech (then famous for its School of Drama). My father, unlike
Bob's, responded (as usual) with indifference, having long since decided,
as best I could make out, that I was some sort of alien mistakenly
dropped into the backyard.

Yet at my mother's insistence, he did take me aside for an unprecedented "talk" about my future plans. By rote, he awkwardly delivered the message he'd been assigned: "You've grown up in a financially
comfortable home; the theater can't provide a steady income; go to
college and study something practical, accounting maybe; then when
you graduate, you can come into the business" (dress manufacturing).
His tone was perfunctory—but I much preferred that to the imperious
posture Bob's father had adopted. My mother (who'd been listening
at the door) later scolded him for not having been firmer, but beyond
that I don't recall any further discussion, not even raised voices, and
certainly no threat of cutting off funds or disownment.

Neither of my parents was remotely tyrannical. My mother might
plead and implore, but even to *threaten* rejection was unthinkable. It
was understood by all parties that final decisions about my life were
mine to make—a gift of incalculable value that would stand me in good
stead, imbuing the assumption that *I* was in control of the direction
of my life and that if I stood my ground, roadblocks could ultimately
be circumvented. I would meet many an obstacle and some defeats in
the years ahead, but none that, if I persevered, would permanently turn
me off course. Parenting is a brutally difficult job, and my parents, like

most, would in some areas prove inept—but never cruel. My mother especially gave me the gift of self-assurance—*not*, I like to think, mere stubbornness or arrogance, the rigid counterfeits of self-confidence (and not, I believe, central components of my character). My parents—my mother, to be exact—encouraged in me the confidence to pursue what would sometimes prove a difficult path and, when caught in the thickets, to continue to struggle for a way around—or through—them. My mother might vocally oppose my choices but would never dream of trying to break my spirit.

There was nothing ill tempered in her attempt to discourage me from skipping college. Both my parents viewed education as the only way of escaping from the minimal options that had confined their own lives. My father, a semiliterate Jewish farmworker, did manage, when still in Russia, to become a foreman on a beet plantation. When drafted into the army, he'd deserted, made his way to Frankfurt, and traveled steerage to the United States—all by the age of twenty-two. Landing in Manhattan, he soon became a low-level cog in the garment industry (earning seven dollars a week), mastered the art of cutting fabric, lived close to the bone, saved his money, and eventually became moderately successful in the dress manufacturing business. He fell in love with my mother, who was a beauty, and *her* mother pronounced him "a responsible man who would always look out for her." In 1923 they married.

My mother, from a second-generation Austrian American family, had managed to complete high school—but only by working as a secretary during the day and taking classes at night. She and my father were determined that my older sister Lucile and I would have an easier time of it. When my father's company began to prosper, and when I was still a youngster, we were able to move from an apartment on Manhattan's Upper West Side to a house in the nearby suburb of Mount Vernon. For the early grades I attended local schools, but by the time I reached high school my parents were able to send me to the private Horace Mann School in Riverdale, a small but prestigious school for (mostly) prosperous second-generation Jewish boys. Many years later, it greatly expanded and became coed.

I had no sense of privation growing up. If my parents had to cut corners in order to send me to Horace Mann, they never said so. My mother was a thrifty housewife always on the hunt for a bargain—a reflection, I suspect, more of her aborted creativity than her concern about money. We were able, at any rate, to afford vacations that alternated between Grossinger's and Florida, and for me to take piano lessons as well. If I wasn't schooled in denial, nor was I brought up to covet luxuries. Still, my sister and I took for granted the middle-class basics that my parents themselves had never had when growing up: a comfortable home, plentiful food and clothing, a good education. I myself never pined for anything more. As a child, having a bike and a fort full of soldiers marked the outer limits of acquisitiveness. My mother stressed the importance of "security," not maximizing income; plus she had a well-developed sense of humor that did a lot to leaven life's unwelcome surprises. When I later chose academia over business, I was well aware, and indifferent to the fact, that the inevitable corollary would be a financially modest lifestyle.

My mother, gifted, energetic, and attractive, exemplified the lot of her generation of women. Boxed into domestic routines, she lacked even the feminist's later vocabulary for formulating and expressing her resentment. Many years later, after my father's death, she moved to an apartment in Westchester and opened a tiny resale shop, Treasures and Trifles. One day she proudly showed me a small article that had appeared in the local newspaper and had mentioned her shop. "Well, Mart," she said, "I finally made it, huh?" Those words have long haunted me.

Like most women of her generation, my mother embraced her prescribed domestic roles with little overt complaint. Yet over the years, lacking any satisfying outlet for her energy or a feminist movement that might have expressed and channeled her mounting discontent, she gradually mutated into the stock figure of nagging complainer, though offset by a large capacity for laughter. My father, having long since fallen out of love, for a time fastened his attentions on my mother's sister, Florence, begging her to run away with him. Flo had no interest in either him or his proposal.

If my father did ever have affairs—somehow I feel sure he lacked the drive—I never got a hint of them. He settled into his lifelong domestic role of quiet disengagement—he was the man in the armchair, an abiding stranger, who read the paper at night and didn't talk much. I never heard tales of his earlier life in Russia, or of his travails as a penniless immigrant. His emotional disconnect freed me from the dictates of an authoritarian figure, but also from a sense of nurturing affection. He was the opposite of a macho bully, a role that implicitly requires intense and ongoing involvement. My father was simply detached, not involved enough to express sustained pleasure or displeasure. That, at any rate, was how as a youngster I experienced him: he rarely bestowed his attention—let alone affection.

After I became old enough to theorize, I came up with a more charitable explanation for our disconnect: for my profoundly "foreign" father to have even briefly opened the door on his past would have been to risk reliving past torments. He had enough to contend with in the present. In my more mature view, he never recovered from a severe case of culture shock that attended migrating from a Russian beet plantation to the utterly strange world of Manhattan's tenements and skyscrapers—a shock reinforced when he was unaccountably presented in 1930 with a blond-haired, blue-eyed Anglo-Saxon-looking—and ever more educated—son. Regrettably, that more empathic interpretation of my father's detached role in my life wasn't available to me as a youngster seeking affection and acknowledgment.

I have no idea how my mother succeeded in derailing my plan to become an actor (in truth I can't really recapture how profound my own determination actually was). All I know is that in the fall of 1948 I found myself a freshman at Yale—*not* enrolled in Carnegie Tech or the American Academy of Dramatic Arts. It must have been a triumph of tact on her part since it left me with no bitter sense of defeat.

From the first, I was happy at Yale, my fervor for the theater slipping quietly underground. I was soon buried in new books and making new friends, as well as gradually entertaining the notion of a possible career as a historian. The groundwork had formed early: growing up I'd been able to win release from the taut unhappiness of the dinner table by claiming schoolwork, and it had become second nature for me to disappear into my room to read in contented isolation.

Academically I did well at Yale from the start. Then, in my junior year, I was elected to Phi Beta Kappa and graduated near the top of my class. I hadn't gone near a stage for four years, but I *had* somehow located an appealing alternative arena: my professors told me that I had the potential to follow in their exalted footsteps and urged me to pursue a doctorate at Harvard.

A scholar was born. And the fit was good, the needed aptitudes precociously in place: a large tolerance for solitude, a perfectionist's need to learn *everything* about a subject, and an early penchant for writing down my thoughts. (From age four I'd been composing little stories, usually with stark moralistic messages: "Alice learned that her mother knew best. From then on she did as she was told.") After completing my BA I went directly—following one last parental effort at resistance—to Harvard to begin work on a PhD in US history. It was there that the theatrical embers briefly flared: I directed an undergraduate production of *The Italian Straw Hat*.

I had no problem with the minimal creature comforts that graduate school offered. For a time I lived in a tiny motel room, with the bathroom down the hall. Later I upgraded to a musty room in a rundown Victorian house—the bathroom this time on the floor above. In my third year I was elected a fellow of Adams House, one of Harvard's residential colleges, where I lived rent free in a small bedroom, a slightly larger living room—and a bathroom all my own.

Soon after arriving at Harvard I'd managed to acknowledge—if not accepted—my sexual orientation. I somehow learned of Boston's only two gay bars, the upscale Napoleon Club and the unsavory Punch Bowl. It was at the Napoleon that I met (and that same night had sex with) Leo Bersani, my first gay friend and fellow graduate student—and later an eminent queer theorist. That core friendship would deepen over the years, despite occasional bumps, and even while at Harvard it gradually grew to include a few other gay graduate students. Within that small circle of friends, I became particularly close to Dick Poirier (who, like Leo, would become a prominent literary critic).

Leo and I specialized in long lamentations about how our homosexuality blighted our human prospects, dooming us to truncated lives, and we both embarked on long careers as analysands desperate to escape from our blighted futures. In these years, the profoundly conservative '50s, homosexuals were all but uniformly dismissed and mocked as "perverts"—a condemnation most of us internalized. We recognized with relief that academia was one of the few environments where, if circumspect, we could find a degree of esteem, solace, and accomplishment, and could live relatively productive, relatively protected lives. The theater was another such environment, and its pull on me would remain for many decades, interweaving with my scholarly life and periodically preempting it.

After completing my doctorate in 1957, I became an instructor in American history at Yale, and again descended—though without any remembered sense of deprivation—into a rented room in somebody's attic. In my second year of teaching, I was elected a fellow of Silliman, one of Yale's residential colleges, and provided with a luxurious set of rooms, complete with maid service and free meals in the dining hall. Unused to so much space and unable to afford any additional furniture beyond what the college provided, I initially rattled around—a problem solved by permanently closing off the huge living room.

In the years since, I've always lived comfortably, and over time in better-than-modest quarters. Yet I never developed much interest in possessions; I was into "cozy," not "costly"—comfortable, not expensive or modish. I didn't want a car, a boat, a trip to Majorca, a country "getaway." To me these things represented disagreeable interruptions not pleasurable additions to my comfortably routine life, burdens that required too much upkeep. I was puzzled but not envious of friends who longed to get away, to fly off to St. Croix—or to afford shopping at Bergdorf's. I felt happiest when staying put, when rooted. I liked teaching, research, and writing, and felt no need to escape from those activities, to interrupt my work or to change my surroundings.

It was just as well, since my decision to become a scholar was, in those years, a decision to remain on the margins—not only of prosperity but of mainstream ambition. Today academics, especially at prestigious universities, often command substantial salaries and deferential respect. Not so in the '50s and '60s, when I was an untenured neophyte with a decidedly modest income. At the time, the Yale History Department had no open tenure-track lines, so when Princeton offered me an assistant professorship in 1962 at the astounding salary of $8,500, I unhesitatingly accepted. (To track my academic income just a bit further: As late as 1968, by then a tenured full professor, my annual salary at Princeton had "climbed" to $14,500. And that—as I'll elaborate anon—was meant to be punitive. I was being punished for my maverick ways—that is, for writing plays, for living in New York and going light on administrative chores, and for experimenting with "nonauthoritarian" teaching—hell, let's just say it: for being queer.) A decade later, when I moved on to an exalted distinguished professorship at the City University of New York, my salary more than doubled, skyrocketing to $33,775. For a single man, that was regarded as the equivalent of winning the lottery. I could buy theater and ballet tickets (which I *did* want), take taxis, and afford good medical care. My needs may not have been extravagant, but I didn't have to stint on them.

Once in a while—through my forties and for the bad-boy reason of being too blithe about money, of forgetting that it was one thing not to have extravagant needs and quite another not to pay ordinary bills—I *would* now and then suddenly find myself "short." That would mostly be due to the dual discovery of cocaine and the male hustling circuit, but also to some extent to my monthly tithing. Especially during the Vietnam War years, I sent off a percent of my income every month to left-wing organizations and publications, mainly *Liberation*, SNCC, and WIN. Once the war was over, I tithed myself less but distributed the money more broadly, especially to gay causes.

When a minor financial crisis *did* erupt, I had a fail-safe fallback cushion: I could always borrow a few hundred dollars, at no interest, from my generous, loving aunt Theresa, my mother's sister "Tedda." As my income increased over time, so did my debts—which I usually claimed to find "mystifying." To clear up my messy accounts, I several times had to take out bank loans, which, as a good security risk (White, male, and middle class), I had no trouble procuring. For a while I dispensed entirely with the need to manage my income, turning it over to a financial adviser. But that experiment was short lived. He turned out to be a scoundrel, as even I quickly recognized, and I soon left him—my embezzled money *not* recouped. Only a small sum was at stake; I hadn't been one of his truly prosperous clients.

One illustration of my cavalier attitude toward money is the day, hurrying down Madison Avenue, I happened to glance over at one of the street-level art galleries. It brought me up short. In the window were sample works of the artist currently being shown, and my eye fell instantly on a riveting side-view portrait of a dwarflike figure, hands resolutely folded on her bloated stomach, a bright blue "Renaissance" cap perched jauntily on her head, and her steely, beady eyes daring you to approach. "I'm coping," was the message, "but don't even *think* about fucking with me!"

When I went inside, I learned that the artist's name was Fernando Botero, that he was still in his twenties, and that this was his first show in New York City. Putting on my best gee-whiz voice, I explained that the painting had stopped me in my tracks, that I'd fallen instantly in love with it, and was hoping against hope that I might somehow buy it. "I'm still in graduate school," I explained, "but I do have $400 in a savings account. Do you think that would be enough? You can have all of it!" The gallery owner gave me a tight smile, declared himself "gratified" at my enthusiasm, and expressed regret that he couldn't possibly let the painting go for so small a sum.

Crushed but determined—a not unfamiliar state—I noted the date of the show's closing and promptly reappeared at the gallery.

"My" painting, I gleefully noted, was still there; it hadn't been sold. Cornering the owner, I repeated my earlier offer, and he repeated his dismissive snigger. I was ready for him. "Might you possibly be willing to ask the artist himself? Maybe, I mean just maybe, he might be willing to—"

He cut me off. "You certainly are a persistent young man," he said, but then added, with a trace of admiration, "Oh well, why not. I suppose we should try and encourage such enthusiasm for the arts." He phoned Botero, who immediately said, "Sure—let him have it." I wrote out the check, pretty certain it wouldn't bounce (which I *didn't* say), and carted off the painting that very day.

And there it stood above the mantel on my fireplace from that day until 1980 when a recent acquaintance, the art critic Barbara Rose, stopped by for coffee. It didn't take long for her eye to alight on the Botero.

"Marty," she nearly gasped, "that isn't a *real* Botero, is it?"

"Of course it's 'real.' Who would bother to copy it?" I then told her the "Madison Avenue story" and, as her excitement mounted, quickly added that I wasn't anything like a "collector," had bought very little in the years since the Botero purchase, and had no idea what the painting's market value might be.

"I have some news for you. Maybe you'd better sit down. Fernando Botero is now a renowned, world-class artist. That painting is worth real money."

"You're kidding!" Out of the blue my mortgage problem—I was about to buy my first apartment—seemed solved. "Do you know which gallery currently handles his work?"

"The Marlborough Gallery. They're a slick outfit, so be forewarned."

Slick-smick, I should care. No sooner was Barbara out of the apartment than I had Marlborough on the phone. Within the hour, my doorbell rang and up the stairs came an affected, bored young man who seemed decidedly put out at having to come *all the way* downtown to such a déclassé address. I was in no mood. Skipping any offer of coffee, or even a chair, I placed him promptly in front of the Botero.

He let out a deep sigh of disappointment and looked as if he might bolt for the door.

"What's wrong?" I timidly asked. "Barbara Rose—you know—the art critic—"

"—Mmm—"

"—*Barbara* told me that the painting was quite valuable."

"What *Barbara* is apparently unaware of is that it's from Botero's *Blue* Period."

"What does that mean?" I was genuinely mystified.

"The market is *glutted* with Boteros from the Blue Period." He sighed again and moved toward the door, as if preparing to leave. "If *only* it had been from either ten years earlier or ten years later," he sighed, "we might have been able to offer you *something.*"

"Isn't it worth *anything*?" I plaintively asked. "I'm really quite desperate for cash"—surely one of the dumber remarks ever made to a potential buyer.

"Well," he hesitated, "I suppose, as a favor, we *could* take it off your hands . . . it would have to be for a minimal sum, though."

"Like what?" I could hear, but not control, my fevered tone.

"Oh, let's say—and this would be the top figure—*not* negotiable—something like $10,000."

I almost hugged him. "It's YOURS! . . . Absolutely—yes!"

"Oh, very well then." His enervated voice had become a whisper—no match at all for the avid rush with which he unhooked the painting from the wall and headed for the door.

"The *check*," I nearly shrieked. "What about the CHECK?!"

"You want that *now*?" The tone was sheer astonishment, as if I'd proposed burning down the Reichstag.

"Of course *now*!" Even I finally recognized that a potential heist was in play.

"Oh, very well." His voice was a mixture of outrage and petulance. He got out his checkbook, I signed the release and bill of sales forms that he now abruptly produced, and he, like the stealth burglar in a silent film, scurried noiselessly away.

Several months later, a friend called to tell me that my Botero had recently sold at auction—for $900,000.

The *Blue* Period indeed!

Well, I *did* get the mortgage—as I had to remind myself, tearfully, for many a year.

Over the past fifty years nothing much has changed in the number and kind of hoops a PhD candidate must jump through in order to complete a doctoral degree. Along with taking courses and writing a dissertation, at the end of the grueling process candidates have to face what many experience as a traumatic ordeal: the dreaded "orals," in which a panel of professors grills them on the depth of their knowledge and their acuity in analyzing it (though never on their qualifications for teaching the young, or how best that might be done).

Today the hurdles placed in the path of a would-be professional scholar seem all the more bizarre when placed beside the grim fact that the number of full-time university jobs has been declining for three decades. A successfully completed PhD these days too often entitles the young scholar not to the privileges of a tenure-track university appointment but to the low status and security-free job of being an "adjunct"—someone who races from one campus to another teaching an absurd number of courses for minimal pay and with only the narrowest chance of ultimately landing a full-time position. The dramatic shrinkage in tenure-track jobs, especially in the humanities and social sciences, leaves all too many PhDs doing part-time gigs to piece out a living—meaning even less free time for the kind of research and writing that might elevate them to candidacy for a tenured position. It's Catch-22 with a vengeance.

The ordeal of my own orals in 1957 can still stir up a bit of retrospective angst, though the anticipatory terror I felt was *somewhat* offset by the knowledge that the ordeal, once surmounted, at least led to a job market bulging with offers and opportunities. Nonetheless, I dreaded the looming cross-examination—and with good reason, as it would turn out.

My four-person committee was a prestigious one that would have intimidated almost any novice historian. The two senior members of the committee, both born in 1887, were at the time of my exam seventy years old. Frederick Merk, an honorable, cheerful man, had been a student of Frederick Jackson Turner's (*The Significance of the Frontier in American History*) and had inherited his mantle. The other senior member, Samuel Eliot Morison, was a starchy Boston aristocrat whose 1942 biography of Christopher Columbus (*Admiral of the Ocean Sea*) had won the Pulitzer—despite the way it minimized the slaughter of the Indigenous population. Morison's views on race were at the time commonplace among professional historians: slavery, to give one example, was widely seen as essentially a "benevolent" institution.

Morison's contemporary, the Yale diplomatic historian Samuel Flagg Bemis (also a Pulitzer winner) represented the historical profession's mainstream views in its defense of American imperialism for spreading "the blessings of democracy and Christianity." When I was an undergraduate at Yale, I took Bemis's course American Diplomatic History, and one day, after Bemis had described our annexation of extensive Mexican land as "good for everybody" and "entirely justified," I somehow summoned the nerve to ask what the legal grounds were for confiscating Mexican land. Bemis roared with laughter. "So whaddya wanna do—*give it back?!*" The class howled in support of Bemis's put-down. I squirmed in silence.

The two junior members (though both tenured) of my orals committee were Arthur Schlesinger Jr., age forty, and Oscar Handlin, two years his senior. Schlesinger had initially been my thesis adviser, though I grew tired of always having to catch him on the fly. By 1957 he was already much sought after—and far beyond the campus—having skyrocketed to fame at age twenty-nine when he won the Pulitzer for *The Age of Jackson*. Three years later, Schlesinger staked out his centrist views in *The Vital Center*, in which he criticized the Progressive Party and its 1948 presidential candidate Henry A. Wallace for advocating coexistence with Communism—and himself became a political figure. By the '50s Schlesinger had become a leading speechwriter for Adlai Stevenson during his 1952 and 1956 presidential bids. (At the time only a semiconscious liberal, I too supported Stevenson.) Given his multiple projects, Schlesinger was a bad bet for idling away the hours talking to PhD candidates or reading their earnest thesis chapters. I could never get to see him for more than a few minutes, and often not at all, and finally decided to switch to Oscar Handlin as my adviser.

If possible, Handlin proved even more inaccessible, not because he was a national figure but because he was a hooded Buddha, enigmatic and remote. When himself a graduate student at Harvard, Handlin had been denied the vice presidency of the Henry Adams Club because he was Jewish. Yet he went on to become one of the few Jews up to that point in Harvard's history to become a tenured full professor. Given the fact that I too was Jewish, I thought for a time that Handlin might keep special watch over me, even if my self-identification as Jewish was tenuous. (*He* looked the part; blond and blue-eyed, *I* didn't.) My mother's side of the family never regarded our Jewishness as other than an accidental, irrelevant act of birth. (We were "Yom Kippur Jews"— people who went to temple only on the High Holidays.) My father came from more Orthodox stock, but my mother made sure that contact with *his* relatives was kept to a minimum. He was rumored to "sneak off" now and then to his Brooklyn brethren, but to my knowledge he never openly disagreed with the goal of full assimilation or complained about our limited contact with his Orthodox relatives. In any case, Harvard's politely subterranean anti-Semitism never directly impinged on my consciousness, as it had on Handlin, and was never overt enough to mandate any alliance between us based on religious grounds.

As I should have known, having taken a seminar with Handlin and watched him nod off during many a student presentation, he had little interest in students or in teaching. He enjoyed being regarded as a mentor—overall he "advised" some eighty doctoral dissertations during his career—yet was unconcerned with actually doing the job. "Benign neglect" perhaps best characterized his attitude. Each time I turned in a chapter of my thesis (a biography of Charles Francis Adams) to him, the same pattern would repeat: I'd wait several weeks for a response that never came, would then politely ask for feedback, and would be brusquely told to "keep going."

When Yale offered me a full-time job in 1957 as an "instructor" in history, I asked Handlin what I should do.

"Take the job," he said.

"But my thesis on Adams is only halfway completed!"

"Your thesis? Where's your thesis?" Handlin scanned the piles of typed pages that littered the floor of his office.

"Uh—I handed in each chapter as I finished it. They must be here . . . somewhere."

That prompted Handlin, quite unruffled, actually to rise from his chair and start glancing through the piles of paper on the floor. "Ah!" he finally said, retrieving one of the stacks and dumping it in my lap. "Here are your chapters. Go get them bound. You're done."

"I'm done?"

"After your orals you'll have completed the PhD. Later you can complete the biography."

And I did; Houghton Mifflin published it in 1961. When it was still in manuscript, I sent Handlin a copy, along with a note asking for his comments, daringly reminding him that he'd never given me any significant feedback when serving as my official adviser. "I have no criticisms of substance to make," he wrote back, except that the manuscript "is simply too long." After it came out as a book in 1962 and was well received (the *New York Times* put it on the cover of the Sunday *Book Review*), Handlin grew more expansive: "I am very much impressed by the skill with which you have put the whole thing together." That was Handlin's version of rising to the occasion.[1]

Handlin and I never reconnected. As my politics through the years moved steadily leftward, his moved to the right. He denounced the New Left, publicly supported the war in Vietnam, and then in 1988 helped to found the conservative National Association of Scholars. That organization still exists. According to its official literature, its mission is to promote "virtuous citizenship" and to oppose the current "politi-cization of the classroom," with its "over-emphasis on issues of race, gender, class and sexual orientation." Even Handlin's early pioneering work on immigration (the Pulitzer Prize–winning *The Uprooted*) has come under sharp scrutiny for his assertions that Black Americans do not face unique obstacles to achieving assimilation, and that segregation has not seriously impeded their progress.

Is it any wonder that this twenty-six-year-old graduate student was shaking in his white bucks when, in 1957, he faced his board of four Pulitzer Prize–winning examiners? While Handlin dozed throughout the oral exam and Schlesinger made scant effort to conceal his scribbling away during the two hours on some article or speech he needed to complete, Morison took the reins and started to grill me on the War of 1812, about which I knew little and cared less. The topic had nothing to do with my thesis on Adams, nor with my declared primary interest in the subjects of slavery and antislavery. I presumed that the War of 1812 was being featured because Morison had reached that event in the fifteen-volume history of US naval operations he was writing.

When my abysmal lack of knowledge about the War of 1812 became apparent—which was immediately—both Schlesinger and Merk did briefly intervene to deflect Morison's determined pursuit, but neither was insistent enough to succeed. I know that we discussed more than the war during the grueling two hours, but I got so rattled over the War of 1812 that every other topic has long since drowned in the remem-bered sweat of my discomfort. When the two hours finally came to an end, Handlin told me to wait in the corridor outside the exam room while they discussed my fate.

And wait I did, as the minutes dragged by and steadily mounted. After what seemed an eternity, and after I'd concluded that I was doomed, Handlin emerged from the exam room, closing the door behind him.

"We've decided to pass you," he told me, his face expressionless. Without another word, he turned on his heels and went back into the room. *Somebody*, I decided—my guess was Schlesinger—must have said the equivalent of "Look, he *does* have potential, despite his disastrous performance. Let's pass him and be done with it." My further guess is that Morison at best abstained, at worst was outvoted.

Anyway, I'd somehow squeaked by, managing a borderline pass. But the grim experience left a lasting mark. To explain, I need to jump briefly to the mid-'70s when I held the exalted title of distinguished professor at the CUNY Graduate School. Having become active by then in the gay liberation struggle, I proposed to the History Department that I give a seminar on lesbian and gay history. The response was to the point: "The subject matter," I was told, was "not a legitimate field of inquiry." Furious, I told the department that if I was, as their rejection implied, "contaminated," then they would surely not want to unduly expose their graduate students to my odious influence. Accordingly, I said, I would no longer advise doctoral theses, sit on PhD orals, or teach any other, more "respectable" subject matter. I announced my resignation from the Graduate School and made it clear that henceforth I would confine myself to teaching undergraduates at Lehman College, one of CUNY's affiliated undergraduate campuses.

That stalemate held for fifteen years and was finally broken as a by-product of the changing climate of opinion. In 1986, in the midst of the AIDS crisis, with attitudes about gay people now far more sympathetic, I gathered a group of lesbian and gay scholars to begin planning a formal Center for Lesbian and Gay Studies (CLAGS) at the Graduate School. It took five years to put CLAGS together—*that* story lies ahead—and to then get approval from the CUNY Board of Trustees. When that victory was finally won in 1991, I rejoined the Graduate School History Department and "graciously" repeated my earlier offer to teach a seminar on lesbian and gay history. This time around—the department had grown more liberal over the years—the offer was accepted. But with a caveat: I was warned that the course was unlikely to draw the required enrollment of eight students, in which case it would automatically be canceled. In the upshot, it in fact drew forty-two students, and to accommodate the crowd I had to break the group into two separate seminars.

Pleased though I was at the outcome, rejoining the Graduate School meant that I'd once again have to participate in the still-unchanged rituals of the PhD orals. When my own turn came to play Grand Inquisitor, I tried not to repeat the barbarous exercise I myself had been put through, and I did what I could to make the ordeal as informal and friendly as possible. But with few faculty allies, I couldn't make any headway in completely toppling the noxious ritual. One oral in particular stands out in my memory, perhaps because the candidate was himself belligerent about what he clearly regarded as an antiquated and downright cruel procedure. I'll call him "Paul," and his examiners—there were only three of us on this occasion—"West" and "Posen."

West was a specialist on the colonial period in American history and led off the discussion. At its conclusion he announced that he'd found Paul woefully unprepared. Instead of bursting into tears, Paul (to my delight) became combative. He boldly told West that he hadn't rattled off a string of bibliographic citations in colonial history for a simple reason: he wasn't interested in it. He could see no reason, he said, to memorize material that he knew perfectly well would remain in his head for a few weeks at most. It was a waste of his time, he argued, time better spent on grounding himself more deeply in subject matter likely to be useful in his future research.

I defended Paul's position. The best historians, or the best anything, I argued, pursue what interests them and exclude what doesn't. West was quick to respond and, I had to acknowledge, did so rather cogently. "Why did Paul accept the conditions of a PhD oral, knowing its traditional parameters?" West asked. "And why did he agree to present the colonial period in the first place, when he could have chosen other, more congenial time periods instead?" West had a point, though I knew that Paul's aggressive personality, which sought and enjoyed controversy, would never acknowledge its legitimacy.

What I said instead (somewhat airily, I confess) was that Paul, after all, was much like the rest of us: he wanted to live comfortably, as professors did, and knew that getting his academic credentials was a necessary prerequisite. If, I added, his unorthodox way of preparing for the orals was to read only in the areas he found germane to his interests—well, that unorthodoxy could be viewed as a refusal to follow archaic rules, and that in turn suggested originality and independence. What I didn't say, but what I knew from talking to Paul on the outside, was that he was a left-wing activist who scorned the ancient order of self-serving scholars and refused to abide by the hidebound guild requirements of the university system.

When Posen and I proceeded to jointly examine Paul on African American history, his primary field of interest, he turned in a vibrant, trenchant, and knowledgeable performance, even in the face of Posen's needling pedantry. In the subject that he cared about, in other words, Paul proved as bright and well informed as any of the several dozen PhD candidates I'd previously encountered. It didn't wash with West and Posen. When Paul—like me before him—was finally ushered into the corridor to await our verdict, Posen declared the candidate "weak on bibliography," even in his own chosen field. Ignoring that arguable point, I tried to persuade my colleagues that for all Paul's admitted defiance—yes, even arrogance—he was a bright, alive, valuable person, a scholar, potentially, of much-needed originality. To which West acidly replied that although Paul disapproved of what he'd called "credential mills," he seemed to have no qualms in pursuing credentials himself—though alas, not by meeting the necessary "standards" but by "fudging them." The vote, predictably, went against him two to one.

Personally, I didn't much like Paul, but I did recognize our similar distaste for the desiccated rituals of the university—and our shared defiance of them. Like me, Paul made feints at dropping out and feints at joining up. Unlike me, he refused the in-between ground: trying to retool the credential mills from within—which meant getting inside them first. Paul couldn't quite snub his nose at the university world yet refused to do the work that might have allowed him to become part of it—from which perch he might have helped to change it. Which to be sure is easier said than done. As I myself had learned, the older academic generation was so entrenched in its prerogatives and rectitude that no tactic was clearly available for dislodging, modifying—or even circumventing—their traditional hold on what a "proper" education meant.

As far as I've been able to learn, Paul never became either a full-time academic or an independent scholar, nor a fully committed political activist. I lost track of him years ago, though the trauma of his PhD orals has remained vivid in my mind—a stand-in for much that has become oppositional in my own relationship to the traditional university (of which more anon). Perhaps what has stayed with me longest is the uncomfortable sense that none of us can confidently outline the essential ingredients that produce a "good" education—even more, how little most of us seem to care about exploring the subject. The assumption of a Posen or West—still dominant in the university world—that blithely equates a "good education" (undefined, along with the subdivisions of "valid" scholarship and "enriching" teaching) with optimal preparation for a satisfying, productive life *and* the responsibilities of citizenship is a subject—at times a passion—that over the years has perplexed and engaged me, but since I've already written a good deal on the subject, I'll try, for now, to turn off the faucet.[2]

———————

Even before I finished *Charles Francis Adams*, my own scholarly interests had rapidly coalesced around the mid-nineteenth-century abolitionist movement, itself the offshoot of my identification with the burgeoning Black struggle for civil liberties. One entry (September 30, 1962) from the sporadic diary I kept at the time epitomizes the intensity of my connection:

> Kennedy has just finished appealing on the radio to the "courage and integrity" of Ole Miss. . . . Not one word about the courage and integrity of [James] Meredith, though *here* the words actually apply. . . . Kennedy [appeals to] Ole Miss [to] obey the law [regarding school integration] because not to do so would be to sully her splendid traditions: namely, as specified by Kennedy, her prowess on the battlefield and the football field—as if zeal to kill and maim could in any way be related

to a respect for human beings or for those rights which the law, ideally, is meant to sanctify. What a sad, revolting spectacle.

By that point I'd already centered my scholarship on the antislavery struggle, and in particular its radical wing, the much-maligned abolitionist movement. I summarized my revisionist view in an essay, "The Abolitionists and Psychology," which the *Journal of Negro History* published in 1962. A strenuous defense of the abolitionist cause—*immediate* emancipation and without compensation to slaveholders—the essay hit a nerve among a number of young, politically engaged historians; I then encouraged them to write up their own views, which I edited into a book, *The Antislavery Vanguard.* It appeared in 1965 and rather rapidly displaced the older take on the abolitionists as misguided fanatics with an appreciation of their immense contribution to the struggle to end slavery.[3]

In the next few years, I further elaborated my views in a number of additional articles, along with the successful play *In White America*, that pointedly connected the abolitionist struggle against slavery with the contemporary struggle to end Black subjugation. I put special emphasis on the example of William Lloyd Garrison, who'd initially championed *gradual* emancipation followed by "colonization" (that is, the deportation of formerly enslaved people), but had soon shifted—in part due to pressure from already-free Black abolitionists themselves—to demanding unconditional and uncompensated emancipation, along with the full rights of citizenship. During the latter part of the 1960s, as Black militancy deepened (along with my sympathy for it), I put special emphasis on the parallels between the abolitionist movement and the rise in the late '60s of Black Power—how both endeavors shifted strategy in response to shifts in the contemporary climate.[4]

In regard to the Black struggle during the 1960s, I argued that during the early stage of the civil rights movement it had emphasized nonviolent direct action, which was itself the product of rising expectations rather than rock-bottom despair. But then, civil rights victories became increasingly met by rising White resistance, and that produced a decrease in the number of pacified liberals and an increase in the number of Black activists, especially among the young who demanded more militant tactics. A *Fortune* magazine survey from the late '60s revealed that twice as many Black youths as their elders rejected "integration" as neither possible nor desirable—proof perhaps that radicals are not born but made. Yet only a small number of Black Americans ever sanctioned violence and an even smaller one sympathized with the Muslim call for a separate Black state.

A similar pattern—from moderation to militancy—can be traced, I further argued, in the histories of many Black Panther figures. Stokely Carmichael, for one, did not begin his career as a "revolutionary." At the start of his political odyssey Carmichael called for nothing more than integration; indeed, as a teenager he'd been so tentative that he'd actually opposed student sit-ins in the South. Like so many others who later became militant, Carmichael initially called for "pragmatic" reforms and gradual timetables. But when his moderate appeal was met with White indifference or outright violence, Carmichael's rhetoric shifted from "reform" to "revolution"—a shift best explained *not* by some genetic predisposition for "fanaticism" but by the inflexibility of White resistance.

When the social order turns a deaf ear to reform or gives it reluctantly in the form of tokens—when it scorns or toys with moderate pleas for justice—it must bear the bulk of responsibility for the disorder that follows. If society remains in denial after a moderate Black movement has irrefutably revealed that our urban institutions are riddled with racism and with a corrupt, criminal indifference to the plight of the poor, it becomes ever more apparent that "the system," not the citizenry, is responsible for the escalation in protest. If the Black population had *not* become notably more alienated in 1968 than in 1962, one would have to wonder why.

As I wrote in a preface to Leon Friedman's 1967 civil rights reader, "For a brief time it looked as if white America was about to face up to the hollowness of its official morality, was ready at last to convert the ringing expressions of equality in our historic state papers into reality. We now know that such hopes were excessive. Like the First Reconstruction of the 1860s, the second one of the 1960s stopped tragically short of the hopes once held out for it." At the end of the '60s, 80 percent of White children in first grade were still attending schools that were 90 percent or more White, the unemployment rate among non-Whites had doubled, average Black earnings were half that of White workers— and most Black workers were still being held to unskilled or semiskilled jobs. Residential segregation too was increasing, not receding, with the polls revealing that by a large majority southern White Americans still objected to a Black family moving next door.

In my view the basic ills of our society were national phenomena requiring national resources for their solution—but the will for enacting such legislation was, alas, lacking. A survey by the Harris Poll in 1966 found that 70 percent of White respondents thought Black people were "trying to move too fast." At both Yale and Princeton, I got into disputes with "liberal" professors who argued that "we cannot legislate against prejudice." Perhaps not, I'd reply, "but we *can* curtail its outward expression—*can* insist that people obey the law regardless of their feelings about that law." There was even evidence that in the long run legislation can affect the prejudice itself ("compulsive bigots" excepted).

Yet some grounds for hope remained. As the psychologist Gordon Allport put it, "I believe that the racial bigotry of most [White] Americans is counterbalanced by their belief in Christian and democratic ethics, and the resulting tension between their prejudices and their values produces the guilt which can creatively respond to egalitarian legislation." But far fewer Americans agreed with Allport's analysis at the end of the '60s than at the beginning. One thing was certain: we could hardly rest on our laurels—pitiful as they were.

After my first book (the biography of Charles Francis Adams) won the Bancroft Prize in 1962, followed by the success of *In White America* (about which more anon) in 1963 and *The Antislavery Vanguard* in 1965, a wide variety of offers began to come my way. Carey McWilliams, the legendary editor of the *Nation*, asked me "to contribute an occasional piece" to the magazine. (I of course said yes, the *Nation* being close to my political bible. Soon after, he also asked me to cover the NAACP convention, but that I declined, not feeling qualified.) By 1965 I was regularly fielding requests for a range of radio and TV interviews; one highlight (of sorts) was a "conversation" between me and Paul Goodman on the local TV show *All Things Considered*. It was neither pleasant nor informative: Goodman puffed on his pipe, ostentatiously blew smoke in my face, and patronized me throughout ("Surely as a historian, Mr. Duberman, you should know that . . . "). Reviewing the event, the *New York Times* critic referred to my "losing battle to persuade Goodman to clarify" his distinctive views, for which I received only "involuted" answers.

The popular *Steve Allen Show* featured scenes from *In White America*, and was soon followed by a 1965 production of the play in Paris starring Gordon Heath (of *Deep Are the Roots* fame). A mutual friend reported that Robert Oppenheimer had attended a performance and "talked with great enthusiasm about your play." Janet Flanner ("Genêt") wrote in the *New Yorker* that "the evening was much commented on in the Paris press . . . [it's] one of the few valuable national productions so far given here . . . [it was] effective and affecting." That helped me digest the report that Massapequa High School on Long Island had banned the play on the grounds that, to quote the local school board, "it might create a controversial situation" (apparently unaware that the "situation" had long since become "controversial").

The variety of offers kept coming. Joan Ganz Cooney (this was before *Sesame Street*) persuaded me to host two special tributes on Channel 13, one on the life of Norman Thomas, the other on A. Philip Randolph. I've never felt comfortable, then or since, on TV; the blinding lights and frenetic atmosphere usually distract me from putting my two-minute slot to good use. The Thomas and Randolph specials were much lengthier affairs, but weirdly (residual terror?) I remember little about either event, other than a bathroom break that had me standing next to Norman Thomas in adjourning urinals. Apparently awestruck at the proximity (not to mention the dangling penises) I gushed some half-assed compliment about how vigorous he seemed for a man his age. "You don't understand," Thomas sighed. "I only do these shows because they give me a boost in vigor."

I was also getting a steady stream of feelers from various historians to write one of the volumes in some sort of series they were editing, and from universities offering high salaries and full professorships to move to their campus. Perhaps for that reason alone, Princeton promoted me in 1965 to the rank of associate professor with tenure—which made me at thirty-four the youngest such appointment to date in the social sciences, or so I was told. (Oh, how they would come to regret it!)

But to return to *In White America* and the phone call that instantly put all other requests for my services in the dust: Cindy Degener, an agent at the Sterling Lord literary agency, called to say that the agency had decided to try the experiment—unheard of back then—of taking on a few scholars as clients. Cindy thought I might be a likely candidate. Was I interested? Well, yes, I said, but felt the need to add that scholarly books rarely sold well and the agency was unlikely to ever make a dime off me.

Did I per chance, Cindy went blithely on, have any experience writing for the theater—or know of any historian who did? That perked me up. Cindy explained that she was asking because a Broadway producer named Jay Julien had recently contacted the agency asking if they could put him in touch with a writer who combined a knowledge of history with some playwriting experience. Inspired by the current British mega-hit *The Hollow Crown*, a stage work about the history of the British monarchy, Julien wanted to put together a comparable production on the history of the American presidency.

Well, I offered, eager but irrelevant, I *have* toured in summer stock as an actor and, well, I've also recently completed my first full-length play, *The Martyr*, about the abolitionist publisher Elijah Lovejoy, murdered by a proslavery mob in 1847. I quickly added that *The Martyr* was "pretty primitive" and the few people I'd showed it to hadn't been enthusiastic. (If a copy still exists somewhere, I hereby disavow in advance all ownership.)

Cindy thought I just might do, and within days had set up a meeting between her, me, and Jay Julien. To everyone's surprise, it went well, and we decided to schedule a second one. Then, only days later, while I was on my way to the second meeting, lightning struck: instead of a tedious evening about the presidency, I thought, why not instead do a documentary play about what it's been like to be Black in White America? After all, I was already teaching Slavery and Antislavery at Princeton and had also published a fair number of reviews and articles relating to the current Black struggle, about which I felt passionate.

By the time I arrived at the meeting I was aflame with enthusiasm. I mounted my soapbox and ardently pressed for the substitute assignment, pointing out (this was 1963) that the civil rights movement was daily mounting in intensity—lunch counter sit-ins, Freedom Rides, the murder of Medgar Evers, preparations for the March on Washington—and I myself longed to make some contribution to the struggle. Julien sat through my zealous oratory with stone-faced indifference—and then rejected it out of hand: "incendiary, much too controversial; no one would come." Cindy hemmed and hawed.

I was adamant. I told Julien to find somebody else to do "the American presidency." I was fired up with my own idea and determined on pursuing it. And I did—with such concentrated intensity that I completed the entire script in the summer of 1963. At which point Julien read it—and dismissed it as "not commercial." Cindy read it and loved it. The very same day she sent Julien packing (he never did do "the American presidency") and offered my play to Judy Rutherford Marechal, who, though still in her twenties, had already produced several off-Broadway hits. She proved my match in the hundred-yard dash: she read the play overnight, formally optioned it the next day, and booked the Sheridan Square Playhouse for an October opening.

And open we did, though it was a close call. A few days before the curtain was due to rise on the first preview of *In White America*, the stagehands, owed several weeks' pay, went on strike. I raced home, borrowed the money from my mother (somewhere in the neighborhood of $500, if I remember correctly), and the curtain went up on schedule.

The reviews were mostly ecstatic—the (then liberal) *New York Post*, for one, called it "one of the finest and I think most moving off-Broadway shows of recent years." The conservative *New York Daily News*, oppositely, adamantly refused even to send its critic, telling Cindy that *In White America* was "incendiary." Nonetheless, the play became a hit, and even won the Vernon Rice/Drama Desk Award for the best off-Broadway production of the year.

Most important, the Free Southern Theater performed *In White America* during Freedom Summer in 1964 at thirteen different locations in Mississippi, on makeshift stages in churches and improvised backyards—one was in the middle of a beanfield—and usually before standing-room-only crowds. Many had never seen a play and kept interrupting the actors with shouts of "That's right!" and "You tell it!"

Howard Zinn, who was active in Freedom Summer, wrote me from Jackson, Mississippi, to say that he'd seen the play performed in "a ramshackle wooden church" and had to tell me that it was "an overwhelming experience . . . people were standing five deep, every vacant spot filled between, behind, beside, the wooden benches where others sat—and more outside looking in. At the end, no one wanted to go home—and they stayed for an hour longer, singing freedom songs . . . seeing it in New York was thrilling, but this was far more so."

Mario Savio, who was teaching during Freedom Summer at a school for Black children in McComb, Mississippi, was another enthusiast. (In the fall he would emerge as the leader of the Berkeley Free Speech Movement.) On August 1, 1964, he wrote his girlfriend that he'd seen *In White America* performed that night "outside the Freedom House in McComb, with people from all over the area attending, hanging on every word. . . . I won't make the slightest attempt to describe the performance," Savio wrote, "but I plead with you, Cheri, to buy the record. It will tear at your insides, but it will have been worth every moment."

Not everyone agreed. I learned about one performance where some two dozen members of the Indianola White Citizens' Council appeared just before curtain time, sat mum throughout the performance, and after it was over told an audience member, "It's just what we expected—a piece of Communist trash." Despite that predictable reaction, the play after its extended run in New York twice toured the country doing some 150 performances in seventeen states during 1965–66, often to a tumultuous reception.

A separate production in London drew all the heavyweight English critics—Harold Hobson, W. A. Darlington, Clive Barnes, and Bernard Levin—and all of them raved ("magnificent, fierce, compelling," wrote Levin), though the *Financial Times* all but accused me of trying to start a race riot: "History should not be cited to inflame current prejudices." To this day I still hear about local productions.

Though I waived all royalties from any performance connected to the movement—like those done in Mississippi during Freedom Summer—I nonetheless, thanks mostly to the two cross-country tours, did earn $7,500 in royalties from the play, which from the beginning I split fifty-fifty with the Student Nonviolent Coordinating Committee (SNCC). I like to think that conscience had a hand in my SNCC contributions, but so of course did wanting to see myself as one of the "good guys." I periodically tortured myself over my "mixed motives," even though I'd long since decided that a patchwork of impulses accompanies all gestures of social protest—that pure altruism is a pipe dream, at best a fantasy aspiration rather than a live option in our flawed lives. To await the arrival of a purely unselfish set of motives is to indulge in fake sainthood—as well as serving as a standing rationale for never engaging in political work. In the mid-to-late '60s, as "Black Power" emerged at home and the war in Vietnam heated up abroad, the preoccupying vanity of the self was not so much usurped by politics as refracted through it. And that was OK. The canny response to smears and sneers against the motives of do-gooders is to ignore—or openly laugh—at them.

And the little matter of whether all the attention and praise had given me a swollen head? I'm not the best candidate for making that judgment. But nor, strangely, am I necessarily among the worst. It's like this: much good fortune has indeed come my way, and my being an educated White male has surely had a great deal to do with it. Yet from at least my sexual awakening in adolescence I'd also been carrying around a pretty nasty amount of self-disgust, having internalized the current consensus that homosexuality was a pathological disability. That common opinion had in my case been somewhat balanced out by unconditional mother love, but even that (as my sister enjoyed reporting) became compromised as I grew older by my mother's angst over my lack of girlfriends and her growing awareness that I might be "one of them," one of those damaged and despised weirdos that the profoundly homophobic culture in those years had all but unanimously convinced the general public were unfit for close association. When I wrote to one of my oldest, dearest friends in the spring of 1964 that I'd been feeling much happier of late and was actually thinking about calling a halt to psychotherapy, she wrote back in horror that she and her husband "both felt terribly sad" at the news. "What will happen in five, ten, fifteen years' time? Are you really opting out of the possibility of a wife & kids?" The friend was a highly educated, liberal-minded academic who I didn't doubt cared a good deal about me—she was merely echoing the gruesome consensus of the day.

My euphoria, in any case, didn't last, and before long I was again lashing myself to the alternating masts of either celibacy or guilt (after "having a slip"). Despite all the attention and praise I'd recently been getting, the profound conviction that I needed "fixing" resurfaced. My recent string of career successes did allow me to see myself in a better light, but the light refused to stop flickering, as I went back and forth between sexual "acting out"—the common psychiatric term for destructively discharging anxiety that needed to be husbanded for "analysis"—and the alternating charade of concealing my homosexuality and pretending to be one of the boys. Deep down, deeper than any career success, I still thought of my homosexuality as a personality "disorder," as intrinsically disturbed.

The sense that I was pathologically "less than" is probably the basic reason I didn't get much of a swelled head from the gobs of praise that had come my way of late. Even in my diary I dutifully discounted my accomplishments, writing on March 7, 1964, that "my biography of [Charles Francis] Adams is a compilation of data—the result of diligence. A virtue, perhaps, but not an uncommon one. My 'play' is essentially a skillful job of editing. A talent, no doubt, but not of a very high order." Minimizing my accomplishments was a subtle way, amid a shower of alarming praise, to reassure myself of a permanently disabled future. I couldn't even locate the willpower—to my therapist's ill-concealed contempt—to avoid homosexual contact and to fight the good fight of matching up my outer camouflage with my inner lust.

When I joined the Princeton faculty in 1962, I quickly came to dislike the smug, complacent tone of the place. "Everything," I wrote a friend, is "too well-manicured to be real." I gave as one example the southern-born undergraduate who had no compunction about arguing in class "that putting Negroes on the welfare rolls only encouraged their 'laziness,' destroying their 'incentive' and 'self-respect.'" Another student argued, with high seriousness and to general applause, that social security legislation was "immoral"; this son of inherited wealth had the gall to openly admonish Black people for not doing more to "raise themselves up" to a place where "they might better *deserve* equality." To him, suffering was an abstraction; he didn't believe it was widespread, and where it did exist he was sure that the remedy for it lay entirely within the reach of the sufferers themselves. My missionary zeal helped me to control my anger; perhaps I was already aware that I'd soon discover at least *some* liberal voices on campus among both students and faculty—but I was horrified at the glib dismissals, the lack of simple compassion for those less fortunate.

Isolated, depressed, and angry, I went into New York now and then to decompress, but the city wasn't close enough for an impromptu escape (at one point in the early '60s I went without sex for fifteen months, a bout of hepatitis and on-again, off-again herpes being contributory). Fortunately, I began to meet a few congenial Princeton faculty members—in particular, Amélie and Dick Rorty—and in my seminars, which were more pliable than my large lecture courses, some of the students proved even more unhappy with their so-called education than I was. Together, we began to explore alternatives. By 1963, my second year at Princeton, we began to strip away the authoritarian structure that then typified (and often still does) the university classroom. Over the next half-dozen years, especially from 1966 on, we turned the traditional seminar inside out—took turns at sharing leadership, made collective decisions about discussion topics, and disposed of the traditional role of the professor as the dispenser of grades, exams, assigned topics—and Truth.

In the spring of 1964 I made the decision to move to New York City and commute to my Princeton classes. I told the History Department that as a "bachelor" (I left the definition to them) I needed the variety of city life—naming as examples group therapy and theater, but not of course the still more important gay social and sexual circuits. At a meeting of the History Department, I fully acknowledged that I'd be on campus less often than before and thus much less available for administrative chores. I argued, though, that every professor engages in three functions: teacher, scholar, administrator. No professor was equally active in all three areas. I myself was far *more* intrigued and involved with teaching and scholarship, and far less with administration, than were most of my colleagues. Since none of us, I argued, were or could become strenuously involved in all three areas, we all prioritized. I myself, I argued, was deeply involved both in teaching and scholarship, so I had to go light in regard to administrative duties. If they disagreed, I said, I was entirely prepared to resign my tenured professorship and seek employment elsewhere.

No, no, they insisted: it was perfectly *fine* to redefine my relationship to Princeton in the terms I'd laid out. They had no problem with it—none at all. I should feel free to proceed according to the redefinition of my role as I'd outlined; the new arrangement was entirely satisfactory to them.

I think we actually did believe what we said, and for roughly two years everything went relatively smoothly. But by 1966 I'd taken a deep and fascinating dive into trying to destructure the traditional autocratic classroom. I was careful to distribute to my History Department colleagues detailed proposals for their formal approval that explained and defended each experimental step in our classes—and slyly noted that both the experiments and writing up of the proposals consumed far more time and energy than I'd anticipated. Yet my scholarship, I stressed, had recently become *more* demanding since, after a somewhat slack period, I'd plunged into a massive research project on the history of Black Mountain College. I did not mention that somehow in my rigidly tight schedule I was managing to squeeze in a burgeoning social life in New York, which put the kibosh on finding time, other than rarely, to sit in on one of the History Department's mandarin marathons about matters of miniscule interest to me. Nor did I add that I'd recently been elected a member of the New Dramatists and was now free to use its facilities, of which I was taking full advantage, to stage readings and workshops of several new plays of mine in progress.

I hung in at Princeton for another five years, rumbles of disapproval rising ominously louder, until the point came early in 1971 when the department actually vetoed my latest proposal for classroom experimentation. The dean of faculty rejected my appeal and Princeton's president, Robert Goheen, refused even to grant me an audience. I resigned in 1971.[5]

To jump back for a moment to 1966, the year my third book, *James Russell Lowell*, was published and subsequently announced as a finalist for the National Book Award. New York's liberal literati doubled down on its invitations to wine and dine me, and a number solicited contributions to their literary fiefdoms—to *Dissent, Daedalus*, the *Atlantic Monthly*, the *New Republic*, the *Nation*, *Book World*, and the *Village Voice*. I was also increasingly invited during the late '60s to join various symposia to discuss such hot-button topics as the turmoil on college campuses, the Black struggle for civil rights, and the war in Vietnam. As well, a fair number of well-known public intellectuals, including Irving Howe, Alfred Kazin, and David Riesman, wrote me to praise a particular piece I'd published, and to offer lunch or drinks. Still in my mid-late thirties, I was both amazed and of course pleased when Alfred Kazin effusively praised a "splendid" recent review of mine and to propose cocktails, saying that he'd "wanted for quite some time" to meet me. I was no less surprised when Arthur Schlesinger Jr., with whom I'd had a complicated relationship as a graduate student, sent me a congratulatory letter about my "clear and brave" analysis in the *Village Voice* of William Styron's *The Confessions of Nat Turner*.

The symposia were sometimes imposing, and I had to blink twice at the renown of my copanelists: Julian Bond and James Farmer on a symposium to explore "Race Equality and the Bill of Rights"; Norman Thomas, William Kunstler, and William O. Douglas to discuss the 175th anniversary of the adoption of the first ten amendments; and at a *Partisan Review* conference, "What's Happening to America," I shared a platform with a showy array of intellectual stars that included Michael Harrington, Tom Hayden, Susan Sontag, and Diana Trilling on the topic "Prospects for SDS" (Students for a Democratic Society).

At that last event, I used my time at the mike to predict that "only a fraction" of students were ever likely to get involved in SDS, not because they were unaware of our society's ills but because they lacked any *emotional* identification with the suffering, material *and* psychological, of the underprivileged, the kind of identification that *sustains* a commitment to radical change. By the time they did meet with their natural portion of affliction, it was more likely than not that they would spend their energy trying to deny and conceal it; in America, after all, calamity is not considered part of the human condition but rather the result of personal inadequacy. Why *some* middle-class White students *do* manage to identify—and lastingly—with the disadvantaged remains mysterious; could we answer that question, we'd be a long way toward a psychology of social protest. But we can't answer it—not now, and probably not ever.

As my reputation continued to grow and the American Academy of Arts and Letters gave me a "special award" for my "contributions to literature," Princeton duly took note. Yet with diminishing cordiality. As my experiments in unstructured education multiplied, so did the History Department's mounting irritability over my explicit condemnation of the sort of traditional education that Princeton exemplified. And as I continued to write plays, eyebrows were raised about "boundary-crossing" and "moonlighting." Then, when I decided in the spring of 1964 to move to New York and commute to teach, there was open disgruntlement, along with smug astonishment: How could anyone be foolhardy enough to forsake the idyllic perfection of the Princeton community (forget the fact that my research assistant was the *only* Black undergraduate on campus and, until 1969, there were *no* women undergraduates) and settle instead for a shabby apartment in Greenwich Village? The rumor that I was homosexual seemed confirmed.

Given my scholarly track record, it would have seemed downright peculiar if the department had openly urged me to resign. Having early on been given tenure, I was protected from any attempt at outright firing—permissible only in instances of "moral turpitude." Homosexuality, in those years, might have qualified, but they had no *proof.* Still, the department managed, by the late '60s, to send me a clear message: it kept my salary $5,000 below the *average* for full professors—making me all at once the most published and lowest paid.

During my first few years at Princeton, most of the grievances against me stayed hidden; it wouldn't have been seemly, after all, to openly deplore my homosexuality. Instead, disapproval stayed focused on the "impossibility" of anyone teaching in one place and living in another; it *had* to follow, so went the argument, that I was giving teaching short shrift. In fact, the opposite was true: in 1965 I was on the cusp of a series of experiments to peel away the standard authoritarian trappings— exams, grades, etc.—of the classroom and create in their place an "open" environment that allowed for a freer exchange of views. My detractors could have made a case, though they did not, that I was "destroying" education, but not that I'd lost interest in it. I was in truth more passionately involved than ever before.

When more and more reports of disparagement reached my ears, I decided on an open confrontation and took my case to Jerry Blum, then chair of the History Department. "I *need* New York," I wrote him. "I was born there, it represents my pace and style, and I'm only really happy when living there. And personal contentment, I believe, is essential to the quality of my work as *a historian*." I also told Blum, which I hadn't before, that after moving to the city the year before, I'd joined a therapy group—unavailable in Princeton—to help me deal better "with certain problems in my life" (which I left unspecified). I suggested to Blum that he call a meeting of the full department to discuss and resolve the grievances against me; if they were not resolvable, I would voluntarily resign from Princeton.

Blum did convene such a meeting, but it proved a farce. I was roundly praised as one of the department's shining lights and reassured that it fully understood that my involvement in the theater necessitated my living in New York. I knew perfectly well who among my detractors had been leading the charge against me: Lawrence Stone and Charles Gillespie. But since they registered no open complaint, apparently preferring covert antagonism, I had nothing to answer for. Unreality ruled. It would be five more years before matters would finally come to a head—at which point I *would* resign, and gladly.

The attention and applause I was getting *outside* Princeton had a counterbalancing, and complicated, effect on me. In those pre-Stonewall years I veered unsteadily between exhilaration (a finalist for the National Book Award!—I'm *not* a disturbed sicko!—or not solely that . . .), anxiety (how can I maintain this crazy pace?), and gratitude (how nice it feels, after years of belittlement at the hands of the psychiatric profession, to be treated like a person of value). Strange to say, I don't recall even momentary concern that I would be "outed" as gay, that these castles in the sky would be reduced to rubble, that the older I got (the '60s coincided exactly with my thirties) and remained unmarried and childless, the more suspicion would grow that I was an unstable, unsubstantial bit of flimflam who was likely, in the long run, to have a negative impact on the reputation of any individual, organization, or movement that embraced me.

The paradoxical fact was that, behind my own back, as it were, I was *myself* spreading the word of my sexual orientation: following *In White America*, my plays—especially *Payments*, which depicts the world of gay male hustling—had taken a decidedly salacious, "immoral" turn. I was preparing myself—the process at most semiconscious and the route circuitous—for the day when I *would* come out publicly. Before I could fully embrace—and announce—my homosexuality, I had to give up once and for all the notion (in the '60s still common) of a "cure"—including the self-torture of psychotherapy, which had had long insisted that "conversion" was both possible and necessary. The essential precursor to "coming out" openly—as I can see only in retrospect—was the emergence, *post*-Stonewall, of an explicitly gay movement, and community. I had to face the likelihood that the varied honors being heaped on my head would stealthily but remorselessly steal away once I publicly declared that I was queer—which would indeed turn out to be the case.

The seeds that would make it possible for me to take the leap had been planted early on. At the deepest level the most profound influence—strange as it may sound—had been my mother's unconditional love. For many people besides me, such love is the essential ingredient that makes it possible for an infant's squalling demands for total attention and instant gratification to gradually recede over time, giving way to acknowledgment of the equal claims of others. From there—if unconditional love has done its job of nurturing rather than punishing our affiliative nature—basic acceptance of the needs of others can appear, develop, and be negotiated, and an affective social bond satisfyingly formed.

That summary, oversimplified, is the theoretical argument that the psychologist Gordon Allport put forward in his 1955 book, *Becoming*. Over the years, when I've occasionally been asked which books have most influenced me, I almost always cite *Becoming*. It's a silly question, of course: we lack the exquisite self-consciousness, as well as the precise measuring tools, to chart even approximately the inner journey of the self. Rather than rudely say as much, I've usually responded politely to the question, often adding two other books to Allport's: A. S. Neill's *Summerhill* (a 1960 distillation of his long-standing experiment in running a noncoercive English boarding school), and Norman O. Brown's 1959 *Life Against Death*.

At the height of its influence in the'60s, *Summerhill* was a considerable force—it sold three million copies. The popularity of *Life Against Death*, on the other hand, was more circumscribed, though in intellectual circles, profound. I, for one, found it remarkable—and especially the section on the pleasure principle. Reading Brown, I decided (playfully) that if I applied his "reality principle" to my own circumstances, I could discard my overdone penchant for self-recrimination and shift the emphasis to counting my blessings. I could view myself, as Brown might put it, as one of the privileged few able to avoid the pressure put on the vast majority of heterosexual adults to conform to a "principle" that mandated repression and could act out instead "dreams of omnipotent indulgence." *My* ontology need not recapitulate phylogeny to the extent true of most people—an attractive rationale for indulging what I'd been taught to believe was *mere* sexual pleasure (that is, nonromantic and multitudinous).

Giving further, if inadvertent, encouragement to Brown's analysis, the sexologists Richard Green and John Money, in their 1969 book, *Transsexualism and Sex Reassignment*, argued that sexual orientation was psychosocial rather than biological in origin, yet was as deeply imprinted as any genetically derived trait and could not, in whole or in part, be reversed. Allport, Neill, Brown, and Money—they put me well on the path of questioning a whole knapsack full of "truisms" with which I'd been raised.

There was only one trouble with these cheerfully expansive bouts of speculation: Was I in fact fit to inhabit the brave new world that the speculations of Norman O. Brown and others were trying to encourage into being? Did my much-praised professional accomplishments in fact mask a temperament that sometimes veered into depression, curtailing the buoyant optimism that I at other times exuded? Was it, in short, too late for me? *Theoretically* I was now opposed to "mandated repression," but embedded beneath my own burnished surface lay a thick layer of damaging self-distrust engendered by a homophobic culture and periodically manifested as bouts of disabling loneliness.

Years later, in the mid-'70s, when I was thinking of writing about the tortured period when I'd bought into the psychoanalytic insistence that "conversion" was my only hope for a satisfying life, I asked two of my closest friends from graduate school days to write down their impressions of me back then. Both were straight, one male, one female. In his response Rick itemized "two perceptions": despite (or was it because of?) all the psychoanalysis, "you did not really know yourself very well," yet back then he saw me as "being healthier, saner, and better balanced than most people who are ostensibly 'healthy' . . . you were someone who did love others . . . you were a warm and affectionate friend. I know that you cared about your friends. I know that I always felt great affection for you." My other friend, Joan, with whom I was deeply connected (and remain in touch), emphasized "the sheer *intensity* of the emotion" between us and how much "I loved your openness & warmth . . . it was possible for me to talk about anything."

Their responses were written in 1976, long after I'd rejected the traditional psychoanalytic view of homosexuality as a pathology and become active in the post-Stonewall liberation movement—better able, as it were, to accept Rick's and Joan's upbeat memories of me. Yet I would never claim, down to the present day, that the process of self-acceptance has triumphed; the homophobic culture—not just psychotherapy—has left too deep an imprint. Here, as one more example, are some scattered notes I scribbled down in the fall of 1962, when I'd just begun to teach at Princeton—in other words, *later* than the graduate school years Rick and Joan had described:

> I'm sometimes astonished at how well I can function both socially and professionally at the same time that I'm feeling empty and wretched inside . . . these past few weeks I've been more painfully aware than ever before of the rigidities of my life

and how my frantic need to stay busy neither satisfies in itself nor successfully conceals the deep loneliness beneath . . . no close friends nearby, and neither alcohol nor sex to provide transient feelings of contentment. Only work remains, and I'm now so aware of the way I use that as a painkiller, that it no longer has the same curative effect. Still, working hard is a superior form of evasion—superior because it isn't obviously destructive; on the contrary, it results in "achievement" . . . the fact is, I enjoy my work, aside from its neurotic component; if I didn't, it's unlikely I'd be able to use it successfully as a distraction from unhappiness. Still, it's strange to me that I can teach classes with my usual zest and alertness, and can spend evenings with comparative strangers chatting amiably away. Unless I'm more self-deceived than I think, strangers would pick up in me few outward signs of discontent or disturbance. Perhaps they sense a too-eager desire to please—one marker of unhappiness—but I doubt it. Not that I care if it comes through. Perhaps my depressions are no more than mild melancholy. Deep or extended depression, it seems to me, isn't compatible with functioning as well as I do.

One acid test against which I measured my well-being in these years was the orgiastic watering hole of Fire Island. I'd first gone there in the mid-'50s, along with my closest friend at the time, Leo Bersani. We were both still in graduate school at Harvard, and having little money, we rented a room in a private house in the community of Cherry Grove. In those years the island still lacked electricity; gas lamps reigned supreme and managed to make *everyone* look enigmatically attractive. As Leo and I headed out that first evening to scout the scene, the middle-aged straight woman who owned the house took us aside for a whispered warning: "You seem like nice boys, so you be careful out there. That boardwalk is dark and there are a lot of very strange men around. Perverts, you know."

Managing not to smile, we thanked her for the advice and set out double-time to find those strange men. These were the years when barely anyone was publicly "out." I was not only "*in*" but was still laboring under the psychiatric definition of me as "sick" and working dutifully in psychotherapy to change into a functioning heterosexual. The most pronounced side effect thus far had been not dawning self-acceptance but guilt-ridden body shyness. The psychiatric injunction in the late '50s was not Norman O. Brown's advice to rid myself of "mandated repression" but to throw off the "yoke" of homosexuality.

I was not, in other words, a likely candidate for indulging in, let alone enjoying, the outdoor sex scene in Cherry Grove known as the Meat Rack (campily referred to as the Enchanted Forest). My need for sex—I was then in my midtwenties—was insistent but hindered by bodily self-consciousness that put orgiastic oblivion out of reach and far removed from what I ingenuously assumed was the heterosexual's jaunty, lighthearted pursuit of pleasure. The therapist I was then see-ing ponderously warned me that if I continued to "act out" sexually, it would be impossible to achieve the healthy goal of heterosexuality (monogamous, no less).

Judging from photographs of me from the '50s, I was a physi-cally attractive young man, yet my body shyness was so entrenched that I was unable to take off my T-shirt on the beach—not even when alone with a boyfriend. Sad but true—*very* sad. Fire Island, whose specialty was the display of the buffed male body, was for me an environment designed to evoke maximum discomfort. Over the years I would periodically go back to Cherry Grove or, later, to the upscale Fire Island Pines (for wealthier White men and their invariably stunning young guests). But I went reluctantly, and never felt comfortable enough to consider much more than an overnight stay. It wasn't moral scruples that kept me from sexual indulgence (or, for that matter, prevented me earlier from going fairly often to the famed Everard Baths in Manhattan, where the dim lighting made me feel somewhat less conspicuous). In print and otherwise I defended "sexual adventuring" and nonmonogamous relationships as core ingredients of the cultural revolution then beginning. I simply wasn't well equipped psychologically to live comfortably in the brave

new world of unlimited sexual partners that I theoretically championed and *did* believe in.

It wasn't until years later, the mid-'80s, after I'd met Eli, the man
who became my life partner, that was I able—romantically isolated in
our rented house—to feel relaxed enough to spend a full week on Fire
Island focused on him and me and the pleasures of the beach and able
to ignore, with relief, the lubricious attractions parading up and down
it. Prior to that point the longest I'd managed to stay put at the Pines
or Grove was a five-day visit to Leo in the small cottage he rented in
the Pines in the summer of 1971.

That trip stands out as an emotional wringer. On the plus side was
spending time with Leo on a low-pitched, *un*eventful basis, and minimizing my involvement with the known anxiety of trying to compete
in the island's sexual sweepstakes against the horde of fetching twenty-
year-olds. That calm frame of mind was disrupted when I made the
mistake of leaving our hideaway to visit "Stan," a wealthy businessman
I knew from the city who, when I ran into him on the beach, had
invited me to "stop by the cottage sometime."

Big mistake. It was the Meat Rack in miniature—drugs sharing the
foreground with sex. Stan's three winsome houseguests were in varying
stages of tripping and clamorously wove in and out of the living room,
not seeming to know or care which planet we happened to be visiting.
The disconnect was complete. Feeling wretchedly unwanted, I headed
back to Leo's cottage via a solitary, moonlit walk along the beach.

Another mistake. I was swept up by a wave of melancholy as I
bemoaned the fact that I hadn't had a steady boyfriend in nearly a decade
and blamed myself for the lack of any consistent tenderness in my life.
I would never, I told myself, have a mate, would never find the "right
person" to settle down with. And the fault was *mine*. I berated myself
for not *consistently* wanting a partner, and for heeding the therapist's
repetitive demand that I break off a promising affair. Stripped of the
usual insulation of work, I found myself in tears. There is no solution,
I sadly concluded, other than to thicken the insulation, to bury myself
still *deeper* in work. That, and to stop feeling sorry for myself: "No

one has a *right* to be cared about," I admonished. "You earn that right. And by that measure I have more than I deserve: there *are* people who care about me. I always want so fucking much that I'm bound to feel poverty stricken. Perfect intimacy, perfect sex, perfect understanding. It's always the *ideal* situation I pine for, and that's enormously destructive of enjoying the always imperfect but still pleasurable moment."

Self-flagellation did the trick. No longer sobbing, I reached Leo's door.

The next day I left the island and plunged back into the ice-cold bath of scholarship. I'd been making steady progress over the previous three to four years on a history of Black Mountain College, the legendary experimental community in the foothills of North Carolina that from 1933 to 1956 had been the seeding ground, the forerunner and exemplar for much that became innovative in the arts. By 1970 I'd already traversed the country interviewing many of the singular, shaping talents that had been part of the community, and had, as well, been reading through the mound of previously untouched documents at the state archives in Raleigh, North Carolina. It was time to start writing up my findings.

I was also "allowing" myself (the academy generally viewed scholarship as a priestly vocation demanding singular preoccupation) to switch hats now and then and continue to write plays. Several of my one-acters, under the title *The Memory Bank*, opened in a small East Village theater in January 1970. The critics encouraged me far more than my Princeton colleagues. The *New York Times* characterized the evening as "dazzling . . . exquisitely wrought"; others added "utterly fascinating" and "sensationally effective," and Stanley Richards chose two of my one-acters for his annual volume, *Best Short Plays*.

Earlier I had also been elected to the New Dramatists, where I was able to use their facilities to workshop new material, which I frequently did. I also wrote a movie script with Ossie Davis—our working theme was "football as fascism," with O. J. Simpson set to star. It never got made. At one point I even signed on to doctor the book of a Broadway musical (*Soon*) that Gerry Freedman (*Hair*) directed and that included in its young, unknown cast the soon-to-be famous Nell Carter, Richard Gere, Peter Allen—and the already famous Joe Butler of the Lovin' Spoonful. It ran for exactly two performances, and all I learned from the experience was what I already knew: musicals were not my thing.

Even before the 1969 Stonewall uprising, most of the plays that I was now writing included overt or implicit gay material; what I can see in retrospect was that, disillusioned with psychotherapy, I was in fact "coming out" in my own way. But if I had become ready to drop the near universal "gay is sick" attitude in favor of the radical post-Stonewall posture of "gay is good," the theatrical powers that controlled the industry—despite the legions of gay people working in it—were not. I grew used to my agent Cindy's repetitive phone calls notifying me that producer X had thought my new play was "brilliantly" written but had been "turned off" by the subject matter. Several other producers urged Cindy to do an "intervention" before it was too late, to "rescue" my talent, make me come to my senses, and shift themes.

My 1971 full-length play *Payments*, centered on the world of gay male hustling, elicited the most shock. "I found the play fascinating," one director told Cindy, "but I don't think it bisects my own life sufficiently to let me bring much to the staging." After Alan Mandell—at the time assisting Jules Irving in running the Repertory Company at Lincoln Center's Vivian Beaumont Theater—had seen a workshop of *Payments* plus an evening of my one-acters, he invited me to lunch to convey similar sentiments. Before twisting the tourniquet, Alan buttered me up: "along with John Guare, I think you're the most promising of the younger playwrights, and I want you to feel that Lincoln Center is available to you." After lunch we stopped off to "say hello" to Jules, who reiterated his hope that "you'll let me see anything of yours available, since our schedule for next season is wide open."

I was puzzled. They'd seen, read, and liked my stuff, were asking to see more of it, and yet weren't inviting me to help fill their "wide open" schedule. What gives? Mandell came clean at a second lunch. Having seen my long one-acter *The Electric Map*, he solemnly told me,

"I thought you were on the verge of doing a 'profound' play, but then when I read *Payments* I was dismayed to see that what you've chosen to pursue is not the interaction of past and present suggested by the Civil War theme in *The Electric Map*, but rather the homosexual subtext in the quarrel between the two brothers. I think you've made the wrong choice, but recognize it might have been a necessary one. I hope you've written that phase out and can now move on." I thanked him for his interest and concern—and presumed that was that.

But to my surprise, I got a call a few weeks later from a member of Mandell's staff (I'll call him Kenneth) urging me to submit some of my one-acters for a possible production at Lincoln Center's new Exploration series. I did so promptly. Soon thereafter, Kenneth called a second time and, after forty-five minutes of hemming and hawing, told me that "the management" felt that my one-acters were "too good, too mature and authoritative" for the Explorations project. Still, he and Mandell were willing to submit them to Jules Irving "as a candidate for the fourth Forum production," which remained unfilled. Knowing that I was a member of New Dramatists, he suggested that I book a production slot there in case Irving's verdict was negative.

In other words, another turn on the merry-go-round. I told Kenneth that I resented Jules and Allen repeatedly telling me how much they admired my work—and repeatedly deciding, after repeated dangles, that they couldn't find room for it. "You'll do endless productions of *Mary Stuart*," I told him, "but won't take a chance on contemporary American playwrights you *claim* to admire." The New Dramatists, I said, "has been good to me and I don't want to reserve precious space on their schedule and then leave it vacant at the last minute." I made it clear that I'd very much like a Lincoln Center production, but I needed a firm answer one way or another: "The next best thing to a 'yes' is a 'no.'" Misplaced bravado? It didn't feel that way at the time. But all these years later, with a number of my plays still at the bottom of a chest of drawers, I'm less sure. In any case, that was that. I had no further word from Kenneth, Allen, or Jules, and a year later Jules resigned his post at Lincoln Center.

My one-acters did find somewhat more favor than my full-length plays, possibly because their content was less overtly homosexual. They got assorted readings, workshops, and marginal productions, and actors like Bob De Niro (not yet super famous) and Bill Macy were even willing to come over to my apartment to take part in reading aloud a play I'd recently completed. It was one of three due to be shown (with the overall title *Dudes*) first at New Dramatists in January 1972 and then that summer at the John Drew Theater in East Hampton (with Edward Albee coproducing). Each of the three plays centered on an unconventional young man in his early twenties, and De Niro wanted to be triple cast in all three roles. At which point in telling my "De Niro story," I can always count on a jaw-dropping reaction along the lines of "What?—don't tell me you said no?!" Alas, I did—even though De Niro, in an effort to persuade me of his range, took me back to his apartment after the reading to look at the portfolio of character roles he'd already played. Impressed though I was with his chameleon-like talent, I felt I had to tell him (he was then in his thirties) that I thought the stretch was too great! *Not* one of my more astute judgments . . .

In the early '70s, one or several of my one-acters did get performed at places as varied as the Actors Studio, the Manhattan Theatre Club, the Dorset summer theater, and Tambellini's Gate. But publishers seemed to like my work more than theatrical producers did, in part, perhaps, because they tended back then to be less commercially minded. In the '70s three separate publishers issued volumes of my plays: Dial's *The Memory Bank*, Dutton's *Male Armor*, and Little, Brown's *Visions of Kerouac*. In contrast, no producer offered a full-scale production, though there were a few close calls.

I mostly had to settle for workshops. Since few of them pay their actors and since the scripts are performed only once or twice before actual audiences, the available pool of talent is limited. Additionally, I often came away from auditions feeling that the actresses—even from my unglandular perspective—were more striking and talented than their male counterparts. Moral? I can't even begin to think of one, given the way my right eye for talent and my left eye for pulchritude refuse to align.

At any rate, when we were casting for a New Dramatist production of *Payments*, we auditioned endlessly for the leading role of Bob, which called for an athletic young stud as physically magnetic as he was emotionally evasive. Several hustlers I knew would have been ideal in the role—two or three were even actors—but I decided that mixing my several worlds was not a wonderful idea.

Desperate, I called my friend Joe Chaikin (who headed up the Open Theater) and got the address of Ray Barry, a troupe member whose erotic charms I'd earlier noted. Barry, I decided, would be perfect as Bob, and I dashed down to his apartment with a script. After reading only a few pages, he declined: the material "isn't," he said, "my cup of tea." Big surprise. We finally had to give the role to "Ted," an inexperienced twenty-one-year-old still studying at the American Academy of Dramatic Arts. Alas, the closer we came to performing before an audience, the more Ted froze. The material terrified him; instead of "emotional evasion" we got one-dimensional ice. A mummified Bob, devoid of sexual *heat*, made it impossible to read him as a sexual magnet, which ruined the play's central dynamic. The one marginally interested producer disappeared into the night.

I might add, as an aside, that ordinarily I found the process of casting a play enjoyable, though I doubted if it was good for my character. Even when auditions yielded little talent, I took pleasure in hearing my words read aloud (and sometimes got ideas for changing them). I also enjoyed the unequal power differential at play and, as a subdivision of that, the eagerness of all those humpy twenty-five-year-old males to win my approval—a situation somewhat comparable to the power dynamic of university teaching, and quite different from the more routinized exchanges, not to mention rejections, of daily life. I knew that "holding the reins" wasn't good for me, and I did my best not to exploit the position, but shit—who could not enjoy all those beautiful eyes batting at you?

Let me immediately add, even at the risk of further extending this rambling sidebar, that in more than five decades of teaching I've never had sex with a student. Lord knows I've found any number of them physically attractive through the years, but in only one instance—long after the student had graduated—did he and I make a single, stumbling attempt. With "Rich," another ex-student with whom I'm still in touch, we talked—and talked—about whether we did or didn't want to proceed from affection to sex, but never did. The content of what we talked about instead—this would be in the mid-'70s—was rooted in the ethos of the times and for that reason might be worth recounting.

After graduating from Princeton, Rich had gone to live in a commune, and from there had enrolled in graduate school. Unsettled and disgruntled, he stopped by my apartment in Manhattan one day to see, as he put it, "if anybody in his life was still there." We spent a long afternoon together, went to yoga class, walked, ate, and talked and talked. Rich told me for the first time that he'd earlier had sexual fantasies about me and that one night when he'd stayed over at my Manhattan apartment had hoped we'd sleep together, though he'd never had sex with a man. In the upshot, he hadn't made a move, perhaps sensing that I wouldn't be responsive. Talking more about it, we agreed that neither of us felt any significant lust for the other, though we both did want more physical affection, more hugs—which we again agreed could conceivably, but no more than that, eventuate in sex, though it would be a mistake to push it.

And that, I thought, was that. Yet on a subsequent overnight visit, much to my surprise, Rich pushed overtly for sleeping in the same bed and having sex. It seemed clear to me that some sort of displacement was going on—that sex was *not* what he wanted (nor did I)—and I suggested talk rather than action. I pointed out to him that he'd pushed for sex right after he'd finished telling me about his recent breakup with his current girlfriend, and what bad shape he was in emotionally. I said I thought he needed solace, not sex, and added, in the gentlest way I could, that I simply didn't feel lust toward him. Weeks later he insisted that we give it a try; in the upshot, he was unable to get hard—and apologized.

In all the long years of friendship that have followed, we've never again attempted to have sex, nor has either of us "achieved" bisexuality.

Back in the late '60s and early '70s, under the sway of the countercultural nostrum that we both strenuously bought into at the time, we thought it imperative to "unblock" our "residual puritanism," the "one-sided" sexuality (me entirely gay, Rich entirely straight) that was preventing us from reacting to *individuals* rather than genders. We viewed "exclusivity"—being *only* gay *or* straight—as the enemy, the pathology. During the height of the Age of Aquarius fifty years ago, I once jotted down my fantasy definition of what constituted an ideal sexuality: "the one free-est from hang-ups, guided only by the fluidity of desire . . . one endlessly spontaneous, unpatterned; no return to known comforts, no reliance on previous formulations." Even back then I sensibly added, "It's a foolish fantasy because insistent on incompatibles: perfect balance plus continuous change." It was a young man's fantasy. Today I'd more likely characterize it as "giving nihilism a utopian gloss."

Where Rich and I differed by the mid-'70s was that I, at forty, felt more confirmed in my core patterns than did Rich, still in his mid-twenties. By the mid-'70s I'd come to doubt whether countercultural models for optimal living would hold up any better than had the prior insistence on, say, lifetime heterosexual monogamy. I was less convinced that there was any natural (if blocked) progression from men freely hugging other men to yearning to suck their cocks, or that the progression had to take place before caring could be certified. I'd grown dubious about whether Norman O. Brown's undifferentiated infant sexuality could long survive the socialization process that *mandated* repression and destroyed the dream of "omnipotent indulgence."

Yet part of me is still tempted in 2023 to argue against what remains the dominant view in the culture (less so among the young) that insists one is *either* gay or straight. Via the mails, I had a brief epistolary debate with Eric Bentley over his assertion in an essay that bisexuality is "almost invariably used as an evasion." That wasn't true, I wrote him, "of most of the bisexuals I know," and added that it seemed weird for "an exclusive homosexual" (me) to "defend the 'naturalness' of bisexuality" and for "the bisexual (you) to defend it only as a form of serial progression"—which had in fact been his own history.

The either/or view, in any case, is based on the unproven essentialist conviction that sexual orientation is biologically determined, and that those who insist they "swing both ways" (a '60s term) are deluded, cowardly—or both. This commonplace argument has thus far failed to convincingly demonstrate that genes and hormones (biology) are determinative in establishing sexual orientation—though some would concede that the early imprinting of sexual desire, regardless of the blueprint, is difficult if not impossible to modify. There's no consensus, however, as to how and when the process of imprinting takes place—nor to what extent the formation of patterns of desire is linked to particular patterns of parenting.

In any case, the earlier theoretical battleground on sexual orientation has given way to an intensive debate about the gender binary, a shift from challenging the either/or nature of sexual desire to a profound assault on the "unnatural" divide that separates traditional maleness from femaleness. The burgeoning trans movement has spearheaded a debate that has thoroughly destabilized fixed notions of "male" and "female"; it views gender not as a physiological given but as a signpost of evolutionary progression.

———

Approaching my fortieth birthday—half a century ago!—I elegiacally wrote that I was feeling "more conscious than usual of time passed, of its fierce, unexpected hold over me, of my not unbounded future. Aging and its angst—a new topic with me." I smile in disbelief. Not solely at the posturing, but at the notion that forty marked a major milestone in decline.

Aging, in any case, isn't a topic that stayed with me for long, certainly not back then. Two sentences later, I switched over to pondering the odds of the new boyfriend and me making a go of it. One side effect of my intense involvement in the gay movement that marked my coming out in 1971 was meeting many more people than I recently had been; there was a sizable uptick in candidates for a "significant" relationship. One boyfriend in a series of them I met at a cocktail party inaugurating the Lambda Legal Foundation. He looked like Chopin, was twenty-seven, and was completing a PhD at NYU. Soft-spoken and affable, he was sensibly modest in his demands on the world, content to tailor his expectations to an intuited sense of their likely fulfillment. Here was an available, peaceable companion. A near paragon. A textbook prospect for undramatic closeness. Not even a suggestion of jagged intensity, not a soupçon of turmoil or tumult. Put another way (my way), he was boringly bereft of amplitude.

We drifted on for a few months—until I finally decided that his unvarying blandness would never give way to a genuine eruption of feeling, and called it quits. I even managed to avoid the standard Long Talk designed to "try and work things out." Instead, I told him that neither of us should have to apologize for who we were or swear to "change" to meet the other's expectations. We were both fine; we simply didn't match—it was nobody's fault.

"Chopin" was but one of several short-term affairs that briefly flourished—then bit the dust. Each for a time seemed full of promise, an "appropriate" partner (meaning *not* yesteryear's undereducated, finely muscled hustler). First up after "Chopin" was the epitome of a conventionally proper mate: a thirty-year-old Jewish accountant who turned out rather quickly not to be appropriate at all. He was capable of precisely two moods: bland, self-absorbed evasion (much smiling, little listening), and rage—whenever I suggested we talk through some disagreement. I lurched away, and into the arms of Stefan, a Romanian political refugee who claimed total devotion, and ended up a disciple of the Reverend Moon.

Next up was a recent graduate of Amherst named Lane, who'd won the "junior Bollinger Prize" for poetry (was there such a thing?), and whose quicksilver changes from tough street kid to winsome fashion model were briefly enticing. The first night he disdained my horniness as "importunate." (He had a large vocabulary.) The second night—just as I was passing out from fatigue—he earnestly announced that I *could* fuck him, that he "wanted to satisfy [me] completely." When I said

I was too tired, he replied haughtily that he never got too tired. The warning signs multiplied: he was too fancy for my taste—he "adored" wine with dinner, crossed his sevens, preferred Irish setters to yellow labs. The third night in bed he patted me patronizingly whenever I started to get passionate, announcing that I was "too tentative, too spasmodic" in my advances, that my "rhythms" were off. Then came the evening he asked me point-blank to take the strap off his pants and "make me do what you want." I decided I didn't want anything.

More likely, I wanted too much. At forty-two, I reminded myself, I was a bit long in the tooth for romantic love—especially since I'd been developing a conveniently jaundiced ideological position deploring such "adolescent" expectations for anyone at any age. In fact, within a few years I'd fall hard for someone, and that relationship would end only when the other man decided that the Catholic Church, unlike transient love, was the safer harbor. Later still, Eli and I instantly clicked on our first meeting and—through the usual ups and downs of a long-term relationship—are, after thirty-five years, still together.

But I didn't know any of that in the early '70s, and the disappointing outcome of my serial affairs brought on a return of the blues. To abort a full-blown depression, I did what I swore I never would again: I consulted a psychotherapist. Stranger still, I found him impressive: he was not at all dogmatic, had no interest in changing my sexual orientation, and was full of unexpected insights. Yet after a few months I stopped seeing him. Among my "camp" reasons was his view that it had been "inappropriate" for Marlon Brando to use the Academy Awards as an occasion to protest the plight of Native Americans. The real reasons, obviously, went deeper. At forty-two I believed less and less in my ability to envision—let alone to work toward—any life goals not already well established. Besides, I was tired of paid sympathy, and of being encouraged yet again—this time benignly, intelligently—to view myself as a collection of symptoms to be ameliorated rather than as a unique individual needing help in actualizing his potential gifts.

Approaching middle age, I'd become far less optimistic about the possibility of reshaping my core being and had finally become convinced that psychotherapy lacked the instrumentalities to achieve basic shifts in personality. When I said all of that to the therapist, he actually—to my surprise—agreed with me. But "some of the structures learned," he added, "may not be synchronic with your preexisting genetic disposition; therapy can help us to see the difference and to eliminate the disharmony."

"Genetic disposition?" I told him I didn't believe in it. Besides, if my core disposition *was* a genetic phenomenon, years of the talking cure hadn't managed to budge it, let alone succeed in eliminating my "learned disharmonies." The "core," I insisted, was too deeply imprinted, was impermeable to other than marginal change. We were at an impasse. He shrugged. We parted amiably.

————————

My major project during the six-year period from 1967 to 1972 was researching and writing the history of Black Mountain. Over the course of those years, I interviewed dozens of people, though personally took to only a few. I was particularly drawn to the writer Francine du Plessix Gray, who'd been a student at Black Mountain. I liked her immediately—her grace, her integrity, her ingratiating combination of elegance and shyness. As is the way in New York, friendship is a sometimes thing, and Francine and I never got to see much of each other. But at lunch one day she referred to writing her book *Divine Disobedience* as a way of avoiding the "mess" of her own life. Perhaps she was settling for fashionable shorthand. I, for one, found it hard to believe that this splendid woman was in (or saw herself as in) a "mess"—but that disbelief, of course, derives from the cliché of "satisfied others."

Some people, I've learned, have a comparable cliché about me: that I've glided serenely through life, with minimal obstacles easily sidestepped, success piled on success. As a subset of that view, people commonly think that I roll with ease from one book to the next. Purportedly I always have a topic on the drawing board, words pour effortlessly out, my agent—a loyal mother hen, a paragon of perspicacity—never has trouble placing one of my completed manuscripts and indeed is invariably besieged with glamorous offers, and I, wallowing in riches, swiftly and effortlessly polish off book number forty-seven, greeted like all its predecessors with a chorus of hosannas. If only. This isn't to suggest that my actual publishing history is anything close to a sob story; many unpublished or minimally published writers would give their eyeteeth if, like me, they could lay claim to a steady run of publications and respectful reviews.

Still, the consensus that I never suffer from serious writer's block ignores the fact that I've frequently mucked about for months trying to settle on the "right" next project. One such period of producing no book-length work in fact ran for more than a decade, though it was partly explained by my absorption during those years with writing and workshopping plays, as well as shifting the focus of my scholarly interest to the new field of LGBTQ+ studies. It's true too that for two extended periods, well-connected and savvy agents Cindy Degener and then Frances Goldin represented me, yet in recent years I've left several agents after brief tryout periods revealed a mismatch, and over the past two decades I've usually represented myself, approaching various acquisitions editors directly. As for advances, when publishing with a university press or a nonprofit left-wing one (home to more than half my books), I got the usual measly $2,000–$8,000, and several times got nothing at all. Only twice—for my biographies of Paul Robeson and Lincoln Kirstein—did I get substantial advances (above $100,000), both times from Knopf.

Once a contract is signed, the process of getting a manuscript into final shape can be a prolonged, edgy struggle—that is, if you're lucky enough to connect with a genuine editor, a dying breed it seems. More often than not I've been left with the *acquisition* editors who signed me up and who are more interested in increasing the number of notches on their belt than in sentence structure. In terms of angst, though, nothing compares to waiting for, and then having to read, the sometimes bizarre reviews that greet a new book. I've never understood writers who insist they don't read reviews of their work and who, above the fray, claim that Time Alone is the only judge that matters (apparently certain that their ultimate elevation to the pantheon is guaranteed).

Which isn't to say that it's less than excruciating to wade through the complaints of reviewers who know in advance (though never admit) that they disapprove of your politics or your sexual orientation and proceed to scan the pages of your new book looking for confirmation of what they hated about your last one. I've never taken solace, as some writers claim to, in mocking the "stupidity" of a negative review or confidently announcing that its bias is transparent to one and all. Being sliced up *right now* has never done a thing for my mood; even if the reviewer is an incompetent fool, I'm aware that many readers will conclude otherwise.

The critical reception of my books over the years divides rather neatly into two contrasting periods: before I became active in the gay movement, and after. My earliest work—traditionally written history dealing with standard subject matter—was greeted with acclaim, culminating in my biography of James Russell Lowell being named a finalist for the National Book Award. But by the late '60s, the world had changed, and me along with it. The Black civil rights movement activated me politically, leading to my first play, *In White America*. It also affected my scholarship, leading me to challenge (in *The Antislavery Vanguard*) the consensus view among historians that the abolitionists had been meddlesome fanatics who, in the pre–Civil War words of Daniel Webster, "bound the slave's chains more tightly than before." To the contrary, I argued, far from being irresponsible malcontents, the abolitionists had been the ethical barometer of their generation, the few Americans of their day who were clear sighted and fearless enough to attack head-on the monstrosity of human slavery.

Ironically, though, we've rehabilitated the antislavery cause without—in the public mind, at least—rescuing its champions from the one-dimensional role of "hero." The more prominent the reputation, it sometimes seems, the more likely the individual will disappear under a simplistic label, with complicated figures like William Lloyd Garrison being buried under an easily digestible cliché. Maybe that's what fame comes down to: the substitution of a single characteristic or action for the unsalvageable intricacy of the whole person. In lusting after fame, it's tempting to say, one lusts after obliteration.

Like so many others initially radicalized by the Black struggle, my activism soon branched out to question other established pieties and institutions. By the late '60s I'd developed an extended critique of the structure and methodology of university education, with its automatic deference to the purported expertise of an authority figure—the professor—who graciously condescends to pass on to the properly passive student the received wisdom of the ages, the wisdom itself unquestioned. The university classroom, I began increasingly to argue both in print and in the way I destructured my own seminars, needed to democratize—to scrutinize authority and to generate questioning citizens rather than, as currently, dutiful parrots.

I also began to view with increasing skepticism the traditional practices and pretensions of historical study itself. Over and again, I argued that the inescapable paucity of historical evidence, in combination with the historian's inevitable subjectivity in evaluating it, demands that we "come clean" about the incomplete, tentative conclusions we draw. Paradoxically, we can also be more forthright in claiming for historical study a unique virtue. The very limitations of evidence, along with the inherent personal bias we bring to our evaluation of it, are potentially a singular strength. An honest admission of the strictures of historical study inescapably reveals that our view of the past, rather than being a body of absolute truth that remains unchanged through time, always reflects the values of the period that produces it. Of all the social sciences, the study of history is particularly well suited to teaching the lessons of limitations and humility: we, too, will be only fractionally remembered, will become mere fragments barely visible in the blinding dust storm. That distinctive, if melancholy, feature of historical study strikes me as perhaps its primary value, though far too often historians defeat that potential by drawing—as we do in ordinary life—confident conclusions from what in truth is woefully incomplete and contradictory evidence.

By the mid-'60s, I became active in the mounting protest against the Vietnam War. In addition to sending off a set percentage of my income every month to antiwar and civil rights groups along with left-wing publications, I also signed a "complicity statement" in support of those refusing the draft (swallowing hard over the section warning that "your signature could lead to five years in prison and a $10,000 fine"), joining as well those pledging to withhold their federal taxes—though my own first attempt proved something of a farce when it turned out that I was due to get a refund and had no tax bill to renege on.

Dick Poirier, the literary critic who'd become my closest friend, thought all three sorties nonsensical, even unproductive, though he strenuously opposed the war as well. He pointed out to me that tax refusal was possibly the least effective protest available. First of all, he said, it wouldn't work: I had a salary that could be attached. Besides, the gesture, confined as it was to fringe groups, would go unreported, thereby exerting zero pressure on the government. Finally, Dick reminded me that the government had retaliatory powers that were both extensive and subterranean, all but guaranteeing the kind of harassment that would disable me from carrying on other activities, including antiwar ones— not to mention the fact that the FBI wouldn't have to turn over many rocks before they found enough material regarding my "degeneracy" to disgrace me publicly, and possibly lead to the loss of my professorship. Though Dick unnerved me, I went ahead—ineptly, as it would turn out—and also became active in the antiwar group REDRESS, spending one whole night in jail after getting arrested during a sit-in on the Senate floor.[6]

Along with increasingly writing articles against the war ("Vietnam and American Foreign Policy," etc.), I wrote in these years on a wide range of topics—"Black Power and the American Radical Tradition," "On Misunderstanding Student Rebels," "The Relevance of Anarchy"— that appeared in a variety of publications, including the *Village Voice*, the *Nation*, the *New Republic*, the *Evergreen Review*, *Liberation*, and the *Atlantic Monthly*. Enough of my political essays had accumulated for Random House in 1969 to publish them as a book, *The Uncompleted Past*.

During the late '60s a considerable number of Americans came to sympathize with the broad critique of American values then agitating the body politic. Far from being widely denounced for my views, I was—as the Random House imprimatur attests—widely praised. Invitations to speak and write arrived from the four corners; even the *New York Times* let me know that anytime I felt like doing a book review for them, all I had to do was ask, as long as I wasn't personally acquainted with the author.

Then, following the Stonewall riots in 1969, I turned another corner, into a neighborhood far less inhabited and where most of the store-fronts were shuttered. Increasingly and publicly, I began to question the assumptions that had long equated homosexuality with pathology—and for years had kept me in determined pursuit through psychotherapy of a "cure." By 1971 I'd junked that whole misguided enterprise, come out publicly, gotten strenuously involved in the emergent gay movement—and was rather precipitously dumped by the heterosexual cognoscenti.

It took years in fact for the news fully to sink in that my once-crowded dance card had become conspicuously bare—that invitations from the straight world to write an article, review a book, sit on a panel, or give a talk on *nongay* topics relating to race, culture, politics, and theater declined in tandem with my deepening involvement with gay liberation. A slew of offers were withdrawn: PBS dropped its invitation to write a play about the life of Emma Goldman, a near-finalized contract to make a movie based on *In White America* disintegrated, the actor Harris Yulin never got back to me after initiating a possible collaboration on a documentary about Dan Ellsberg, and the tentative suggestion that I write a film to be shown at the Democratic convention had no follow-up. I did finish *Mother Earth*, my play about Emma Goldman, but a day later—literally—PBS withdrew from the project, informing me that the White House had become upset about the station's "radical" programming, and since *Mother Earth* was "the *most* radical" item on the agenda, it had to be canceled.

Not one to pull in my horns, my involvement with the fledgling gay movement accelerated, and I also restarted my long-standing project, begun in 1967, to write the history of the experimental Black Mountain community. I'd recently put that project on hold, dissatisfied with my inability to capture a prose style that did justice to Black Mountain's unorthodox ways. The second time around proved more satisfying: my distanced academic stance gradually morphed into a more subjective, emotionally nuanced engagement with the community's story.

Contributory to the shift was the near simultaneous workshops I'd been doing on several of my plays; the theatrical emphasis on emotional immediacy and direct engagement energized my prose, along with my growing conviction that subjectivity was an unavoidable ingredient in any attempt to reconstruct historical events—a truth that needed to be embraced, not suppressed. In retackling *Black Mountain* I made a conscious effort to demonstrate how historical reconstruction inescapably involves the dynamic intersection between the story and the storyteller—and should be openly revealed and embraced.

One significant result of adopting a more personal tone when dealing with historical material was my coming out within the pages of the Black Mountain book itself. A particular episode in the community's history all but mandated the decision. One evening in mid-June 1945, Bob Wunsch, who taught drama at Black Mountain, was arrested while having sex in his car with a marine. Such "crimes against nature" at the time carried a mandatory prison sentence in North Carolina, but some of Wunsch's influential friends in the Asheville area interceded with the judge and he was let off with a suspended sentence. Though Wunsch hadn't had sex, or tried to, with anyone at Black Mountain, he became an instant pariah. It was strongly hinted that he should resign immediately, and he did. The very night of his release from jail, as he went up and down the stairs packing his belongings in his car, not a single member of the community came forward to offer help or to express regret. Wunsch was allowed to steal away silently in the middle of the night, without an embrace or a word. At the close of my narration of the incident, I appended these lines in the book:

> It's hard to think well of a place that could cooperate as fully as
> Black Mountain did in an individual's self-destruction—indeed

to have assumed it as foreclosed. But perhaps I exaggerate—a function of my own indignation as a homosexual, a potential victim. It may well be that Wunsch would have had it no other way. And it may well be that communities, no less than individuals, are entitled to their aberrations.

When the book appeared in 1972, a number of reviewers leaped on that paragraph with barely disguised glee. The *New York Times* reviewer dismissed my coming out as a vaguely unclean bit of business, "merely" confessional, a "tendentious" personal intrusion at odds with a scholar's obligation to remain detached. The academic journals were more emphatic still: "Duberman," one review concluded, "has thrown the cardinal principles of historical writing to the wind by letting himself get 'personally involved' with his subject."

The favorable critical reception given my earlier books gave way to a much more muted mix, with moral outrage a prominent new ingredient. Probably the most surprising—and hurtful—of the negative reviews was the James Leo Herlihy (*Midnight Cowboy*) piece in the *Village Voice*. Jim was a friend who'd been a student at Black Mountain, had never concealed the fact that he himself was gay, and had been the very person who'd originally urged me to do a book about Black Mountain. Yet in his review Jim sternly proclaimed that "what I want is for each of us to mind his own sexual business, historians included."

A number of prominent reviewers—preeminently Edgar Z. Friedenberg in the *New York Review of Books* and Judson Jerome in the *Saturday Review*—did write glowing reviews, but it was the homophobic ones that stuck in the craw. I hadn't, of course, expected reviewers to ignore my coming out, since I myself had provided the information and had intended it to have impact. But I had hoped it would be discussed in the spirit in which I'd finally, agonizingly, decided to include it—as a function of my enlistment in the gay liberation struggle and, as well, of my conviction that historians must *openly* interact with the events they describe—must "come clean" about the inescapable subjectivity inherent in writing about the past. All of which was perhaps too grand and high-minded—and more than a little naive.

From this point on, I became vocal and active in the burgeoning gay movement. In the immediate post-Stonewall years, my political activism had remained focused on protesting the war in Vietnam, and until 1971 I did little more than stick a toe into the two New York City gay organizations—the Gay Liberation Front and the Gay Activists Alliance—that arose in the immediate aftermath of the Stonewall riots. But after coming out publicly in *Black Mountain*, I rapidly joined up, helping in 1972 to found both the Gay Academic Union and the National Gay Task Force; I was particularly active for five years as a board member of the Task Force. Later, in the mid-'80s, I came up with the idea of creating a university Center for Lesbian and Gay Studies (CLAGS). I thought the time was ripe, that enough new scholarship had accumulated to justify the legitimization and encouragement of gay studies. CLAGS would prove a tougher sell—first at Yale, then at CUNY—than I'd anticipated, and it wasn't until 1991, after we'd jumped through multiple hoops and survived a rampage of internal squabbling, that CUNY's Board of Trustees would finally agree to the establishment of CLAGS as an official center at the Graduate School. (More on CLAGS shortly.)

Up through the '60s, like many gay people, I'd internalized the going view of homosexuality as pathology, and rarely challenged the corollary: that I was disordered, second rate, unworthy. Ironically, until I came out, and *unlike* many homosexuals, I was seen as a standard-issue White, middle-class male—the essence of normality, the embodiment of privilege. Nor had I been notably discriminated against, neither legally persecuted nor socially ostracized. Though a nonpracticing Jew, I'd never felt that opportunity was closed off to me, advancement barred, or personal contact shunned. My gender, race, and class had always been apparent (and approved); my sexual preference had *not*—that is, until I chose to announce it.

Many closeted homosexuals *have* been more readily visible—in gait, gesture, voice, whatever—*have* suffered discrimination in housing, education, and employment, while also experiencing daily belittlement and aggravation. As have all Black Americans, many Jews, and most women. To the degree they've been able, like me, to "pass," many sexual deviants have felt less discrimination than have other minorities—though not, however, necessarily less oppression. The effort that goes into "passing"—into escaping detection—itself derails inner confidence, saps self-possession.

In becoming active in the gay movement, I wasn't fully aware of the likely consequences—for example (as I've already mentioned), no longer being asked to write for the various mainstream media to which I'd previously had access. In their eyes, and despite my prior left-wing credentials as a widely published "public intellectual," my homosexuality disqualified me from objectivity on that subject—and made me unfit to comment on any other. It was only as an "out," active "gay liberationist"—someone pleading a cause and not expected to be an impartial witness (yet still useful as a convenient target)—that I was now called on for an opinion.

A case in point was the nationally televised *David Susskind Show*. When the host's handlers decided to do a segment on "gay liberation," they invited me up for a preliminary discussion of what sorts of things I might want to talk about—a kind of pre-interview. It was not a success. The Susskind people grilling me instantly flared when I suggested that homosexuals just *might* have light to cast on such general matters as monogamous lifetime pair-bonding; two of the staff members reacted to the suggestion as if I'd set off a stink bomb. Their condescension had a familiar ring. It was that old "liberal" refrain: "We *may* let you join us, in whole or in part, but you have nothing of interest to tell us about our own lives." Their attitude typified the kind of "public service" broadcast that trashes the victim in the guise of exploring his plight. I told them I wanted no part of it, that I had no confidence the subject would be treated with respect or in depth, and I had no wish to serve as part of that week's titillation.

Within the gay movement itself, the same sort of refrain sometimes sounded: differences of opinion were sometimes dismissed out of hand rather than fully and considerately aired. This wasn't exactly surprising, since the so-called gay community, unified in its defense of same-sex love and lust, was otherwise riven by divisions of race, class, and gender. When anger erupted, say, over men dominating discussion, it was often expressed directly, but on other issues resentment would usually appear in disguised form. Much later, for example, when we were debating various matters attendant on establishing the Center for Lesbian and Gay Studies (CLAGS), I found myself, as executive director, being denounced directly not for being male or White (though I was decidedly resented in some quarters for both) but instead for attending either too few subcommittee meetings ("as director you need to keep abreast of *everything* that's going on") or too many ("you're trying to concentrate all power in your own hands"). *Some* secondary grounds were always available for challenging primary objections that couldn't be comfortably addressed—like race or class. I thought I'd freely acknowledged my privileged upbringing, yet some folks on the CLAGS board continued to feel that I overlooked the actual depth of that privilege. I took comfort in the fact that at the same time a number of *conservative* gay White men were hotly denouncing me—to the university authorities, no less—as a far-left zealot, even a confirmed Marxist.

Still, the benefits resulting from becoming politically active in the early '70s far outweighed the drawbacks. Long schooled in apologetics, I now relished the emphasis on self-affirmation. Where solitude had been my chosen state, I was now unstoppably busy—raising money, planning conferences, traveling widely to spread the good tidings. I met gobs of intriguing people who, given my stay-at-home habits, I never would have otherwise known. As an out gay man, I found that people would often turn to me for advice, or to guiltily explain their own *inability* to come out, or to share their harrowing personal experiences, both past and present.

Their stories were poignant and varied. A sociologist wrote to me from a college in the Midwest to say that while he admired me for coming out, he himself "could not make public what you have made public since I have chosen to go the route of having a family about which I am deeply fond." I assured him that I understood, that our circumstances were different, and that both our choices suited our needs. A woman who taught at a college in Wisconsin expressed her eagerness to follow my example, yet wrote me that she felt hesitant. Responding, I told her that I too had vacillated before making the move and urged her to wait until she felt ready. "It's hard for me, even in retrospect, to understand the motives behind my own decision," I told her. "An 'accumulated urgency' is about the best way I can put it—urgent for self-acceptance—and for expressive necessities as a writer."

I stressed, though, that I'd acted from "a protected position": there seemed little chance, given the security of tenure and a long list of publications, that I was risking serious repercussions. But, I added, I would certainly not generalize from my own situation. "This is New York," I wrote her, "and I don't think it's merely provincial to feel that New Yorkers tend to be more enlightened than even big city dwellers elsewhere. Maybe I underestimate mid-America, but my guess is that a national referendum would at the least deny us the right to teach." That advice may today sound unduly cautious, but in the early '70s comparatively few people had come out and there had been a number of university firings. One college president was stupid enough to put his reasons up front, declaring openly that he did not want "a known homosexual" teaching the impressionable young. The National Gay Task Force (on whose board I continued to sit) won that case—but in those early days a win was rare.

I especially prized the phone call I got one day from New York mayor John Lindsay's former health commissioner, Howard Brown. He said he'd been "inspired" by my coming out, wanted to do the same, and asked to talk. We hit it off instantly and that first afternoon talked for hours, and soon became good friends. He told me that he'd had a serious heart attack, very much doubted if he'd live to be an old man (he in fact died a mere year and a half later, at age fifty), and wanted to use the time remaining to work for gay rights. Soon after our meeting, Howard came out—an event featured on the front page of the *New York Times*—and then, in the fall of 1972, he combined forces with Bruce Voeller, Nath Rockhill, and Ron Gold to form the National Gay ("and Lesbian," tellingly, was added only later) Task Force.

Howard's death from a heart attack early in 1975 came as a shock. I hated it when people said how "glad" they were that he'd completed his book (*Familiar Faces, Hidden Lives*) or that he'd "done everything he had wanted to do." What crap, I thought. As if death ever catches us "completed." The brouhaha that developed over Howard's memorial service made me feel still worse. NYU, where he sometimes taught, announced that it would hold a memorial service for him—as did the gay community. The "competition" infuriated the straight male brass at NYU, and they announced their intention to boycott the gay event. I went to both memorials, and found the NYU service repellent. Five White men spoke—no student, no woman, no person of color—and the three straight speakers ran true to form: desiccated spiels, résumés about their own accomplishments, point-scoring at Howard's expense. Only one of the three expressed any feeling for Howard the *person*. If any proof was needed that the gay community had to do its own memorializing of Howard's sweet, gently exuberant soul, the NYU event provided it.

I may have been overdoing the indignation. Euphoric at finding a political outlet for grievances long stored up, I could occasionally shoot from the hip. Something of that dynamic may well have been at play in my interactions with Susan Sontag, though at the time, still enveloped in missionary zeal, I didn't think so. Over the years I tried to enlist Susan in the "cause," asking her to lend her name or presence to this or that gay fundraiser. She never turned me down—she simply never responded. Part of the reason may have been that she became convinced early on—so she told our mutual friend Joe Chaikin, director of the

Open Theater—that I didn't like her. That came into the open one evening when Susan unexpectedly joined Joe and me for a movie. After it, Joe managed to whisper to me, "Susan thinks you dislike her," and he appealed to me "to make things right."

From my point of view Susan and I had never seen enough of each other for anything to have gone wrong between us, though I'd taken note that whenever we did meet, her reactions to me never ran much more of a gamut than rude to aloof. Anyway, to please Joe I gave it one more shot. Joe had told me that *touching* "is the only communication she'll believe."

"*Sontag!*—you're kidding!"

No, he wasn't. So following instructions I gently touched and slightly caressed Susan's arm. It worked, at least momentarily. Susan almost immediately began talking about the "inexplicable" tension she felt between us, and how we should make some effort to get to know each other without intermediaries. She was about to set off for the summer, but suggested we get in contact when she returned in the fall. I was startled and moved: the ice princess had become a forlorn waif. But come fall, she transmogrified back into the same detached and chilly Susan of yesteryear, which I uncharitably ascribed to my having shown compassion for Susan the waif.

I had a similarly truncated but much pleasanter relationship with Ned Rorem. We'd first met in the '60s but were always too dissimilar through the years to seek each other out. It didn't help that on one occasion, when invited to Ned's apartment for a dinner celebration of his birthday, I appeared on the wrong night—the party had taken place the evening before. (Ned's brow furrowed at the unexpected sight of me, but his essential good nature—or was it timidity?—quickly blanketed his annoyance.) On the rare occasions when we were alone together, we chatted away amiably (mostly surface gossip), Ned insisting, for example, that Tennessee Williams's *Memoirs* were "unreliable."

Though already in his early fifties during the brief period we occasionally met, Ned in appearance and manner still threw off glimmers of the gaudy youth. But I was always struck at how little actual vanity he

had (due, perhaps, to his solid Quaker background). His campy comments about other people—pervasive enough—weren't aimed at hurting them but rather at getting you to like *him*. Curiously, despite his
having accumulated a lifetime of plaudits, I never sensed much ego in
Ned, and suspected there had never been much. I doubt he'd ever had
enough settled self-regard actually to internalize the abundant compliments thrown his way. He had a real sweetness to him, along with a
certain fragile skittishness. Frank but not forceful, even a touch dainty,
he struck me as essentially a sexless man—there was no weight at all to
his presence; touchingly, he seemed in constant danger of being blown
away. We never became more than distant acquaintances.

An altogether more enlivening example of my new burst of sociability
was Richard Avedon's phone call one day inviting me to an impromptu
lunch at his studio, a former carriage house on the Upper East Side of
Manhattan that was also his home. I hadn't seen him since we were
both arrested during the REDRESS sit-in on the Senate floor to protest
the war in Vietnam, but I'd heard the rumor that he and the director
Mike Nichols were sometime lovers—which, following the death of
both men, has been openly debated.

Nichols wasn't there that day. It was simply me, Avedon, and Luis
Sanjurjo, a gay Harvard-educated lawyer who I'd known for several
years. (He died of AIDS in 1987.) Luis had at one point in a checkered
career been Mike Nichols's executive assistant and had then gone on to
become a literary agent for, among others, Arthur Miller and Tennessee
Williams. Luis had earlier told me that Dick wanted to renew contact
with me, not (as I'd hoped) because I'd come out and he was thinking
about doing the same but simply because he much admired a recent
essay of mine, "An Experiment in Education."

It was a delightful, if somewhat cagey, afternoon, full of mutual
backslapping and gossipy tidbits, including Dick's strange tale that the
night Diane Arbus killed herself, a large *stone-grounded* lamp crashed to
the floor in Avedon's studio (psychic tales having already become the
rage, I feigned a sense of wonderment). As we chatted away, my eyes
kept wandering to the huge, stunningly theatrical photographic panels

that surrounded the walls of Dick's studio. One of the three was the famed portrait of Warhol's Factory, including a nude Candy Darling, penis front and center, as well as Joe D'Alessandro, whom I used to see off and on before the movie *Trash* made him a Warhol superstar. Featured on another panel was a group portrait of the Chicago Eight defendants, their eyes soft and sweet—excepting only Jerry Rubin's angry intensity. A third panel was what Dick called the "War Council," designed to look like a police line-up, with the focus on the sinister, smug-looking Ellsworth Bunker, a leading hawk during the war in Vietnam. Yet another wall highlighted a superb if discomforting portrait of the pianist Oscar Levant, which Dick had shot days before Levant died. Addicted to drugs and often committed to mental hospitals, Levant had once said that "there's a fine line between genius and insanity. I have erased this line." Avedon caught that precise moment.

Though we skirted intimacy (other than Dick and I commiserating over our mysterious bouts of diarrhea), there was no direct reference to being gay. He did say that he'd been separated from his wife for some time and had concluded that he was one of those people "who should always have lived alone." Luis later told me that Dick had long ago decided that he wouldn't allow his sexual orientation to define him, and he stayed determinedly in the closet. Yet he did agree to the news being revealed after his death—as it subsequently was.

On the subject of the "closet," I had, during this brief period of playing the social butterfly, a much less pleasant run-in with Dotson Rader, author of *I Ain't Marchin' Anymore*. We'd first met when he and the actress Ruth Ford came to see an evening of my one-act plays at the New Dramatists, declared themselves "mad" for them, and swept me off to Oscar de la Renta's, where a rather bizarre (to my sheltered scholar's eyes) collection of jet-setters had gathered for drinks and dinner. A few years later I again ran into Dotson and Ruth at a party in their fortress-like Dakota co-op on Manhattan's Central Park West. Ruth looked—nearly walked—right through me, and Dotson only stopped long enough to say, in a tone of aggrieved compassion, that he "disapproved of what I'd been doing lately," that I'd "painted myself into a

corner with 'the homosexual thing'"—then sailed by. I was too astonished at the haughty dismissal to get off a proper reply.

My friend Dick Poirier was also at the party and I told him about the
encounter. Angered on my behalf, and with me trailing in his wake, we
went over to where Dotson was standing and put a few hard questions
to him. Did he think it was possible, I asked, "to get the anti-sodomy
statute off the books in New York without a political movement to
protest it?" Dotson's response was that "those statutes aren't meant
to be used against homosexuals only." Following that inaccurate non
sequitur, he haughtily told us that he disapproved of the entire gay
liberation movement. Though Dick had never been particularly political, Dotson's supercilious tone annoyed him—and when angry, Dick
could be formidable. He told Dotson that his "inauthenticity as a person" accounted for the falsity of his writing. That got Dotson's hands
noticeably trembling—and Dick and I lost stomach for further combat.

I later realized that Dotson may have thought we were hell-bent on
forcing him to come out, which would have likely led to Ruth Ford's
showing him the door. We weren't; publicly "outing" someone, Dick
and I both felt, should be reserved for those right-wingers doing overt
harm to gay people while concealing their own proclivities. Up to the
early '80s and the onset of the AIDS pandemic, comparatively few gay
people had left the closet, and still fewer had become openly political.
In that earlier time Larry Kramer gave voice to what most White male
homosexuals felt, especially among the more privileged, when he openly
scoffed at activism as not "chic." It was certainly not popular. Every year
for fifteen years, starting in 1971, nearly the same small contingent of
gay activists would present a bill to the New York City Council calling
for equality before the law for gay people—and every year it would be
voted down.

Dick also inserted himself into a budding dispute between me and
Norman Mailer, which, tangentially, again involved Dotson Rader. In
that same year of 1974, the new gay magazine *Out* put on the cover
of its first issue a photo of Norman's head fastened onto a facsimile of
the famous shot of a blast of air shooting up Marilyn Monroe's skirt.

The cover was meant to illustrate Andrea Dworkin's article inside the magazine titled "Why Doesn't Norman Mailer Become the Woman He Is?" Norman was not amused and, on the false assumption that I was involved with *Out*, wrote me an angry letter. That led to a mini-correspondence in which I lowered the heat, told him I wasn't connected to *Out*, and suggested that we both get back to work.[7]

Dick knew Mailer far better than I did (he'd written a book about him) and, licking his lips, joined the fray. He pointed out to Norman that his "Mailer book is dedicated to Marty. And it might have been supposed that you wouldn't easily believe the worst of him for this if not for any number of other and better reasons, especially on information from a veritable fount of rumor [i.e., Dotson] . . . you probably figured that if you wrote a letter of simple inquiry to Marty this might be construed to mean that you had some doubts, for Christ's sake, about Dotson. So what the hell, send a letter of accusation." Norman responded—with what Dick, in his own reply, characterized as "the prose of an erect spinal column," expressing wonder "why the most lampooned literary figure in America should be so exercised by yet another spoof, and guessed that you'd have been less bothered, if at all, had it appeared on the cover of *Esquire*." Dick then praised my coming out as an "exemplary kind of candor . . . made in the progress and as an inevitable result of the highly innovative kind of history he was writing in the book *Black Mountain*," and closed by contrasting it with the "phoniness" of Dotson's initial attack on me at the Dakota party. After a few more exchanges on all sides, the powder went belatedly dry.

If the Mailer contretemps was mere literary byplay, it did, in a minor way, represent the country's pronounced and ugly swing to the right by the mid-'70s. Los Angeles police chief Ed Davis spoke out publicly *against* extending civil rights to gay people, referring to us as "predatory creatures." The famed Chicago *Daily News* columnist Mike Royko published a piece he called "Banana Lib" about a new organization of "men in love with monkeys" who were suddenly "coming out of the cage" in droves. The Toronto police raided the offices of Canada's leading gay publication, the *Body Politic*; vandals ransacked the feminist Diana Press in Oakland; and Florida governor Reubin Askew—known as a "liberal"—announced that he "wouldn't want a known homosexual teaching [*his*] children."

A low point of sorts occurred when, on March 19, 1976, the Supreme Court (in *Doe v. Commonwealth's Attorney for City of Richmond*) upheld— over Thurgood Marshall's outraged dissent—a Virginia sodomy statute that criminalized "crimes against nature." According to the court, personal privacy did not take precedence over a state's right to regulate morality. I happened to be in DC at the time for a production at the tiny Back Alley Theater of my play *Payments*. Shocked at the decision, I saw it as reflective of a much wider backlash.

Payments, my play about gay male hustling, was an early casualty. Though dozens of people were being turned away from every performance—even though Back Alley had no money for advertising and no staff to accept advance reservations—the management made an abrupt decision to close the run. The *Washington Star*, which had taped an interview with me, canceled its publication with the offhand remark that "we've printed too much of 'that stuff' lately." As well, the gay movie theater in DC abruptly shut its doors, several gay bars were raided, and I heard a rumor via the activist Frank Kameny that "the big discos are next." A friend called to tell me that back in New York "Brad," someone I knew slightly, had gone out on his very first call as a male escort, ended up in the arms of a cop, and was then jailed. The charge was "prostitution involving a minor" (which Brad was not—nor, certainly, was the customer). One day later, the Indiana state legislature, which had earlier dropped "sodomy" from its criminal statutes, voted to reinsert it. The furtive '50s were returning with a vengeance.

Meanwhile, the all-night dance parties continued uninterrupted on Fire Island, its participants resolutely inactive on behalf of their own civil liberties. The prosperous contingent of career-oriented gay people mistakenly equated their individual success with general toleration, refusing to understand that *selective* toleration is itself a convenient blind for passionate distaste. With friends like that, the gay movement needed no enemies. Which isn't to say that overt enemies weren't plentiful, nor that they felt inhibited about loudly voicing their enmity. On TV, Matt Troy, the Queens Democratic leader (who later went to jail on charges of larceny), scornfully compared homosexuals to "lepers." Bill Buckley, the acidic aristocrat, wrote a vicious "let's face it" column, declaring "they're sick"—and then a few years later, after the AIDS plague had descended, strenuously advocated branding gay men who tested positive on their buttocks.

In the early '70s on the East Coast, both post-Stonewall activist organizations—the Gay Liberation Front and the Gay Activists Alliance—had by the end of 1973 gone belly-up. By then, the Gay Academic Union (GAU), which I'd helped to start, had been taken over by a small retrograde group of gay White male conservatives who were openly hostile to feminism and deplored as "Marxist" any political position left of Barry Goldwater. By the late '70s, Wayne Dynes, a professor of art history and a leading spokesman for gay male conservatives, was denouncing GAU in the *Advocate* (the national gay magazine)—while deploring the prominent feminist quarterly *Quest* as "shlock Marxism" and its leading theorist Charlotte Bunch as "virulently man-hating." When I wrote a letter of protest to the *Advocate* (I was a friend and admirer of Charlotte), Dynes in response urged me to "examine the sources of your own gallantry towards women (whom by your own acknowledgement with which you will not sleep)."[8]

Only the National Gay and Lesbian Task Force and Lambda Legal Defense, both of which I'd had a hand in founding, were left standing, though hardly flourishing. When the Task Force sent out a fundraising appeal to gay doctors calling on them to help support the move within the American Psychiatric Association to remove homosexuality from the list of "psychiatric disorders," we got almost no response. I got an equally indifferent reaction when I tried to raise money for *Gay Sunshine*, the lively, daring West Coast political and artistic journal edited by Winston Leyland. I personally sent a fundraising letter soliciting help for *Gay*

Sunshine to some two dozen prosperous people I knew (mostly in the arts), thinking friendship alone might mandate a gift. No way. Only four of them responded at all, and only Dick Poirier actually sent in a donation. The other three ranged from lukewarm to hostile. Arthur Laurents (*West Side Story*) was straightforwardly blunt: "I can't share your enthusiasm for GAY SUNSHINE . . . [it] seems rather provincial . . . no sense of humor, no depth, no style, no illumination, etc."

———————

I used to commonly hear from people who themselves identified as *either* gay or straight that bisexuality was a fiction, a self-description employed by those either too cowardly or too confused to take on a burdensome label. It's a debate that goes *way* back: to see homosexuality and heterosexuality as *in opposition* to each other is a core feature of Judeo-Christian ideology, and was even the dominant view in the various liberation movements that arose in the late '60s. I vividly recall that when some of us in 1973 formed the Gay Academic Union and were planning its inaugural conference, "The Universities and the Gay Experience," a heated argument broke out about whether to include bisexuals. I myself had early on been drawn to the countercultural models of gender fluidity and pansexuality, though I was unable to incorporate them to any significant degree into my own life. I lamented the paralysis of will (if that's what it was) that prevented me from joining the polymorphous parade, and chalked up my behavioral rigidity to the deep imprinting inflicted on me during my formative years of traditional views on gender, sexuality, and romance.

Still, if not a participant, I *had* become a partisan of the countercultural attempt to destabilize standard notions of gender and sex, and thought it exemplified the brave new world that seemed about to come into being. And I said as much during the prolonged debate within GAU, arguing against those who denounced bisexuality as a fake identity, primarily adopted to avoid the onerous repercussions of coming out publicly as gay. As one prominent feminist put it during the GAU contretemps, "I've passed through my bisexual phase. The current pressure to be bisexual should be resisted as a cop-out, as a failure of nerve." She went on to say that anyone who claimed to find a great deal of pleasure from bedding down both men and women was suffering from "lower consciousness," an inability to come to grips with their essential homosexuality. I thought that view patronizing in the extreme, a symptom of *her* refusal to come to grips with her own potential bisexuality. Yet when it came to a vote in GAU, the count went against our side by a 2–1 margin; self-identified bisexuals were *not* formally included in GAU's descriptive literature nor in its official statement of purpose.

Yet over the years evidence has continued to mount that confirms the validity of a bisexual identity—to the point where today, at least among the young, those who openly reveal their romantic and sexual feelings for individuals of both binary genders (and the "nongendered," too) are likely to be greeted with a yawn. And along the way, the "experts" have been overturning any number of assumptions that once supported the denigration of bisexuality as the preserve of cowards and poseurs.

Within just a few years of the debate within GAU, Philip Blumstein and Pepper Schwartz published a wide-ranging study of bisexuality in the *Journal of Social Issues* that included a variety of socioeconomic groups. They reported that 61 percent of the males and 32 percent of the females interviewed recounted some same-gender sexual experience. At nearly the same time, the sociologist Laud Humphreys published *Tearoom Trade*, his report on casual male-male sexual encounters in such public or semipublic places of assignation as men's rooms. Humphreys found that 54 percent of the men involved were married and, tellingly, he could find little evidence that their marriages were significantly troubled or unstable.

Then, in 1979, Masters and Johnson published *Homosexuality in Perspective*, their study over a twenty-year period of the sexual fantasies of four subject groups: exclusively homosexual men and women, and exclusively heterosexual men and women. Some of their findings were so startlingly contrary to conventional wisdom regarding bisexuality

that Masters and Johnson, staunch defenders of heterosexual monogamy, did their unsuccessful best to downplay them. Their single most
astonishing observation was that in all four groups they found a high
incidence of "cross-preference" fantasies. What made the finding so
explosive was that the heterosexual subjects *in their behavior* were overwhelmingly Kinsey 0 (that is, exclusively heterosexual); during repeated
face-to-face interviews, moreover, they'd described same-gender sex as
"revolting" and "unthinkable." Yet their *fantasies* contradicted their
stated views. The same men and women who vitriolically condemned
homosexuality showed in their uncensored fantasies "a significant curi-
osity, a sense of sexual anticipation" for sex with members of their
own gender.

I, for one, had no trouble at all crediting the Masters and Johnson
data. My own experience (until I settled down in the mid-'80s with my
life partner), included hooking up fairly often with heterosexually married men who were uninhibited in bed and who—with the few I got to
know well—usually described themselves as content in their marriages
and attached to their wives and kids. That was certainly true of my
deep infatuation with at least one married man—I'll call him "Andy."
Ours may not have been a love match but it was surely sexual—and
painfully obsessive.

Andy was a rugged, tattooed short-order cook who I met on the
street, and who lived with his wife in Queens. My politically unsound,
fantasy ideal come to life, Andy had no inhibitions in bed; no one had
notified him that it was contra-macho for him to get fucked or to rim
his partner, that sexual abandonment was for demented faggots. Andy
and I even went dancing one night in a gay disco (it was a first for him),
eyes popping at his bulging muscles, mouths agape at the infatuated
way he nuzzled and kissed me on the dance floor. I could imagine the
comments of the onlookers: "So *that's* what Marty's into: Neanderthal
man, rough trade." Or: "Aha—the E. M. Forster syndrome—university
intellectual living happily ever after with milkman, local cop, lumber-
jack." One acquaintance managed to hijack me long enough to whisper,
"He's a sailor, isn't he?" "No, Phil," I answered with mock severity,

"not everyone with tattoos is a sailor." (This was before tattoos became nearly universal.)

In regard to the "E. M. Forster syndrome," I wasn't so sure myself. The standard explanation then current for a relationship marked by significant differences in age, class, and educational level leaned heavily on unproven assumptions: that the Forsters (or Martys) of the world, fearing intimacy, avoided engaging with men who shared their own background or, more simply, disliked the snobby disdain of fellow Oxbridge types. Social scientists commenting on class disparity (and who themselves live primarily in their heads) will not see, or will claim not to believe, the simple appeal of firm young bodies. They insist instead that the Forsters of the world can only feel comfortable when in a position of socially defined superiority; either that, or they can best fulfill their masochistic wish for "debasement" with a certified tough.

Such views seem to me unduly neat paradigms invented to avoid crediting the straightforward claims of lust (on the older man's part) and the appeal of stepping up in the world or getting a bit of cash (on the part of the younger man). Besides, temperamental affinities can transcend differences in age and class—Christopher Isherwood and Don Bachardy, for example. Andy's enthusiasm for gay disco might come out as "super great" and mine as "marvelous," but the enthusiasm is not only on a comparable level but the result of shared responses (for example, liking or disliking the same songs). Deep compatibilities in, say, how one reacts to music—or to people or to events—can be obscured by surface differences resulting from class indoctrination during childhood. *Differences* in experience, moreover, can—for the adventurous—themselves be a source of attraction. I liked hearing about Andy's mountain-climbing exploits; he liked hearing about my archival discoveries relating to gay history.

Although I may not be drawn to older men whose bodies are going to pot, someone like Andy might eroticize the fact that flab is more likely than muscle to come attached to social status, book knowledge, sophistication, and money. Andy—and in my experience many working-class men—are more comfortable with their bodies, its pleasures and uses, than are middle- or upper-class males, who tend to define their worth instead in terms of verbal and analytical skills. Opposites *do* attract, even if *similarities* provide the glue for lasting commitment. As I've written elsewhere, "To move from temporary infatuation to sustained love may well require the presence of significant 'likenesses.' Opposition gives the spice, similarity the substance." Similarities, however, can exist on levels not gauged by first impressions or summarized by fixating on surface distinctions.

For some of us it's only when looking back that we're able to see a pattern to our erotic life that earlier eluded us, or that at the time we were unwilling or unable to trace. The pertinent questions are simple: What turned us on when we were younger? Is a distinctive pattern discernible early on, and if so does it change through time? Are we, at any age, retrospectively imposing a consistency that never existed, though we insist on it as a way of blaming our younger selves for having been "weirder" than in fact we were, and of comparing our callow youth to what we'd like to think, as we enter the twilight years, is a developmental narrative that ended in sound maturity?

———————————

By the time I'd reached my midforties, I'd pretty much stopped going to gay bars and discos. The odds of finding sex or romance in the hangouts of a youth-oriented subculture weren't good, and my packed schedule left little room for time-consuming mating dances. Nor did the sped-up stops on the orgy circuit—the piers, the trucks, the Anvil, the Mineshaft—appeal; I was too self-conscious, and self-deprecating, about my body. Besides, though disembodied cocks and asses *could* appeal, anonymity wasn't for me usually a turn-on.

Occasionally a friend would insist that I was giving up on the bar-hopping scene too soon, that I was still good-looking and could pass as younger than my years. Now and then I'd also hear that so-and-so found me attractive, but I deflected the compliment with disbelief. If they *had* sent up a signal, my antennae, for some reason, didn't pick it up. Maybe because I'd become a workhorse, and preferred it that way.

I *liked* research and writing, liked being super busy; the process could sometimes be tedious and the isolation painful, but the tangible results were often gratifying. Besides, staying busy depleted my energy, usually leaving little room for brooding self-pity or complaint. The subliminal message I got from being productive was that I *had* to be OK if I was able to function well in a variety of arenas. My self-esteem fed on my ability to juggle scholarship, teaching, playwriting, and political activism.

And relationships? Love affairs? Lasting companionship? Ah—a complicated story. In my twenties I had a five-year relationship that ended only when, with the encouragement of my psychiatrist, I took a teaching offer in another city. For the following two decades a different pattern emerged: a series of short-term affairs interspersed with a deepening involvement during my forties with the hustler scene. Affairs were more emotionally than sexually intense; with hustlers it was the reverse (though several of my most profoundly emotional, if erratic, involvements were with younger men I met through the hustling circuit).

One or two examples should suffice. For short-term affairs, I'll let "John," who I met at a cocktail party, stand in for others. He was a fellow academic completing his doctorate in sociology at CUNY and working days as a computer analyst. He had all the purported qualities for matehood: patient, gentle, sweet, affectionate, loyal. Stated positively, he was affable and contented. Stated negatively, he was alarmingly bland, placid to a fault, difficult to arouse—except sexually.

Peaceable companionship, I told myself, was exactly what I *should* be searching for. But my cock wasn't persuaded; it remained resolutely soft. John was patient, unaccusing. Not me. I told myself—falling back on barnacled Freudian assumptions—that "I become paralyzed at the prospect of a mutuality I claim I want," that "I'm stiff pricked only in pursuit of invulnerability," that "I lament the discontinuity of my sexual and social lives, but run from the peaceable companionship that could combine them," and so on.

With John, after several false starts, strong grass and his enthusiasm for being screwed helped us establish that deplorable sex-role bipolarity that can do wonders for short-term functioning. Temporarily comfortable in my dominance, I was nervously aware that to always play the "top" failed to do justice to my variegated fantasies. John continued to bask contentedly in his "bottom" role, while I fretted increasingly (to myself) about how tedious I found its restrictions. Since neither of us brought up the subject of exclusivity, I decided to work in an occasional hustler to ease the pressure. For a while that worked.

But over time, it became clear that the John in bed and the John out of bed were one and the same: unvaryingly, boringly bland. And pretty smug about it too. Content in the role of "he who gets fucked," he saw no reason to alter our assigned "either/or" roles. And if he sensed *my* discontent with the unvarying scenario, he never commented on it or made any move to modify it. Six months in, I decided to end the affair. Considerate and unaccusatory to the end, John departed with surface pleasantries.

The hustling scene was far more colorful—in a few instances, dazzling and dangerous. In the former category, Dave ranks high in the vaults of memory. I was struck dumb at the first sight of him: muscular, mustachioed, colorful headband wrapped tightly around his forehead, a Woodstock superhero come to life. The sex was so good that we arranged for a rematch a mere two days after first meeting. That second evening, my head *somewhat* cleared, I managed to notice track marks on his arm. Yet denial immediately kicked in. I told myself I was imagining it—his eyes were clear, and he was impressively *present*.

Not so the third time. When I opened the door, Dave was leaning against the archway, his speech slurred. I let him come in, told him he didn't look well, asked if I could help.

"You wouldn't understand, Marty." He managed a wan smile.

"I think I might."

"You're hooked on smack, too?"

"It's not my drug of choice. I take pills to help me sleep."

"Nope, that doesn't qualify." I was amazed at how pulled together he seemed, though more disconnected than during the other times we'd gotten together.

Over the long evening that followed, he told me more of his history. He'd been through three years of assorted detox programs, and at one point had stayed clean long enough to become a "senior coordinator" at Odyssey House, the drug and alcohol rehab center. He said he was desperate to get ahold of methadone—but *without* signing up for a program. He wanted to kick and then "get the hell out of New York," which he was smart enough to know was a dead end for him.

I had a sudden flash: Phillip Hornsby. We'd been friendly in college, had stayed marginally in touch—*and* he ran a clinic in Brooklyn. "There's a chance," I told Dave, "that I can find you some methadone."

The next day I got hold of Phillip, told him Dave's story, apologized for bothering him with it, and (fingers crossed) vouched for Dave's character. Within a few hours Phillip got back to me: he'd gotten Dave into a seven-day ambulatory program in Brooklyn. I was stunned when Dave said he couldn't risk it. That turned out to mean that he "couldn't risk being recognized."

"What do you mean?"

"I escaped from a state involuntary commitment program and the all-knowing computer would nail me in a matter of hours."

I got back to Phillip, who understood and suggested a "proprietary clinic"—an *un*official, pay-as-you-go operation. Phillip, unfortunately, had no names and addresses to pass on and as an alternative suggested a private physician. Apparently, I learned, they could legally detoxify someone, though they could *not* maintain him on methadone.

Yes, I know, I was "acting out" a rescue fantasy that probably said more about my needs than Dave's. Still, after three evenings together I trusted my instinct that he was someone well worth helping. I managed to get the names of several private physicians who did *not* feed into the city computer, but when I called Dave to give him the information, he told me he was feeling much worse and asked if I could let him have twenty-five dollars. I told myself I'd done all I reasonably—or unreasonably—could, yet ended up agreeing that he could come by. I met him outside the building. He was limping and carrying a cane—"stung by a bee," he managed to quip. I gave him the twenty-five dollars and refrained from advice or sentiment. Watching him limp away, I told myself "that was that."

It wasn't. Five days later he called again. He'd been kicked out by the woman he'd been staying with and "needed help bad." He told me he was up to ten bags a day—a fix every two hours—that his leg had become infected from the "bee bite," and that he'd spent the previous night in a doorway. I tried to talk him into seeing one of the doctors I'd lined up or checking into a city hospital. He wouldn't hear of it: "I'd rather die on the street than give up my freedom again." He asked if he could use my pad for a week while he kicked from some black-market methadone he'd scored. He sounded so desperate that I was tempted to say yes, but I managed to stop myself. It was one thing, I told myself, to let my life be ripped up by a close friend, but to let somebody I barely knew do it could only mean that I was more interested in hurting me than helping him. Still, I *liked* him and felt lousy about turning him away. As I watched him hobble down the street on crutches, I came close to running after him—but didn't.

Flash forward three years. Answering the buzzer one day, I opened the door to find Dave standing there. He'd been clean for almost two years, thanks mostly to a guy, he told me, who "made no preachments but simply showed, through his own life, other possibilities for reducing pain." Dave had changed remarkably: the super-macho stud had become almost feminized, his voice up three octaves, his gestures unblocked. He told me that he was now openly bisexual: enjoys sex with men, though "relationships," he said, "are still with women." He'd stopped by because he wanted me to know that he thought of me often during the three years, that the "respect" I'd shown him had been "precious." A rescue fantasy, it turns out, can sometimes actually rescue somebody.

They didn't all end that way. Far from it. Over the years I became emotionally entangled three or four times with rather remarkable men who I originally met through hustling and who I became seriously involved with over a considerable period of time, two of them obsessively so. On the other side of the ledger, only twice did I have unpleasant experiences—not to be confused with sexual disappointments, which were numerous. One of the two incidents involved potential burglary, the other a serious threat to my physical safety.

When an "intermediary" I'll call "Alan" suggested I hook up with "Greg Reese," who was passing through the city, he warned me to "groove on the body and *don't* ask him about his problems." (My reputation as Salvation Nell was apparently spreading.) The warning wasn't quite up to the danger. When Greg rang my doorbell, Dick Poirier happened to be in my apartment. We both silently gasped at what looked to be a prototypical Hells Angel—hulking, tattooed frame, missing teeth, wild eyes, a chain-link belt. After invented introductions all around, Greg started to pace nervously and Dick got up to leave. I walked him to the door and whispered, "Does he strike you as dangerous?" Dick said he doubted it.

When I got back to the living room Greg was still pacing and without prompting started itemizing his problems: eviction, a two-year-old son parked out front with a "woman friend," and their plans to head straight for Arizona. In other words, he had no time to spare. We headed to the shower, where he made the water scalding hot and groaned as he bathed his legs. Then I saw why—they were covered with ugly sores. I was repulsed but knew I had to conceal my reaction. Instead, I "offhandedly" suggested that he might have something contagious, that I'd gladly give him the expected cash but thought we should postpone the scene.

"How much cash?"

"How's thirty dollars?"

"Not enough."

Greg spread his massive arms out from his side, trapping me in the back of the bathroom. I panicked for a second. "Here it comes," I thought. My semiconscious survival mechanisms snapped to attention. Any sort of resistance, I decided (yes, even verbal) would be suicidal.

"OK, sure. If you need more money—sounds like you're in a jam with your son waiting—you're welcome to what I've got."

"How much you got?"

"I think about forty bucks. Come on inside. You can look and see what's in my pants. Whatever's there you can have." (Half a beat.) "And you should do something about that leg infection, man." (Yes, "man" was designed for bonding.) "You got enough on your mind now, what with your boy and all. A beautiful guy like you—you should take care of your health. I think I know the right doctor to send you to."

As I warmed up the paternal bit, Greg gradually subsided. I emptied my pants' pockets in front of him—forty-seven dollars.

"Take it all if you need it. But"—warm smile—"how about leaving a guy something for breakfast?"

He settled for thirty-five dollars, some grass, and Dexamyl. I kept the smooth, concerned rap going nonstop as we dressed, the repressed actor in me busting straight through my terror. Then I deliberately sat down on the couch and casually put my feet up—as if to say I was in no rush to get rid of him. That led to still more talking about his problems, then finally a move toward the door, where he kissed me hard on the lips.

"I'm not a bad guy, man. Next time it'll be free. Get me that doctor. I'll call you tomorrow."

And maybe he wasn't a bad guy—as born in the cradle.

He did call the next day. I explained that my doctor was on vacation and wouldn't be back for two weeks. In the interim, I suggested he go to St. Vincent's outpatient unit.

"I been there. They don't know nuthin'. Said something about parasites. You want me to come by?"

"Not tonight, Greg. I've got an appointment. And tomorrow a houseguest arrives."

"I'll catch you later." Click.

I called Alan and gave him hell. He confessed it was the first time he'd introduced Greg to anyone: "I figured if he *did* turn out to be trouble, you could handle it."

I thanked him for the vote of confidence but said I'd rather not have my talents tested a second time.

"Be careful leaving and entering your building."

"No shit!"

I slept like the dead for ten hours. The next day I felt no after-effects—a tribute either to my nerves or my stupidity.

That wasn't the end of the Greg Reese story.

About a year later, I got word that a sometime friend of mine named Kenny Gordon, who I'd known since our teen years, had been found dead in his bed, strangled with an electric cord. The police were looking for a "Greg Reese"—he was wanted for a string of assaults and murders, all connected to the world of male hustling. I'd not only had my own frightening experience with "Greg," but just ten days before Kenny's death I'd picked up the phone to hear a voice identifying itself as "Chuck Roby." The vaguely speedy, manic cadence sent instant chills through me—the voice was unmistakably Greg Reese. I told him I was busy and pretended to take down his number. He never called back.

———————

The prolonged, agonizing death of my mother from malignant melanoma was psychologically devastating for me. Our relationship had been profoundly symbiotic, yet in recent years we'd seen little of each other and when she died much had been left tangled and unresolved. I felt awash in grief and remorse, and fell into a depression that only occasionally lifted—and would eventually end in a severe heart attack in 1979.

In the many frayed months before her death, friends encouraged me to seek some sort of therapeutic help. I was skeptical. Given my past experience with various psychotherapists, I doubted if still more would be helpful. After all the years of talk therapy, I'd lost patience with words and theory. I was too practiced and skilled in verbal gymnastics, in articulating and analyzing my feelings, to surprise myself with new insights. What I needed instead, one friend suggested, was a nonverbal way to "uncork" and relieve the pain I was carrying around. He specifically urged me to try "bioenergetics"—in particular the Lowen-Pierrakos group, which employed physical exercises to unlock emotional blocks.

With little to lose, I decided to give bioenergetics a try and for a number of months had twice-weekly sessions with a younger colleague of John Pierrakos. I was astonished at how quickly the kicking and breathing exercises helped bring to the surface a brimful of sadness, anger, and grief. Wrenching as the sessions were, the spillover into the rest of my life was immediate. Where evenings had typically meant some form of carousing, the more likely landing spot these days became a movie alone, then home to bed—nerve endings barely battened down. When I went to see *Rocky*, my mind told me it was clichéd, noisome junk—and I cried anyway. Coming out of the theater, I saw a young woman fall on the sidewalk. I rushed to help her retrieve the money she'd dropped, asked if she was OK, nodded, walked on—and burst into tears.

A different kind of example: I'd been dating someone more "appropriate" (as the world defines such matters—a fellow historian, no less) and just as I was beginning to feel hopeful about the relationship, he confessed, sounding annoyingly pleased with his honesty, that truth to tell he already had a lover and didn't want to lose him. He apologized for not having told me sooner and suggested—over the phone—that after some time passed we should try and pick up again, as friends. I agreed. It was all very mature. I hung up and burst into tears, which was becoming my characteristic response to daily life, pleasant and unpleasant.

After I'd been doing bioenergetics for a number of months, my facilitator congratulated me on having made "great progress" and suggested that I was ready for a ten-day "intensive" at the group's Center for the Living Force in Phoenicia, New York. I was skeptical, but with the ongoing crying jags and lurking desolation, I decided that, at age forty-eight, it was now or never.

The intensive proved to be an emotional roller coaster, ranging from euphoria to tearful hyperventilating. I fit into communal life with astonishing ease; my rabid devotion to Manhattan disappeared along with any interest in sex; and my negativity took a hike. The communal vocabulary about the "lower self" could set my teeth chattering, and hushed talk about the "Path" and Eva Pierrakos's ability to fall into a trance state during which a "spirit face" delivered the Lectures (the community's substitute for the Bible) had me wanting to hire a car and drive straight back to Manhattan. Yet I stayed on, lurching back and forth between the certainty that I'd at last found a congenial home and the conviction that I'd stumbled into a full-blown cult, all at once charmed by the simplicity and warmth of the community members while inwardly squirming at their "spiritual" belief system.[9]

No one, I kept repeating to myself, had invited me to join the Path or study the Lectures. My intensive remained focused strictly on the bioenergetic physical exercises, and those continued to open me up emotionally. Following one particularly grueling session, my five-person team suggested a massage, and then sleep. I stripped to my shorts, lay facedown on the mattress, and closed my eyes. They dimmed the lights, put on a background tape of Indian music, and began to massage me with oil. I alternated between periods of deep quiet, tears of varying intensity, and outbursts of joyous laughter. None of which, strangely, surprised me. But then, to my astonishment, I abruptly flipped over into another reality, entered an earlier time span—whatever the right words are. I was a boy back at Camp Idylwold with Morty Offit, my adored young counselor (he was eighteen or nineteen, I was eleven or twelve). He was leaving camp to join the armed forces (1941? 1942?) and my tears flowed. I hid behind a bush, too shy and sad to say goodbye, but just as he was about to enter the car taking him to the railroad station, Morty spotted me, came over, put his arm on my shoulder, and said something loving about how it was "going to be all right."

Later during the massage I was with my twenty-year-old father in Russia after he'd fled the army and was literally walking across Europe to ship out in steerage class for the United States. I could *feel* the cold, his aloneness, his fear, and his bravery. I traveled with him to the United States, to his shabby apartment—incessant noise from the subway outside his window, friendless, frightened. I felt deep compassion for him. Felt in comparison how fortunate *I* was, surrounded by options and support . . .

When the ten-day intensive ended, I was overcome with sadness at leaving behind the profound connections I'd made there, yet also feeling secure in the knowledge that the sadness would give way to renewed activity and connection.

That's not how it worked out. Once back in Manhattan, I fell almost immediately into a paroxysm of desperation and tears, alternating with encompassing rage at yet again being alone, bereft of the encompassing warmth and acceptance that for ten days had been mine. I'd been thrown back, without prelude or insulation, into the stark isolation of my apartment. At the bioenergetics center I'd "melted," laid aside my defensive armor. And yet, said a countervoice, hadn't I also, once more, allowed others, complete with their moronic metaphysics, to pass judgment on the adequacy of my character, my life? Hadn't I confused the genuine physical release of bioenergetics with the skin-deep simplicities of the Lectures as some higher truth? Back and forth I went. Between tears I acknowledged my emptiness, drying them I recognized that a writer's life was inescapably linked with the perils of isolation.

For a few weeks following the intensive, I continued to have bioenergetic sessions in Manhattan, while Pierrakos continued to harp on the need to give up "instant gratification" as incompatible with the Higher Self. The intensity of my "contraction" gradually lessened, the sustaining routines of work, drugs, and hustlers returned, and I stopped bioenergetics. Defeat? Or escape? I still consider it an open question. . . .

––––––––––––

The half-dozen years at the end of the '70s had been the most tumultuous in my life: the torturous death of my mother from cancer, a series of roller-coaster love affairs, the increasing lure of cocaine, the deflated scope of the gay movement in tandem with my decreased participation, a major heart attack in 1979 that put me out of commission for a year, the landslide election of Ronald Reagan in 1980—all had me toying with the fantasy of setting sail for Tahiti. Instead, I settled for the Jewish version: a lingering depression. It was back into therapy, and back into bed.

I lost any urgency to write—which had long centrally defined my life. For a full six months after the heart attack the doctors sanctioned only minimal physical activity (forty years ago, rest and more rest was the prescribed regime): a literal two minutes on and off a stationary bike, and approval to climb the short flight of stairs within my apartment no more than *once a day*. I'd lived alone since college, had never learned to cook beyond the rudimentary hamburger, and didn't even own a TV set (friends eventually provided a used one). I was allowed to read and sleep—and spent long hours doing both.

Having lost any nagging drive to write, I filled the vacuum with stale broodings and interspersed alarms. I tracked every semi-symptom with exquisite care: one skipped beat, one suggestion of chest pain, and I was dialing the doctor's office (to be put on hold, of course, or curtly told to leave a message). I exaggerate, but how else to take the sting out of recalling what in fact were moments of genuine, terrifying panic? Finally, late in 1980, a year after the attack, I underwent the tell-all thallium test. It revealed some ischemia on the right side but none on the more critical left. "A good result," my cardiologist announced. He took me off Inderal and told me that for now he saw no need for an angiogram or bypass surgery.

With that, I exhaled. Gradually, the blues receded. I went back to teaching, and found I still enjoyed it. I began to sort out what (and who) did or didn't matter to me. I became hopeful that a normal life span lay ahead, and zealously vowed (a near guarantee of recidivism) that it would be one "sensibly" curtailed to exclude drugs, liquor, hustler bars, late-night parties—the whole litany of past pathways to theatrical amplitude. As part of my exalted denunciation of the sins of the flesh, I surrendered all attempts, at the absurd age of fifty, to maintain my defiantly youthful appearance: no more working out on the Nautilus machines, no more hyperbolic contests on the squash court with twenty-year-olds.

Henceforth, I pledged, I would seek intimate companionship with a few equally defective contemporaries and forgo fantasies of romance with perfectly formed gymnasts. I would develop placid routines to offset my reckless, willful ways. With work and health no longer dependable, I would yield up to the "natural ebb and flow" of life—as had briefly proved possible during my foray into bioenergetics. Literal survival, I told myself, hinged on being sensible henceforth in all things, even if only behaviorally—how I lived, not what I dreamed. I read May Sarton's *Recovering* and guiltily contrasted what I regarded as her "fortitude and dignity" with the way I crumbled in the face of misfortune and loss.

I told all that one day to my close friend Naomi Weisstein. "Nuts!" said Naomi. "I studied with Sarton. She's a manipulative mess. But she *does* know how to put herself, always, in an attractive light."

"Well," I mumbled—reluctant to let go of my newfound ego model—"at least she isn't a whiner."

"And neither are *you!*" Naomi yelled. "You've shown a terrific ability to cope, alone, with one misfortune after the other this year! You cope so well most people don't believe you when you try to tell them you're hurting! You hand them a plausible excuse for not taking your pain seriously—and most people are delighted to have one, their own pain being quite enough to deal with. Yes, you can be a pain-in-the-ass perfectionist sometimes. Yes, you confuse isolation with strength. Satisfied? Try being gentler with yourself. Not every need is a character defect."

Dear, dear Naomi. I needed more friends like her.

No longer absorbed with routines of recovery, I turned back to my traditional occupations of research and writing. I also made solemn vows, not for the first time, to give up the search for a perfectly formed Adonis with a doctorate in Middle Aramaic studies—plus a culinary degree from Le Cordon Bleu. The pursuit of flawless beauties was, I belatedly decided, an adolescent fantasy originating not (à la Freud) in repressed anger but (à la Harry Stack Sullivan) in an excess of unrequited tenderness (which, to be sure, made me angry).

Not being hydrocephalic I had, at the advanced age of fifty, at least intermittently come to realize that any fantasy about reprograming my core personality, short of gene-splicing, itself belonged in la-la land. I'd come to understand too that contentment wasn't a steady state but a brief and passing interlude, and that you can't get the love you need when giving out signals that you don't feel deserving of it. All true, all firmly acknowledged—yet insight alone, alas, has never yet managed to jam the perpetual motion machine, to disrupt deeply imprinted, repetitive cycles of behavior.

I again briefly tried psychotherapy, and again managed to glean a few additional, and infinitely subtle, insights into my behavior and its origins. Yet the behavior itself mutated no more than a mite (and I wouldn't swear to that much). A stutterer doesn't develop a golden tongue merely by coming to the realization that he has a speech problem. My newest therapist, the latest lighthouse in a long-traversed coastline, failed to persuade me that my professional success had been attained *in spite of* my perfectionism, not because of it. Nor did I take much comfort in his well-worn bromide that feelings of melancholy, grief, and sadness were intrinsic to the human condition. If I could allow myself *and others* to be "average," he confidently announced, I would find more satisfaction both in work *and* love. Ah, that "if."

At just this point, finally feeling ready to launch into a new project, I suddenly had to put on the brakes. My landlord unexpectedly announced that he was hiking the rent on my Greenwich Village apartment from $600 a month to $2,000! That was a shocker: in those years $600 was itself considered a high rent. At first, I thought an increase of that size would be declared illegal, but I soon learned that if an owner lives in a building with fewer than five apartments, no rent controls applied. And my landlord *did* live in the apartment below me. Since there was no way I could afford $2,000 a month, I had to immediately begin the search for new quarters.

Greenwich Village rents, a broker soon told me, had been steadily rising, and he suggested I try looking instead in the Chelsea neighborhood. It was, he acknowledged, still mostly single-room occupancy, but its run-down rows of nineteenth-century brownstones had decided charm and the neighborhood was overdue for an upscale redevelopment. He also suggested that I consider the option of "buying rather than renting"—a startling proposition.

"Really?! But I don't have any capital and usually live from paycheck to paycheck."

"But you said you were a tenured professor, right?"

"Yes, right."

"Which means you have a guaranteed pension fund and a solid health plan, no?"

"I believe so. I haven't checked recently."

"I suggest you do. I think you'll be surprised at what we call your 'bankable options.' Many real estate brokers would consider you a desirable client—you'd almost certainly get approved for a substantial mortgage."

The very next day I headed up to Chelsea. It was indeed run-down and yet to me—who'd never wanted to live in a high-rise or anywhere uptown—the tree-lined streets and rows of brownstones were immediately appealing. On Twenty-Second Street near Tenth Avenue, I came upon a construction crew that had just begun a top-to-bottom renovation on the first building in a row of substandard yet inherently attractive townhouses. Across the street from the row was a spacious if untended park that, as I'd subsequently learn, was currently a drug drop, something of an outdoor sex emporium, and even the scene of an occasional murder (after I moved in, one stabbing did occur on the doorsteps of my building).

The broker had been right: I got a thirty-year mortgage, with monthly payments that were affordable—*if* I could learn how to be more sensible about money (a long struggle). Mortgage in hand, I was the first person to move into that first building in the Chelsea row—even before the renovation was completed.

By early February 1981, the move had been completed and my mood was on the upswing. I was ready for a "new start," though the trumpets, annoyingly, kept refusing to sound. The thought now and then popped into my head that perhaps I was done with scholarship, that the tide had turned and it was time to yank my rowboat off the sandbar. Yet I knew deep down that archival research continued to be a good match for a temperament drawn to solitude and to digging around, detective-like, for disconnected bits of evidence that could eventually be pieced together into a coherent tale (finding the words for telling a story). The *process* retained its hold on me, but I seemed unable to crank up the engine.

Never mind. I was basking in the new apartment and in a more consistently upbeat take on life. I had a new mantra: "I *really* do expect less these days. Less of everything—romance, glory, engrossing work, consistently loving friends." I was now operating, I told myself, in a more realistic ballpark; I'd begun living the life of an ordinary mortal—"due" nothing, responsible for much of my own pleasure and pain, susceptible to the usual number of unexpected, "unwarranted" disappointments, jolts, and rejections. I'd settled down, I managed to persuade myself, to a more realistic and hopefully more attainable set of expectations.

Thus cheerfully deceived, I greeted every social invitation—previously avoided—with a sunny "yes," determined to do more than my usual share of brushing away any looming hint of the blues. First up on my dance card was an invitation to dinner for four at the penthouse apartment of a gay Episcopalian priest (what an opener!). I expected my host, whom I hadn't previously met, to be a kindly sixtyish type, but when he greeted me at the door I found myself staring at a humpy weightlifter poured into jeans and T-shirt. His pompous vacuity, alas, quickly erased his initial visual glory.

Next up on my still-negligible social calendar was my barber's invitation to the New York City Ballet; the astonishing Cynthia Gregory *did* compensate for the dreary restaurant meal beforehand. Several nights after that, I joined an engagingly surface dinner for six at the apartment of an aspiring member of the gay literati. There I met Ed, an uncommonly sweet, decent, bright man, if a bit plump and dowdy. After four or five subsequent dates, I had to reluctantly admit that sterling character was not a sufficient goad to sexual arousal—at least not in my perniciously limited range of erotic fantasies.

Undaunted, I got determinedly back on the social merry-go-round, including a string of benefits for various gay causes—I even gave one myself for Lambda Legal Defense. I primarily succeeded in reconfirming

my jaundiced view that people who enjoy parties don't much like individuals, preferring to deal with them in a chattering cluster where they
present no more threat of intimacy than do a clump of magpies briskly
competing for leftover bread crumbs.

I've gone a comparable route in my scholarly life, preferring the individual biography to the grand-scale if skin-deep narrative. My nominalist
nature distrusts our ability to know *anything* fully—though there's more
chance of knowing *something* in depth if we focus on the individual.
Even then we can't answer all the questions we'd like, since documentary
evidence on a subject's inner life is usually sparse. Most historians are
basically sociologists, preferring to scan the landscape and to avoid the
individuals who dot it and whose idiosyncratic lives interfere annoyingly
with the search for grand patterns, with our ability to generalize.

And much the same is true, I decided, of our own social lives, where
bland conventions command the foreground and the singular, atypical
individual dutifully sinks out of sight, bowing to the unspoken pressure
to share collective platitudes and ignore rude irregularity—the vivid
idiosyncrasy disappearing into a collective void, along with the chance
of learning anything profoundly true about oneself or others.

When I went back for a time to a standard round of socializing
I didn't expect anything more nurturing than a run of pleasantries
blended with time-tested bromides. Which isn't bad unless, like me,
you're hoping for more—more than a host who, in ten-minute intervals,
breaks into a conversation at just the moment when the prattle threat-
ens to become penetrating. There were highlights, nonetheless: sharing
Vito Russo's excitement at the imminent publication of his book, *The
Celluloid Closet*; commiserating with *Voice* columnist Arthur Bell over
his conjunctivitis; learning from Dennis Altman *in detail* the ghastly
logistics of moving from Sydney to Los Angeles; sharing in Catharine
Stimpson's delight at being freed from editing *SIGNS*; puzzling over
the pleasure Charlotte Bunch (my buddy from Task Force days) still
got from the lecture/travel circuit; learning from Emery Hetrick and
Damien Martin (founders in 1979 of the Hetrick-Martin Institute) the
dire needs of LGBTQ+ youth; happily surrendering to adorable Brett

Averill's invitation (he had become editor of the *New York Native*) to write a regular column on gay history.

From my two-month-long dive into the gay social circuit, one person *did* stand out: a thirty-seven-year-old whirling dervish named Nick Rango, who in a few years would build the New York AIDS Institute into the nation's largest state program, and who would die of the disease in 1993. We took to each other immediately, and for a time became friendly. I hazily recall being sexually attracted to Nick, but he insisted on defining us as "soul brothers"—his way of saying that "romance is out of the question." Nick was, in any case, a wondrous handful, a torrent of energy. His vehemence could pulverize the very person he was trying to cultivate, and his bristling confidence helped to account for the "lonesome isolation" he sometimes lamented. Nick's rhetoric of vulnerability collided head-on with his inbred conviction that most people were "more trouble than they're worth." I knew the first time I met Nick that I wanted to see more of him, though he often pierced my eardrums. I knew he felt the same; weirdly, though, neither of us could somehow manage to find the time to invest in a lasting friendship.

It set me to thinking about the purported truism—one I'd long questioned—that gay men are better at friendship than straight men. This isn't, of course, claiming much, since neither specimen of manhood, in my view, holds a candle to the capacity (learned, not inborn) of most women to share more than surface feelings, to acknowledge their own contribution to a disagreement, and to show a willingness to work through it. Yes, I know—such large generalizations are suspect. Still, I'll stick with my intuition—and personal experience. I've found that many fewer male than female friendships are able to survive more than garden-variety intimacy, stress, disagreement, or separation. There's no evidence that the capacity for intimacy and the emotional resilience needed to accommodate inevitable difficulties in a relationship are causally related to genes or hormones; culture is the source, and culture has long mandated a definition of manhood that minimizes empathy and deplores emotional display.

By the summer of 1981 I'd reached some sort of equilibrium. Not exactly peaceable, yet a welcome distance from the conspicuous highs and lows of recent years. I didn't think the odds were good that I'd ever fall in love again, for which I felt as much gratitude as regret. In some moods I still wanted that intimate partner, but I didn't feel desperate at not having one, wasn't on a frantic search to find one, and on good days realized that life could still be quite satisfying without one.

Rose-colored glasses, alas, don't sit snugly on my nose. To sustain something like a placid plateau required a new and consuming writing project. Before that could announce itself, the good cheer dissolved on other grounds: I came down with a full-blown case of hepatitis that had me mostly in bed, feverish and fragile, for several months. Tranquility just didn't suit my nature. It got a further jolt when a well-intentioned bedside visitor, listening to me lament my contradictory hankerings for *both* solitude and intimacy, burst out laughing. "That's not how most people see you!"

"Meaning what?"

"Most people read you as self-contained and formidable, wanting nothing and no one that couldn't be yours if you simply snapped your finger!"

"You're joking!"

"That *is* how you present yourself, whether intentionally or not."

"Jesus! Can't they *see* I'm a vulnerable, cuddly five-year-old?"

"No, they can't. *Show* them!"

My luxurious sorrows soon gave way to tangible fear. A full two years after my heart attack, a pro forma thallium stress test unexpectedly revealed an arrhythmia (skipped beats). Since my cardiologist, Dr. Downey, was a man of few words, I called my friend Penny, a cardiac nurse, and asked her whether the test finding was serious. The crucial question, she said, was "whether the skipped beats were atrial or ventricular; if atrial, you don't have to worry." The heightened arrhythmia, Penny said, was "probably a side effect of the bout with hepatitis. To be sure, you should do another stress test in a month."

When the time came, I performed well. The loquacious lab technician, contrary to protocol, told me that "on the whole, you test out pretty good. But we did pick up several 'pairings.'"

"What does that mean?"

"We don't know. Pairings are double skipped beats. If they show up within a year after a heart attack, they're not good news. In your case—*two* years from the attack—well, that's unusual. We don't know what it means. But then again, you're one of those people who seem low risk for an MI [myocardial infarction] and yet have one. You're an anomaly." (Tell me about it.) "Talk to your doctor."

On the phone the next day, Dr. Downey was his usual curt self. Well aware by then of his limited tolerance for prolonged discussion with a mere patient, I'd carefully prepared my list of questions in advance. No dice. I'd barely begun when Downey cut to the chase: "I'm putting you on Procan. Possible side effects include pleurisy, which means you'll need weekly blood tests. Caroline [his secretary] will set that up. Goodbye."

After conferring again with Penny as well as a few other friends, I realized that it was time for a second opinion. Not all cardiologists, Penny assured me, were as patronizing and arrogant as Downey. She got me the name of a research cardiologist at Albert Einstein College of Medicine, and awaiting his return from vacation, I decided to hold off on taking Procan and instead to resume my limited exercise on a stationary bike. After a mere minute or so, the skipped beats started coming on fast. I remembered an earlier warning that the prognosis is good when exercise *relieves* rather than initiates arrhythmia—and decided after all to fill the prescription for Procan. Weirdly, I felt neither morbid nor depressed and settled down contentedly to watch from dawn to dusk the US Open tennis matches on TV.

To cut to the chase, the specialist at Einstein came through with precisely the diagnosis I'd hoped for. I was so delighted that I took down his words verbatim: "Pairings during a stress test are a negative finding only when in conjunction with other symptoms—like dizziness or angina. You showed none of those. It's at least as plausible to posit that the arrhythmia is a symptom of live cells *within* the scar tissue, cells that are establishing corollary blood supplies—thus producing a *transient* stage of irregular beats." My prognosis was good, he said—and I should enjoy it! "Do whatever you want—yes, grass too, even a snort of coke now and then. All, of course, *in moderation.*"

I was so delighted at the diagnosis that the "moderation" bit barely registered, which I would later come to regret. But for now, hugely relieved, I felt a burst of energy and the sort of carefree spirits long absent. From that day to this—and despite a serious relapse that lay ahead in 1984—I've had only a few scattered and minor alarms. I've never had a second attack—and I am, after all, still plugging away at ninety. (Shush! Recite at once the ancient caution: "Whom the gods would destroy, they first make mad with power.")

In the immediate aftermath of my welcome-back-to-life medical report, I had a sudden upsurge in ideas for new writing projects—and trouble deciding between them. A play about my heart attack? A narrative history of the 1960s? An anthology of the new perspectives that had been emerging in the past decade about homosexuality—something like "Being Gay: A Modern Appraisal," with a running commentary evaluating recent findings and pointing to new directions for further research? The more I thought about "Being Gay," the more it grabbed me, and I decided to take the idea to the gay-friendly editor Arnold Dolin at New American Library, with whom I'd worked on an earlier book.

We mulled over the idea at lunch, and Arnold found it intriguing. He warned me, though, that only a token advance would be possible, and urged me to flesh out a formal proposal. I did, and as I worked on it, my enthusiasm grew. I thought the book could be a valuable summing-up of recent developments and redefinitions—and of my own migration from psychoanalytic "cure" to the celebration of different-ness. In retrospect I can see that the project also marked the point where my form of political advocacy shifted from active movement work to the more distanced yet still valuable focus on politically oriented scholarship.

The shift was both overdue and incomplete. I continued to speak at various movement events and to take part in assorted panels, but they no longer engaged or energized me to the same extent they once had. When I agreed, for example, to do a TV interview with *The Open Mind* in response to what the sympathetic host called the "slanders" of the homophobic Moral Majority, I felt frustrated afterward. I knew I hadn't botched the interview, but I knew too that I hadn't done the razor-sharp job required. In those days it was still rare for the national media to provide a positive forum for responding to the homophobes, and I felt badly that I hadn't been a more effective advocate.

I felt just as dissatisfied with my perfunctory performance on a panel convened to discuss lesbian and gay writing, concluding that the "talkfest" marked no "notable advance in insight or human connectedness." It wasn't that I'd become some sort of knee-jerk cynic. To the contrary, I felt enthusiastic about the emerging "new guard" of younger activists I'd been meeting—people like Brett Averill and the journalist Larry Bush; I enjoyed their energy and admired their commitment. My feeling of political staleness, I knew, said more about my own unsteady state than it did about them.

It was touch and go. At the 1981 Lambda Awards dinner—at the Roosevelt Hotel, no less, complete with hot and cold straight politicos like liberal assemblyman Frank Barbaro and Manhattan borough president Andy Stein—I had enlivening reunions with a host of old comrades: Ginny Apuzzo, Betty (now Achebe) Powell, Morty Manford, Charlotte Bunch, and so on. And Charlotte's keynote speech was marked by her usual acumen: the next item on the political agenda, she told the crowd, was "what the quality and dignity of our existence will be." She underscored the urgent need, as the most vulnerable scapegoat of the New Right, to unshakably insist on our full entitlement to all the rights of citizenship. Yet not even a lively, gossipy dinner with Charlotte a week later was enough to rout my returned sense of lethargy.

And then a nasty little thought wiggled its way to the surface. Hadn't the research cardiologist at Einstein told me that it was perfectly all right, now and then, to snort a little cocaine? I reluctantly recalled too that when I'd put the question to my regular cardiologist, Dr. Downey, he'd responded with a resounding "No!" But since I already distrusted him, it was easy enough to brush aside his opinion. As if on cue, Danny, a hustler friend, called to tell me that his brother-in-law, a dealer, had just received a "dynamite" cache of coke, and asked if I was interested. The planets, I decided, had suddenly aligned. Neither socializing nor political activity, I told myself—no, not even sex—had been able to interrupt for long the slump I'd been in. Couldn't prolonged sluggishness, I cleverly asked myself, give way to full-blown depression? And wasn't it a well-established medical fact that even low-grade depression was a dangerous stressor for a cardiac patient? Since I'd known Danny a long time, I persuaded myself that he'd never sell me stuff cut with a dangerous additive. Besides, I could monitor my pulse rate and at the first sign of a skipped beat stop on a dime. Anyway, wasn't risk-taking a necessary stimulus to the imagination, "playing with fire" central to creativity? And so on . . .

I of course knew from the moment I embarked on that inner debate exactly how it would turn out: I asked Danny to drop by with a gram, just a gram. (I believe a "measly" gram was how I put it.) Danny came straight over with the coke, and though it proved mediocre, it got me going. Within a week I completed a short new play, *The Last Class*, and liked it even when I reread it cold sober. After a dreary, extended period of illness and depression, it was good to again feel vigorous and intact.

Neither liquor nor pot had ever held much appeal for me, but coke, even mediocre coke, was quick to consolidate its charms. I sternly reminded myself—ho hum—that at age fifty-one moderation had to be my guide; I could never return to the Russian roulette that preceded my heart attack, when excess had for a time become my modus operandi. I reminded myself that a mere two years earlier I'd yearned simply to recover a *modicum* of my previous energy and activity. I remembered how thrilled I'd been when I got the doctor's permission to walk *a full block*, how I'd gloried in my first dinner in a restaurant, my first film, my first classes, my first jottings, my first sex—and how I'd sworn to be eternally grateful for and satisfied with a simple life.

And for a considerable time after the attack, I *had* taken good care of myself and *had* been dutifully leading a becalmed life absent of thrills. Only recently had I begun to miss the old amplitude, to long for some edgy excitement. All I asked for, I (perilously) assured myself, was the ability to start writing again on a consistent basis. That much accomplished, I swore to retreat to strict sobriety (loud clearing of voice to reach those sitting in the family circle). For a time, my determination held; I didn't contact Danny to get a second gram. Circumstances helped hold me back: I was already a month behind on some bills. And his coke *was* mediocre.

At that point, while barhopping one night, I ran into Davey Paul, an old friend involved in film production who was in town from L.A. on business. We chatted away, catching up on each other's lives, when at one point—surprise!—the magic word "cocaine" dropped from the ceiling. Davey, it turned out, was a longtime aficionado. Delighted to hear that I liked the stuff, he grandly announced that he'd call his dealer in L.A. and have a gram "of the finest coke there is" flown to me in the morning.

"Flown?!"

"Sure. I put it in the pocket of a piece of clothing and send it FedEx—you'll have it first thing. Been doing it for years when I run out while on the road; never a drop of trouble."

The "clothing" arrived on schedule. I unexpectedly seized up with second thoughts and decided that before plunging in I really should check in with Bill Trevor, the therapist I'd recently been seeing. To my surprise, he seemed rather blasé about the whole thing. Instead of alarm, I got near-explicit encouragement to proceed: "Yes, there's a real risk involved, but on balance it's probably worth it. Writing is at the center of your identity. Without it you feel bereft, worthless. Mind you, I'm predicating this on two assumptions: that the research cardiologist you saw *is* right about you not showing any residual sign of heart disease, and second, that you use the coke *moderately*, and *only* for writing." I refrained from asking him to define "moderate."

Anyway, a few hits of Davey's transcontinental coke settled the matter. It was gloriously pure. I promptly persuaded myself that I'd been blowing up a mild break from routine into a cosmic melodrama. And oh, how welcome the break had proved! There was truly *nothing* like a little coke, I decided, to convince me that being able to lose myself in writing was central to my sense of well-being—that it outstripped even the pleasures of sex.

After a month of taking only occasional hits, I decided I'd passed the double test: no angina or other related heart symptoms had surfaced, and I did dynamite what had been an entrenched writing block. Not least, I recaptured coke's blissful ability to shut out the world, to feel importantly engaged, to spend long hours of exhilarating intensity thoroughly content in my productive isolation, words flowing out of me with no attendant angst. I didn't even much care whether the growing pile of typed pages would turn out to be "usable." Quality felt irrelevant for now. I'd disgorged what was probably no more than a clogged mess of half-thought-out pages, but (I told myself) that cleared the way for something genuinely new to emerge. I felt buoyant and relieved. It was true, I acknowledged, that there had been a few mini-scares along the way, hours here and there where I'd felt vaguely depressed and exhausted, fragile, empty, unable to concentrate. But they'd been transient. And the *prolonged* period of stress and stalemate seemed behind me.

After a month, I took a cold sober look at the pages that had kept pouring out. They fell mostly into two piles: dialogue for the long-stymied play I'd been wanting to write about my heart attack, and autobiographical material designed for the pending anthology *On Being Gay* that I'd signed up for with New American Library. I especially liked what I'd written about the process of coming out, and decided that I'd zero in on the anthology as my next full-scale project. Did I still need to bump up my spirits with coke? Could I afford anything like regular shipments from Davey? Maybe—if I watched my pennies. Or got a bank loan. Or borrowed from my loving aunt Tedda.

That very same week Frances Goldin, my new agent, phoned to tell me that Paul Robeson Jr. had been reading some of my earlier books and, out of the blue, had unexpectedly expressed interest in me as the possible biographer of his father. Should she arrange a meeting? *Of course!* I told her, beyond thrilled at the prospect. Within days, the three of us were sitting in Frances's office for what was meant to be a preliminary meeting, but which went on for six hours. I'd expected some difficult hurdles—not only did Paul Jr. have a prickly reputation, but some major issues had to be aired. The Robeson archives, known to be vast and rich, had up to now been closed to scholars. Was Paul prepared to give me access to *all* the material, and for a long enough period—which at a guess I put at seven years—for the deep research I considered necessary? And was he "prepared to agree—in writing—to a 'hands-off' policy, forfeiting in advance all control over what I wrote?"

I'd expected fairly adamant resistance and feared that a prolonged negotiation might well end in stalemate, with Paul turning elsewhere for a biographer. It was well known that he had long been a belligerent guardian of his father's legacy and held to a rigid view of *himself* as its only reliable interpreter. Yet to my astonishment—and Frances's—he gave way on all the terms I outlined during that first meeting, and with barely a murmur. He'd come to the meeting, he said, fully expecting me to make precisely the demands I had. He'd also decided in advance, he added, that I *was* the right man to do the biography. He asked only that he be allowed to read the final manuscript for possible factual errors.

That seemingly benign request I quickly granted; seven years later those "factual errors" would lead to a full-blown conflagration, itself the culmination of years of unyielding conflict. Having elsewhere written in detail about all of that (see my book *Waiting to Land*), I'll refrain from needless repetition here. Suffice it to say that the cordiality that marked our first meeting in Frances's office hardly typified what was to follow.

One matter does bear repeating. After Paul and I had agreed to terms and settled down to a once-over-lightly discussion of when I hoped to start working in the family archives ("Today, please!"), I told Paul that

I had to clarify another matter that we'd skimmed over lightly: He could see that I was White, but did he know that I was gay and had been politically active for a decade in the gay movement? "I've had you thoroughly checked out," Paul said with a grin. "I think you're going to catch hell," I told him. He agreed—"and especially from [Communist] Party people," he added. "They're hopeless on the issue of homosexuality. I'll deal with it." As it would turn out, Paul would prove pretty hopeless himself. And while it would prove true that a few party people would refuse to see me, it was primarily because they distrusted *Paul's* political loyalties—he'd been on and off affiliated with the party—and assumed that I was his dutiful creature.

From the first I had inklings that Paul would prove a handful, that his seemingly benign willingness to "turn my father over to history" (as he put it), was whistling in the dark. A man who exuded energy, Paul had given up his long-hated job of translating technical journals from Russian to English and had also finished the time-consuming work of putting the family archives in order. Still only fifty-four and a man of intense vigor, he was now bereft of a consuming project— other than, so it would turn out, delivering frequent, passionate, and repetitive monologues that brooked neither interruption nor contradiction, and that even Frances, who'd known him a long time, found exasperating. She warned me to hold Paul at arm's length, accurately predicting that his bottled-up frustration and inner torment could at any point—and probably over some trivial, unpredictable point—erupt in self-righteous outrage.

Over the years that followed I would indeed feel Paul's wrath many times over; finally, in fact, I would have to break off contact in order to avoid his time-consuming assaults. But if I would soon enough experience his repetitive belligerence, the difficulties between us hardly stacked up against my immense enthusiasm for the project. Robeson's story was a momentous, largely unknown one, and I embarked on it enthusiastically, feeling dumbfoundedly blessed at having been handed the opportunity to tell it.

I rejoined my gym, took a vow of (comparative) chastity, gave up compulsive diary writing (I didn't make an entry for two and half years), and shut the door on my recent indulgence in cocaine. I also put aside all other tentative writing projects—with one exception: *On Being Gay*, the anthology under contract to New American Library. I explained to Arnold Dolin that I was sure the point would come several years down the line when I'd want to throw the mountain of Robeson files and/or myself into the Hudson, a fate that could be avoided if I had a secondary project to turn to for diversion. Arnold generously said that he was content to wait.

Though the heart attack had sidelined me for more than a year, I now felt fully restored, and plunged ahead. It would take me, as I'd predicted, seven years to complete the biography, and the obstacles would prove formidable. But the vast family archive, previously closed to researchers, would prove a treasure trove, and my total immersion in Robeson's prodigious and controversial life a hugely satisfying experience.

My embarkation on the biography exactly paralleled the onset of the AIDS epidemic. Beginning in 1981, a strange set of medical symptoms started to be reported among gay men, a syndrome initially given the label GRID, which soon gave way to AIDS. The election of Ronald Reagan in 1980 had marked a new high in the country's shift to the right and, in regard to gay civil rights, a whole series of ballot defeats. As the number of those afflicted with AIDS rapidly increased, the homophobes could barely contain their delight. Conservative Christians led the pack; Jerry Falwell, among the most vocal, described the plague as God's punishment for the "wicked practice" of homosexuality: "You can't fly into the laws of God," Falwell pronounced, "without paying the price." The Reagan administration promptly *cut* the budgets of the Centers for Disease Control and Prevention and the National Institutes of Health.

Throughout the '80s, AIDS proved a double-edged sword: it elicited a venomous pitch of denunciation against gay people, yet also—as the terrible toll in suffering and death mounted—aroused in some segments of the straight public a growing sympathy for those being cut down at the very beginning of their adult lives. But in the early years of the plague, the revulsion far exceeded the sympathy.

The mainstream press initially joined in the homophobic hysteria. The *Wall Street Journal* published a "bemused" editorial wondering why more people weren't advocating quarantine for those infected with AIDS, while the *New York Times*, for its part, printed a letter suggesting that gay people *owed* it to the general population to present themselves for HIV blood tests. But it was the *New York Post* that hands down won the gold medal for venom. It published an inflammatory series of articles that included a false report that hospital nurses were having trouble keeping AIDS patients from having sex with each other, and gleefully detailed the "sick sexual rituals" that characterized the gay male world, featuring the "animal" sexual orgies at the Mineshaft, a gay club. Simultaneously, a slew of pending gay civil rights bills were easily defeated across the country—in Houston by a 4–1 margin.

"Liberals" expressed their distaste in more sophisticated ways, the New York Civil Liberties Union being a case in point. I was at the time a member of the board and had a firsthand view of the telling debate in the mid-'80s over the choice of a new executive director. My preferred candidate (and good friend) was the dynamic and gifted Tom Stoddard, who I thought much superior to the other finalist, Norman Siegel. During the extended board debate on the comparative merits of the two finalists, several members spoke out in easily deciphered code: Tom was "a whiner," "a magical creature" who would be "an unsafe choice." By a narrow margin, the board went for Norman Siegel instead. Tom (and his friends) were bitter at the covert gay-baiting, but he soon put it behind him and went on to play an outstanding role in the struggle for gay rights as the executive director of the Lambda Legal Defense and Education Fund. He later died of AIDS.

The indifference of the Reagan administration to the AIDS crisis was made abundantly clear early on. In a 1982 press conference—after some thousand people had already died of the disease—Reagan's press secretary, Larry Speakes, engaged in an exchange with the journalist Lester Kinsolving that gave callousness a whole new dimension:[10]

> SPEAKES: AIDS? I haven't got anything on it.
> KINSOLVING: It's known as the "gay plague." [*Press pool laughter.*] No, it is, it's a pretty serious thing. . . .
> SPEAKES: I don't have it. [*Press pool laughter.*] Do you?
> KINSOLVING: No, I don't. . . . Does the president . . . look on this as a great joke?
> SPEAKES: No, I don't know anything about it, Lester.

Kinsolving, to his credit, kept at it. As late as 1984, the audio tape of another press conference contains this exchange:

> KINSOLVING: Is the president concerned about this subject, Larry?
> SPEAKES: I haven't heard him express concern. [*Press pool laughter.*]
> KINSOLVING: That seems to have evoked [a] jocular reaction here.
> UNIDENTIFIED PERSON: It isn't only the jocks, Lester. . . .
> KINSOLVING: You mean he has expressed no opinion about this epidemic?
> SPEAKES: No, but I must confess I haven't asked him about it.

It wasn't until September 1985 that Reagan finally deigned to publicly mention AIDS for the very first time.

Yet homophobia, it should be noted, was hardly confined to conservatives. The New York Civil Liberties Union, that bastion of the left, is again a case in point. In the mid-'80s the NYCLU convened a committee—I made sure I got on it—to discuss whether the board should openly denounce the newly established Harvey Milk High School as "officially sponsored segregation." The school had been created to provide a safe haven for sexual and gender minorities who'd found it difficult and dangerous to attend their local school due to continuous bullying and violence. I sat in on all the committee meetings, and

they were disheartening. Opposition to the school clustered around
the argument that if the NYCLU remained silent, it would be seen as
sanctioning the "dangerous" practice of self-segregation. The point *was*
troubling, yet as I argued, it was also tantamount to saying "that no Jews
should be allowed to leave Nazi Germany until we *solve* the problem of
anti-Semitism there." The debate grew heated but to my relief ended
with the committee voting by a slim majority that "no violation of
civil liberties had been found in establishing the school." To my mind
the incident exemplified the inadequacy of reformist liberalism when
measured against the demonstrable need for radical social restructuring.
By then I'd come seriously to doubt if my politics were a good fit with
those of the NYCLU board, and in 1987 I handed in my resignation.

New York City's mayor, Ed Koch, another self-described "liberal,"
also demonstrated the sharp limitations of the "liberal" position when
he staunchly defended his good friend Cardinal John O'Connor after
the cardinal threw the weight of the church against a gay civil rights
bill. Koch publicly reprimanded gay "radicals" for the lack of respect
they'd shown the cardinal. And what of the cardinal's "lack of respect"
in actively working to deny basic civil liberties to gay people? Not a
word of reprimand from our "liberal" mayor. Rumors that Koch was
himself gay had been around for years but had been dutifully ignored
or authoritatively squashed. It wouldn't be until nearly a decade after
his death in 2013 that the *New York Times*, in a detailed account, confirmed that the rumors had been true. A charitable take from someone
like me, who grew up in the same profoundly homophobic time period
that Koch did, might ordinarily be appropriate. But Koch did so much
destructive damage to gay people and during the height of the AIDS
epidemic was so belligerently indifferent to their suffering that silence
is about the best I can summon up.

For both personal and political reasons, I felt it was time to get more
politically active again. On the personal side, I'd had a cocaine relapse
in the mid-'80s that ended in a bleak period of depression—by far the
worst of my life (and described at length in my 2018 book, *The Rest of
It: Hustlers, Cocaine, Depression, and Then Some*). When I finally came

out of it, I dropped all drug use, and even forswore sex—partly out of fear of AIDS but mostly because coke, sex, and hustlers had become so intertwined that a blanket interdiction seemed for a time necessary. (For years I dutifully attended AA and NA meetings.)

After I'd been clean and dry for more than a year, I gradually eased back into movement work, answering the phones one afternoon a week for a number of years at the People with AIDS Coalition. By then, I'd completed a first draft of the Robeson biography and decided to activate a long-standing idea I'd been toying with: to create a university-affiliated research center for lesbian and gay studies. I sent off a detailed prospectus to Benno Schmidt, who'd recently been named Yale's new president and was married to my close friend Helen Whitney, the documentary filmmaker.

Yale did seem a plausible location. Not only did I know its incoming president but I'd gotten my undergraduate degree at Yale and then, postdoctorate, had taught there for five years. In response to my letter, Benno phoned a week later to tell me that he'd sounded out Bart Giamatti, Yale's outgoing president, and Giamatti had immediately objected to establishing a "gay *anything*." "Gay," according to him, was "an advocacy word" and would thus automatically and regrettably risk "politicizing" the university, diverting it from its ancient mandate to remain "above the fray."

Benno admitted to me that he was closer to Giamatti's view than to mine. But wasn't the university itself, I asked him, already conspicuously "politicized"—in fact reeking from top to bottom of class privilege and racial bias? Benno harrumphed and switched course: "Why not think about endowing a *chair*?" he suggested. I asked how much money that would take. "Yale's minimum," he said, "the absolute floor, would be a million and a half dollars." I squelched the impulse to laugh out loud; my bank balance *had* improved—but only to the point that I could now pay all my current bills. No, I told Benno, "a center would be better—it would generate a dozen PhDs instead of anointing a single individual."

We decided to leave it there for the time being, and then to reconfer in a few weeks. In summing up our discussions to date Benno said that he did agree with me that Yale *might* be the right place for the center: it had superb library facilities, a liberal History Department, my personal connection with the university—and its proximity to the large gay population in New York City. But, he warned me, he was far from sure that Yale would be willing, ultimately, to proceed.[11]

The next morning, I put in a call to John Boswell, the openly gay professor of history at Yale and the author of *Christianity, Social Tolerance, and Homosexuality*, which I'd recently given a laudatory review to in the *Nation* and which had gone on to win the National Book Award. I wanted to solicit both John's advice and his support, feeling uncertain about how he would react: not only was Boswell a devout Catholic but he'd never lent his name to any form of political activism. Yet to my considerable surprise, he seemed genuinely excited about the possibility of a gay research center, and I decided to go ahead and invite him and half a dozen other gay scholars to meet in my apartment.

That first meeting on March 19, 1986, comprised only seven of us. Boswell brought along Ralph Hexter of the Yale Classics Department (and later president of Hampshire College), and I invited New Yorkers Blanche Wiesen Cook (later the biographer of Eleanor Roosevelt), the anthropologist Esther Newton, and George Chauncey, a gay graduate student completing his doctorate at Yale with whom I'd become friendly. It was a productive discussion, though I thought John and Ralph talked too much and mostly to each other. We touched widely on a host of matters ranging from the principles that should guide the center's governance to the prospects for fundraising, and at the close decided to meet again in a month with an expanded group of gay scholars. No one disagreed with the overall guidelines I set out at the top: gender parity, representation for the diverse racial and ethnic elements that characterized the gay community, and the inclusion of independent scholars without university affiliation. Our expectations were high and (so we thought) our eyes wide open to the many roadblocks that likely lay ahead.

Literally two days after that first meeting in my apartment, the New York City Council finally passed—after some dozen failed attempts—a gay civil rights bill. Maybe the launch of the research center had stiffened my spine, but I surprised myself with the angry words I scribbled down:

> I don't feel grateful to a City Council which acknowledges that I'm a human being; I don't rely on their authority for my right to exist. I do not long to throw my arms around my cohorts in the antechambers of power and with them tearfully give thanks for a bill that explicitly denies the validity of my lifestyle and implicitly holds me at unequal arms' length; I'm already beyond such patronization. I recognize, of course, that the bill *will* in fact help some gay people save their apartments and jobs. And beyond that, it does send out a useful message to the rest of the country at a time when the momentum is against us.

A context for any discussion of who is or isn't "human" and what is or isn't "normal" was immediately at hand. It was at exactly this point in time—the spring of 1986—that President Reagan, under the guise of a "reproof to terrorism" and with mainstream Americans cheering from the sidelines, gratuitously bombed Libya in a sickening disregard for human life, dropping sixty tons of munitions and killing any number of defenseless women and children. Ramsey Clarke, the former attorney general, acting on behalf of Libyan citizens killed or wounded in the bombing raid, sued the United States for damages. The US District Court for the District of Columbia dismissed the suit as "audacious."

That word would have been better applied to Reagan's continuing refusal, until nearly the end of 1985, even to acknowledge the existence of AIDS, let alone to allocate resources to fight its deadly acceleration. The administration hadn't hesitated in labeling its massacre of the innocents in Libya as "simple justice," yet it refused to extend even basic sympathy to the thousands dying from AIDS. That double-pronged stance hardly qualified them to pass judgment on when the term "simple justice" could legitimately be considered applicable.

Now calling ourselves the "Organizing Committee" for a lesbian and gay studies center, thirteen of us gathered in my apartment in mid-April

1986 to discuss the next step in trying to make the center a reality. It went well on the whole, though Boswell insisted Yale would and should oversee the guidelines for any center carrying its name. Like the proverbial bull in a china shop—a deaf and dumb bull—he even announced his view that minority representation on the Organizing Committee wasn't crucial for the simple reason that we, "as enlightened people," could do the job of representing their interests.

Several gasps later, the anthropologist Carole Vance, tight lipped, responded with a deserved and eloquent rebuke: in our search for legitimization, she suggested, we should be on guard against a rapprochement with traditional academia that included an accommodation to *its* norms. Both the cultural theorist Anthony Appiah and the African American writer Jewelle Gomez expressed agreement with Carole's position, as did I. Jewelle, in fact, made an immediate decision to resign, and wrote me to explain why: "The race, class and sexism issues that are raised by working with such an institution as Yale and its faculty are so complex and so deeply rooted that I would spend most of my time and energy in re-education . . . [which] is not a priority for me. I would be much more likely to support this type of project in an institution that is more accessible and encouraging to those of us who are routinely ignored by the academic hierarchy."

In writing Jewelle back, I expressed my sadness at losing her but said I understood and honored her reasons for withdrawing. My hope, I added, was that most of the men on our Organizing Committee didn't stand in quite so much need of "re-education" as Boswell did, though Yale as an institution "has a huge way to go." Unfortunately, I added, "no other institution has been breaking down the door to get us to locate the Center on its campus rather than Yale's, nor do many others have Yale's legitimizing power." I'd like to think, I wrote Jewelle, "that so long as we adhere *rigidly to our own* organizing principles when negotiating with Yale," Boswell's traditionalist values could be circumvented.

It was hardly encouraging, though, that both of Boswell's Yale colleagues at the meeting, Ralph Hexter and the biologist Al Novick, seconded Boswell and added offensive remarks of their own. Novick managed to reduce the room to stunned silence when he claimed, in defending Yale's "standards," that there was as much prejudice at Yale against scientists (of which he was one) as against gay people. Come again? As had quickly become clear, in our attempt to establish a gay research center we'd be walking a fine line: on the one hand insistent on maintaining the integrity of gay differentness and unbending in our opposition to discrimination based on class, gender, and race even as we pushed for mainstream institutional affiliation that embodied melting-pot "liberalism" and White male privilege. It was an old dilemma in the history of American social reform: how to balance a *radical* vision against the impulse to operate in a broader arena.

In between planning meetings for the center I was, along with teaching, juggling several other projects: putting a book to bed—*About Time: Exploring the Gay Past*, a combination of archival documents that I'd been gathering from my research, plus essays on gay topics that I'd been publishing—and at the same time doing a final round of interviews for the Robeson biography that proved a memorable one, given the unexpected array of people I got to see. *The* highlight was my time with Ishmael Flory, a wise, warmhearted man with a remarkable history.

The elderly Flory had gotten his bachelor's degree from UC Berkeley in 1933, ultimately becoming a prominent Black trade union organizer and Communist Party member. We took to each other immediately and it soon became "Ish" and "Martin." While a graduate student at Fisk University, Flory had been expelled for organizing a protest against the Fisk glee club for agreeing to sing in a Nashville theater where Black spectators were consigned to the balcony. Soon after moving to Chicago, Flory became an organizer for the Mine, Mill, and Smelter Workers, worked with both Robeson and W. E. B. Du Bois in the National Negro Congress, and twice ran on the Illinois Communist Party ticket for governor and twice for senator. "I didn't win!" he told me, roaring with laughter. We ended up spending some ten hours together during which he introduced me to a raft of people I wouldn't otherwise have had access to, and concluding at 10:00 PM in the locker room of a Black gym on Chicago's South Side talking to Chapman Wailes about Robeson's involvement with the National Negro Labor Conference.

The following day ninety-year-old Oscar C. Brown regaled me with stories of Robeson when they worked together in the summer of 1915 (Paul as a waiter, Oscar as a bellhop) at Narragansett Pier. "The things we struggled to learn," Brown told me, "Paul could get them just by rote almost." Later that same day ninety-five-year-old Earl Dickinson told me about working with Robeson in the 1940s on forming the Council on African Affairs, and as well recounted their attempts to promote antilynching and anti–poll tax legislation as a prelude to the formation in 1948 of the Progressive Party. The day ended talking with the pioneering Black actress Etta Moten Barnett, for whom Gershwin had written the character Bess in *Porgy and Bess*. (He had also had Robeson in mind for the role of Porgy, but both he and Barnett turned down the original production.) At the close of our interview Etta gave me the sum of her wisdom: "The secret, honey, is to remember the past but not to live in it."

By 1985 the Robeson project had brought me one lasting friendship and one unyielding antagonist. The friend was Helen Rosen, Robeson's trusted lover from the mid-1940s on; the antagonist was Paul Robeson Jr. On first meeting Helen, I thought her extraordinary—a formidable, elegant woman used to receiving the attention and adoration of powerful men, intolerant of fools, uninterested in trivia, impatient with flattery. She could not be wooed, but she could be won over—if, that is, I showed sufficient determination, integrity, and patience. It took several years, the number of our meetings growing exponentially, along with our pleasure in each other's company.

By 1985, I'd won her trust and, more precious still, her affection. By then she'd pretty much talked herself out on the topic of Robeson, and we'd worked our way into more intimate matters. Yes, including our sex lives. At eighty (or thereabouts) Helen told me that she'd recently turned down a second date with a forty-five-year-old man she'd slept with because she felt "exploited" by him—and she didn't mean financially. Lust, she insisted, was ageless; in fact, she confessed, her sexual fantasies had never been as "extensive" as they were currently.

On another evening, this one stunning, Helen unexpectedly announced that she had "a surprise" for me. She brought down a hatbox from the top of her bedroom closet and spilled the contents—dozens of Robeson's letters to her—onto the living room rug. She invited me to read away to my heart's content and to take as many notes as I wanted. The feast was sumptuous. Paul rarely wrote letters; he was far too cagey to put either his political views or his personal feelings into permanent, retrievable form. Yet during the most torturous period in his life, he did pour out his heart to Helen, and those letters would prove key in helping me to unlock some of the trickiest episodes in his life.

In addition, Helen bolstered my decision in 1985 to hold Paul Jr. at a firm distance. She'd known him for decades, considered him "deeply disturbed," and advised me "to steer clear of him." Frances, my agent and herself a left-winger, had also known Paul Jr. for many years, but—to her dismay—he began showing up regularly at her office to complain about me. Frances confirmed Helen's view, warning me that Paul was "beset by demons" and was also "dangerously homophobic," despite his rhetoric to the contrary. After a lunch with Paul one day in May 1985, Frances phoned me to report that he was currently consumed with the conviction that Vanessa Redgrave had "trapped" his adult daughter "into an affair." He'd also insisted, not for the first time, that I was out to destroy his father by "revealing" (that was Paul's word, not "inventing") his "gay side."

It was Helen, though, who was instrumental in helping me unlock the key to Paul's *actual* relationship with his father. When I completed a draft of the biography, I sent copies of the manuscript to both Helen and Paul for their comments. They could hardly have been more different. Helen declared the draft "thrilling"; Paul, oppositely, declared it a "smear" job, and launched into a counterfactual rant that continued unabated up to and after the book's publication early in 1989.

By then I should have been used to Paul's nonstop vituperations. Yet I remained puzzled by his relentless harassment—even as I felt somewhat touched by the palpable misery that fueled it. Gradually over the years I'd gotten a pretty clear picture of his motives, but it would only be in 1997, nearly a decade after my biography had been published, that Helen finally filled in some crucial facts. By then, indignant at Paul's ongoing—and now public—vilification of me, she said she wanted to make one final tape with me, one that held back nothing. She asked me to keep the tape under wraps until after her death, and then to share it openly. The transcript of that tape, dated May 8, 1997, runs to sixty-four pages and covers considerable ground. Until now I haven't released it—though I plan to put it in my own papers at the New York Public Library.

Helen covered a lot of ground in the tape—she'd been, after all, Paul Sr.'s intimate confidant for more than thirty years. For now, I've chosen to reveal only that portion of the tape that relates to the father-son relationship since it goes a long way toward demystifying Paul Jr.'s behavior, as well as revealing the profound pain that drove his fabrications, especially his frenetic attempts over the years to persuade me that he was his father's closest confidant, the *only* person his father fully trusted. The twisted version he concocted about his relationship with his father was designed to conceal, not least from himself, the actual texture of their connection.

Helen's blunt words on the tape we made tells the story: Paul Sr. "never cared about or trusted Pauli [his nickname]. . . . He was an unwanted child. And as an adult, his father did not like him." To compensate, Helen continued, Pauli told everyone that he was his father's utterly loyal bodyguard—*the* source of access, *the* guardian at the gate—"and he certainly tried to be," Helen added, her tone scathing. "I don't think," Helen said, that "I ever heard him [Paul Sr.] say anything directly, terribly derogatory about [his son] . . . but it was perfectly obvious that there was no love."

A withholding of affection and trust *that* complete had to have been traumatic for Pauli, especially since Eslanda, his mother, wasn't exactly doting, nor much of a compensatory source of affection and concern. Pauli survived the lifelong anguish of his father's dislike, but he never flourished—though even in his wounded state it was easy to see that inherently he was a man of first-rate intelligence and considerable surface charm. He coped with his father's aversion by fabricating a psychic scenario that he himself could never afford to acknowledge. Yet behind his own back, as it were, he strewed enough false clues in my path that, had I pocketed them, would have brought his father down several pegs—even as he was quick to attack anyone else who dared to suggest that his father was less than flawless. In scattering the seeds of denigration, Paul Jr. was secondarily deriving a sense of power over his father's life that in actuality he'd never remotely enjoyed.

During our very first meeting back in 1981, Paul had "casually" dropped the news that his father had been bisexual, and had had affairs with, among others, Sergei Eisenstein, the filmmaker (who *was* gay). To innocent me that came as a remarkable revelation, and I diligently searched for evidence to confirm it. I turned up nothing—except for uniform peals of laughter from Paul Sr.'s several female lovers who I interviewed at length. As one of them put it, "Paul was the most *hetero-sexual* man I ever knew!" When I told Paul Jr. that I'd been unable to verify any such affair with Eisenstein, he angrily denied that he'd ever suggested such a thing. (At another point along the way, Paul "confided" in me that he'd burned his mother's "lesbian letters"; at another, that his daughter was being held captive in California by "a rich lesbian." Those assertions I did *not* try to confirm.)

Several years later Paul added another name to the list of his father's purported lovers, casually mentioning one day that he'd had an affair with the composer Marc Blitzstein (who, like Eisenstein, *was* gay). Once again, I diligently pursued leads in an effort to substantiate this latest "revelation." Much to my disappointment, I couldn't come up with a drop of evidence to support it.

It was then that a new idea belatedly dawned: Could Paul have chosen me as his father's biographer *because* I was gay, expecting that I would swallow whole—as a gift to the gay movement—any suggestion that Paul Sr. had sex now and then with men? Since Paul Jr. was himself homophobic, he might well have thought that the revelation of a male-male affair, or several of them, would prove disastrous in mainstream eyes, and in at least some circles would destroy his father's reputation. I began to think that Paul—probably as an act of unconscious revenge for having been rejected by his father—was the one bent on "destroying" him, though consciously he would have scoffed at such a view as preposterous. Paul's feelings about his father were an unreliable concoction bred of a need to somehow simultaneously confirm his father's greatness and (unconsciously) plant a bomb at the foot of the pedestal. Sadly, that result could have been more effectively achieved if Paul had simply laid out the facts: his father had never been interested in raising children, had never pretended otherwise, and had in fact been a lousy parent—not even a "good enough" one. His son's efforts to win his father's respect and affection had, poignantly, been doomed from the start, and the consequences for Paul Jr. were calamitous.

By 1985, fed up with Paul's false leads and misleading testimony and, most of all, sick to death with being his whipping boy, I'd grown weary of trying to atone for uncommitted crimes. Once—though I realize this will be hard to believe—he had actually threatened me: "I know someone who could put a bullet between your eyes at a hundred yards." Four years of conscientiously responding to Paul's alarums and accusations had left me with little more than accumulated stress, diverting the needed energy for completing the book. I decided to distance myself once and for all and to get on with it. Paul, however, wasn't easy to shake. In the years ahead he'd usually find a way, time and again, to get under my skin and upset my equilibrium. Indeed, some of the more supercharged tangles still lay ahead after the biography had, in 1989, been published.

———————

In 1986 the Supreme Court by a 5–4 decision in the now-notorious *Bowers v. Hardwick* case sanctioned the right of the states to police *private* relations between consenting gay adults. (It wouldn't be until 2003 that the court, in *Lawrence v. Texas*, would overrule *Hardwick*.)

In the 1986 decision, the court cited "history"—limiting it, with typical American parochialism, to what had taken place through time on our own shores—as proof that homosexuality has *never* been tolerated. Had the justices broadened the inquiry to include a *broad* sample of human history, and the findings of anthropology as well, they would have found abundant evidence of cultures (Periclean Athens being the most obvious example) that not only accepted same-gender sexuality, but in some cases *mandated* it.

As is usually the case, the court in *Hardwick* only selectively cited that part of the historical record that conveniently rationalized its own standards of "acceptable" behavior. In a society like ours, wedded to the "truth" of scripture and the existence of an all-knowing God, the story of mere human behavior is readily sidelined as insignificant, of value neither as a guide for daily morality nor for predicting and coping with our fate in the heavenly hereafter. Only secular societies are seriously interested in the *truthful* study of history—in the *full*, variable record of human behavior.

The *Hardwick* decision was a shocking event for the gay community; Tom Stoddard memorably called it "our Dred Scott decision." Already reeling from the accelerating death count from AIDS and coming hard on the heels of a Justice Department ruling that employers were free to fire any employee known to be HIV positive, the combined impact provided an alarming gauge of the depth of opposition to gay rights and seemed to make a mockery of fifteen years of post-Stonewall activism. It was also in 1986 that Congress voted aid to the Nicaraguan contras and the archconservative William Rehnquist took office as chief justice of the Supreme Court. It was difficult to feel hopeful.

The only potential comfort that seemed available after *Hardwick* was to try to take the long view—to convince oneself somehow that skirmishes are always lost in any protracted struggle for social justice. Still, it was a rough moment. I'd been arguing that acceptance of our privacy rights wasn't sufficient—that this entailed tolerating "difference" only if it remained unseen. OK, says the court, so now we'll take away your privacy rights.

It felt vaguely absurd in such a climate—like trying to climb a mountain in a canoe—to continue with our planning sessions for trying to establish a lesbian and gay research center. Yet it felt cowardly to simply throw in the hat. As if timed to boost my spirits, the very same week that the *Hardwick* decision was announced, Benno, after a long silence, finally responded to the formal proposal I'd sent him weeks before about locating the center at Yale. He invited me up to his townhouse to talk further about the center's prospects. We talked for nearly two hours and I left feeling somewhat more optimistic that Yale might provide a suitable home for us after all. Benno made it clear that he could *not* support anything like an undergraduate major in gay studies or even a policy-oriented public affairs institute. He *might* be willing, though, to consider the possibility of establishing some sort of a "research/think tank." Since that was exactly the goal we ourselves had been pursuing, I was able in good conscience to assure him that we were proceeding along the same lines.

Benno surely understood, I told myself, that any center devoted to creating and disseminating reliable information about gay lives was *implicitly* political—designed, that is, to change hearts and minds. What Benno did make clear was his concern that a significant segment of Yale alumni would come down on his head for associating the school's name with any project advancing gay legitimacy. He did sound prepared to face down the opposition—though I suspected that the fine hand of his wife Helen Whitney (my close friend) had been chiefly responsible for his willingness to keep talking.

A few days later, I left for East Berlin to interview the doctors who had treated Robeson at its famed Buch clinic during the worst of his depressive episodes, and also to explore the mysterious "Robeson Archiv" at the Akademie der Kunst, said to house substantial material. I'd been granted access to the archive, and it would turn out to contain far richer holdings than had previously been known. For weeks before my departure, I'd been going over procedural details with both the consulate of the German Democratic Republic (GDR) in Washington and the League for German-American Friendship in New York, and had been assured that I would have no trouble crossing from West to East Berlin. The plan was for me, after an all-night flight, to take a cab directly to Checkpoint Charlie, where I was to request a *day* visa (though I intended to stay for a week). I hated flying and brought along Mahler tapes to blast into my headphones all night—while practicing *not* sighing "oy vey" should the Libyans decide to storm the plane.

Predictably, everything did not go smoothly. Sleepless, I was held up for another four to five hours at Checkpoint Charlie while the border guards searched and researched my one suitcase, periodically glaring wordlessly at me through the taxi window. Finally allowed to cross, I went straight to the Palast, the hotel reserved strictly for foreigners—the staff insulting, the food abominable. Once I was checked in, a hotel clerk curtly told me that I would be taken at once—"no, you cannot have a nap"—to the home of Dr. Alfred Katzenstein, who'd been Robeson's chief physician during his stay at the Buch clinic. On arrival at Katzenstein's home I was thoroughly grilled about my planned biography and my politics. I described myself, accurately, as a left-wing non-Communist.

I apparently passed muster (wasn't Katzenstein a party member?), and he invited me to turn on the tape recorder for what turned into a five-hour conversation. Throughout, Katzenstein was pleasant and thoughtful. Yet I wasn't impressed with either his general analysis or the depth of his information about recent developments in his own field of electroconvulsive therapy (ECT). He insisted, for example, that when he treated Robeson in the early '60s it was "highly unusual" to administer more than ten to twelve ECT treatments. In fact, it was then—and is still today—standard to administer additional treatments for acutely distressed patients like Robeson who were unresponsive to what was then a limited arsenal of medications. I came away from our day together with the melancholy feeling that Robeson had been in the hands of well-meaning but second-rate doctors. That alone was worth finding out. Additionally, I was able to interview several expatriate Black Americans—the most memorable being the gifted cartoonist Ollie Harrington, who had a mine of stories to tell and personally was wonderfully warm and witty.

I also did some limited socializing, thanks to "Irene," an East German resident whom I'd met during a trip she'd made to New York. Irene introduced me to her circle of friends in East Berlin, many of them gay, and they were a sweet bunch—quick to offer help, affectionate, serious, reliable. Some of them spoke fluent English; with the others, I could manage only fragmentary phrases from Bach titles (*Eine Kleine Nachtmusik*) and an ancient course in German (*Vielen dank fur die auskunft*)—which produced general hilarity.

The high point was the night they took me to a *state-sponsored* gay disco, which to my astonishment seemed a duplicate of a Manhattan hot spot—which led Irene, something of an East German booster, to triumphantly shout, "I *told* you there was full acceptance of gay people in the GDR!" Later some of her friends offered a more jaundiced view, including the information that Humboldt University's Professor Günter Dörner was currently being heralded by the East Berlin authorities for his experiments "proving" that the "mistake" of same-gender sexual orientation could be "corrected" through hormonal shots during pregnancy.

I further learned from another of Irene's friends, who'd just returned from a six-month stay in Moscow, that in the USSR homosexuality was against the law—and the law was being enforced. The GDR's attitude, in other words, was the most enlightened in Eastern Europe. Which meant that the United States, despite all our recent setbacks, was far more advanced in its acceptance of homosexuality than most of the world.

In any case, the GDR struck my American eyes as frighteningly drab. The streets were nearly devoid of shops or casual walkers, and were light-years away from the wondrous anarchy of Manhattan's sidewalks. Sameness and security seemed the GDR norm. Irene insisted that, unlike in the United States, nobody in the GDR went to bed hungry and everyone *had* a bed—along with free education and medical care. I had liked Irene's friends so much that I was inclined to believe her overall claim that there *was* a New German: deeply antifascist and egalitarian, still precise but no longer rigidly formal. And it is certainly true that in the thirty-five years since my trip to the GDR, a reunited Germany has faced up to the ghastliness of the Holocaust with a determination that shames our own country's persistent amnesia regarding the genocide of Native Americans, the bombing of Hiroshima and Nagasaki, and the long-lasting aftereffects of Black slavery.

––––––––––––––

The contentious tone that had dominated early meetings of the Organizing Committee to plan for a research center began to get edgier still. I'd naively thought that John Boswell, despite the patronizing attitude he'd exhibited from the start, would nonetheless hang in there. Otherwise, I reasoned, he'd look foolish if the center did end up at Yale and he had to come up with less petulant arguments for not being part of it than he'd been able to muster so far. I misjudged the depths of Boswell's serene sense of entitlement. When, as chair of the subcommittee he headed, he presented us with a suggested set of bylaws for the center, they were shockingly at odds with the guidelines (gender parity, etc.) that the group as a whole had previously agreed on. He topped that off with a proposal for an all-powerful Executive Committee composed solely of tenured Yale faculty—meaning White men, since no out lesbians or tenured people of color were available.

When Boswell finished his appalling presentation, the women at the meeting uniformly protested, with Ruby Rich, Carole Vance, and Carroll Smith-Rosenberg—distinguished all—leading an angry response. Ignoring their complaints, Boswell lapsed into disdainful silence, broken only when, as the meeting was adjourning, he snarled at Larry Gross, "I don't have time for this!" Larry later told us that he'd succeeded in calming Boswell down, but it would soon become clear that Larry's considerable diplomatic powers had for once proved insufficient.

Upon returning to New Haven, Boswell immediately sent me a scorching letter of resignation that reeked of hauteur. He characterized the three-hour meeting of the Organizing Committee as "an almost uninterrupted succession of expressions of mistrust, condescension, grudging envy, or outright hostility to Yale and its faculty." In contrast he offered his own estimate of Yale as "a great and mysterious treasure, not easily understood and perhaps impossible to duplicate." Given Yale's "special excellence," Boswell continued, it was fully entitled "to control concerns bearing its name" and *not* to defer to the plans for governance that the Organizing Committee had devised—"viewpoints inimical to Yale and even to academic enterprise." At the close of the letter, he let me know that he was sending a copy directly to Benno, along with the advice to have nothing more to do with us.

I responded in kind: "Your resignation is accepted. The Committee's deliberations were confidential and privileged. People felt free to air some of their deepest fears: as women against a traditional bastion of male power; as blacks and Latinos against an elitist white institution; as unaffiliated scholars against traditional academic snobbery. No-one wanted those fears (conversations) transcribed and handed over to Yale officials; our sessions were in the nature of a catharsis, not an ultimatum. No-one gave you permission to hand them over—in exaggerated, inflammatory form no less—to Benno. I think your behavior has been unconscionable."

Boswell felt much the same about me. "I am stunned," he wrote back, "that you reacted with such hostility and vehemence. . . . I am deeply shocked by the suggestion that the committee had some secret purpose which would be compromised by my 'handing over,' as you put it, information to Benno. Had I understood the committee's relations with Benno (or anyone else) to be anything less than candid and open I would have withdrawn long before."

Refusing to give Boswell the last word, I sent him yet another rebuttal: "There has been no 'secret purpose.' Only someone lacking in political experience could mistake the needed catharsis of free-wheeling discussion for a 'plot.' Only someone disdainful of other people's needs would then 'hand over' those private rumblings as evidence to be used against them. You bet I'm vehement—as I would always want to be when private agendas threaten to overwhelm the common good."

Soon after that, Benno called me to dot the i. He solemnly summoned up his best baronial voice to announce that certain "sets of traditions must be respected . . . there should be no misunderstanding about Yale's need to require the usual institutional/faculty responsibility [i.e. control] over the center . . . I simply can't proceed, Marty, without the support of Yale's 'gay star.'"

Swell, I thought, all the prima donnas have now done their dances—and the greater good of a center may well be lost.

As if in confirmation, and all but simultaneously, the committee lost its two most prominent nonacademic members, Joan Nestle and Jonathan Ned Katz. Both were community scholars who against heavy odds had done pioneering work in reclaiming and preserving gay and lesbian history. I'd invited them from the beginning to be an integral part of the center. Yet from the start they seemed uneasy, mostly sat on their hands, and after attending a few meetings resigned, citing their discomfort with academia. Their dislike of the traditional university was for a lot of the right reasons, including its patronizing attitude regarding issues relating to race, class, and gender. Still, many of us felt they were using those legitimate grievances as a cover (perhaps even from themselves) for protecting their own turf. As one of our group put it, "They feel threatened at the prospect of 'their baby' taking any steps out of their line of vision."

Gay studies *did* owe much to those grassroots pioneers who lacked the perks of academia and yet had turned out seminal work. But although their contributions had been indisputably important, so had the work of a number of academic scholars (Boswell, for one) who did have a university affiliation. Acknowledgment could and should have been mutual, but they didn't see it that way. At one of our early committee meetings Jonathan had said flat out that "integrating non-affiliated scholars and empowering minorities seemed to be at odds" with legitimizing gay studies at a place like Yale. "I make my living," he said, "as a secretary: how would setting something up at Yale help people like me?" An organization independent of academia "would not have these problems."

Joan Nestle wrote me a two-page letter reviewing the splendid grass-roots efforts, independent of both the government and academia, that had eventuated in the Lesbian Herstory Archives in Brooklyn. "We represent different visions," she declared, and "I could not be part of [the committee's] . . . vision without betraying my own." Joan and I went way back and I marveled, as I wrote her, at "the heroic work you've done." I assured her that "I don't want any semblance of a quarrel with someone I admire and like so much," but I did need to say that "I don't accept that you and I have 'different visions.' We have the same vision—to better the lot of gay men and lesbians—though perhaps (at the moment) different paths to accomplishing that vision. I do not see how the attempt to extend gay studies to a university (*any* university; Yale is merely a temporary means to an end) can be said to 'betray your vision.' . . . Would you also prefer never to have Women's Studies discussed and pursued in an academic setting?" I urged both Jonathan and Joan to stick with us, and suggested that we try and talk things out over lunch or dinner. Neither responded.

Even post-Boswell, enough divas remained on the committee to produce fairly regular flare-ups in the years ahead. In the face of repetitive accusations and discontent, my spirits would sometimes sink and occasionally I was myself tempted to quit. Though the committee had swelled to twenty by 1988, and attendance at meetings was usually high, in between meetings, scant energy seemed available for the less glamorous work of seeking out potential donors to keep us afloat or investigating a possible home for us on some campus other than Yale. Too many of our "organizers" seemed reluctant to take on the mundane tasks essential to actual organizing.

When in a downswing, and trying to explain it to myself, I often thought that it was a case of our timing being off, that given the AIDS crisis, we were, understandably, too low on the gay community's list of priorities to generate enough enthusiasm for putting the essential building blocks in place. In the late '80s, after all, the community's energy and resources were necessarily concentrated on trying to ameliorate the horrors of AIDS. In the face of governmental indifference and public hostility, gay people themselves had to pick up the pieces. The community's current preoccupation was rightly focused on confronting public indifference or outright hostility, and attempting to care for the mounting numbers of those who'd fallen ill, *not* with creating some pie-in-the-sky scholarly enterprise of dubious relevance to most people's lives.

All of that was undeniably true, yet I still wanted to believe that we could carry off more than one enterprise at a time, that enough energy and resources were left over for supporting an agenda essentially grounded in the conviction that scholarship was itself a powerful political tool for changing hearts and minds. Scholarship and activism in my mind went hand in hand, stimulating and informing each other; the more truths we could learn about the varying lives and cultures of gay people, the better we'd be able to counteract the entrenched antagonism to our very existence. Information about the diverse patterns across time of sexual behavior and gender identity would better equip us to combat mainstream stereotypes that claimed "normality" has always been, and must continue to be, defined as monogamous, lifetime pair-bonding between one man and one woman—the only path, purportedly, to a satisfying life.

Such "truisms" could be defended only if the findings of recent scholarship were ignored. To learn, for example, about classical Persian literature—the poems of, say, Rumi (who died in 1273), which were replete with homoerotic allusions—is to have at hand a thunderous rebuttal to Iranian president Mahmoud Ahmadinejad's absurd claim in 2007 that "in Iran we don't have homosexuals like in your country." In combating Uganda's Anti-Homosexuality Act of 2014, Marc Epprecht's scholarly *Heterosexual Africa?* provides abundant evidence that same-gender sex was well established on the continent *before* the invasion of the White man. In opposition to the insistence that binary genders—one is *either* male or female, the two are *biologically* dissimilar *and* complementary—have always been and must remain the universal norm, contemporary anthropology has discovered any number of places in the world, including the hijras in India, the fa'afafine in Samoa, and the muxe in southern Mexico, where third (or more) gender figures have long been part of the cultural norm.

The abundant new scholarly evidence about sex and gender has provided a growing challenge to the parochial insistence that current "norms" have been unchanging through time and are universally valid. Yes, Ronald Reagan considered homosexuality abnormal—but Alexander the Great did not. Vladimir Putin despises men who lust after men, but Michelangelo fell in love with them.

Americans tend to be ahistorical; they know little about human behavior in the past and see no reason for learning more. Only the present matters. The past is an old building to be bypassed—or demolished. Most Americans have scant awareness that the past offers evidence of rich variations in human behavior, and that knowing about them can liberate undreamed-of possibilities within ourselves. To many Americans, scholarship is how antiquarians—impotent old men—pass their meaningless lives. Yet scholarship is more accurately seen as a powder keg—precisely the ammunition needed for storming the barricades and defrocking the priests.

For a time, I blamed myself for impeding the establishment of the center. I began to wonder if playing the central role might be something of a disservice, that resentment of Big Daddy—I was some twenty years older than most of the members of the Organizing Committee—was impeding the mobilization of energy in trying to find a new home. Many committee members, it seemed, both wanted me to continue taking on most of the grunt work and resented me for doing so. My special entrée to Benno may have justified my taking the lead initially, but with that venue closed off, some form of *revolving* leadership might be the best path; the center should be viewed less as *my* project than as *ours*.

Besides, I resented the common attitude that "Marty will do it"—it wasn't as if I had an assistant on whom I could palm off some of the shit work, or a vast amount of free time to squander. I wanted to complete the Robeson biography, I wanted to accept the 92nd Street Y's proposal that I head up a lecture series, Homosexuality in Society, and I wanted to continue volunteering at the People with AIDS Coalition.

I became so uncertain of what role would best serve both my own needs and those of the committee that late in 1986 I decided to put the whole issue on the table. I told the group at the November 2 meeting that I needed more time for my own work, which meant enlisting others to pick up some portion of it. I also felt that I should be less prominent. In terms of our own principles of gender parity and minority representation, I said, it simply wouldn't do for the same White man to go on initiating and chairing every meeting. The minutes of that November 2 meeting still exist and describe the response I got: "Marty suggested that he step back from his present role in the group to encourage others to share the leadership. Group members made eloquent statements and testimonies to the wonderful leadership Marty has provided in the past, and urged him to continue to occupy a central role for at least a transition period [the period's tenure was not specified]. It was widely acknowledged that without Marty's leadership this group would not have continued."

A pat on the back worked its usual wonders. I stayed on, and for a time some of the others did take over various jobs. The group agreed to form half a dozen committees to handle various aspects of our organizing efforts (fundraising, programming, membership, outreach, etc.), with rotating chairs for each committee. At periodic meetings of the whole, each committee would henceforth report on its activities and recommend various courses of action, which we would then discuss and vote on. At my suggestion, meetings would no longer be held at my apartment and a woman would become cochair.

Within just a few months, we set up the new committee structure, and it would prove to be of salutary and lasting value; that alone took considerable weight off my shoulders. We also set in motion promising negotiations with the CUNY Graduate School as the possible new home for our work. For toppers, letters of support arrived from several committee members who lived out of town and could only occasionally make a meeting or take on a task. They expressed regret at their inability to do more, cheerfully took on the new title of board members "at large," and insisted that they valued highly our effort to create a gay and lesbian research center. Barbara Smith sent me a cheerful note dismissing Boswell's "skewed priorities," and Adrienne Rich wrote from Stanford to express her "strong hopes for this project" and enthusiasm for locating the center in New York at CUNY: both the city and the school, she felt, have "a flourishing progressive gay and lesbian community," and the center "seems like a natural outgrowth of those resources, none of which is a duplication of what the center proposes to be."

We now seemed pointed in the right direction. Over time, of course, a certain amount of slippage would take place and we'd fall back a bit from the crest of commitment. Once or twice in the years ahead, I'd even start groaning again about too many tasks being dumped in my lap and again come close to resigning. But for now, it was full steam ahead.

PART II

1987–1999

At a party in mid-1987 celebrating the ACLU's new gay rights project, I met Eli Zal, the man with whom I still live (and about whom I will *not* be writing, at least not at length). Almost exactly paralleling that major turning point in my life, I completed a first draft of the Robeson biography. It was, for sure, an annus mirabilis.

After doing another revision, I turned in the revised draft to Knopf late in 1987. Given the length (1,243 pages), the demands of a meticulous editorial process, and Paul Jr.'s disruptive attempts at interference, it would take a full year before the manuscript would be ready for publication. Fortunately, I landed from the start in the editorial hands of Barbara "Bobbie" Bristol, a superb, demanding editor (and delightful human being) who over many months gently marched me, line by line, through a rigorous yet enjoyable fine-tuning of the manuscript. In the end the book came out in late 1988 and ran to 804 printed pages, some 250 of them devoted to scholarly notes. In the introduction I explained why the "apparatus" needed to be so full: having been given unimpeded access to the vast family archives, which made it possible for the first time to chart Robeson's extraordinary life in close detail, I had the obligation, as I wrote in the book, to do "all that I could [through careful documentation] to alert other scholars to the possibility of variant interpretations."

Completing the book might have been cause enough for celebration, or at least relief, yet (you know me well by now) the dominant
emotion was dejection. Having a consuming project, one that ideally
would leave zero time for smelling the flowers, was essential to my
sense of well-being. To fill the immediate gap, luckily, another dust
storm gathered force in the planning sessions for the research center.
"Marion," one of the new committee members, was widely known in
the gay community as a champion complainer; corrosively self-righteous,
she was expert in stirring up discontent. Looking around the room at
her very first meeting, she scowled at the majority-White faces and
launched instantly into a lecture on our failure to be "a people's center that takes into account all segments of community viewpoints and
meets all expressed needs." (That's a verbatim comment; I wrote the
words down at the time.)

Several committee members tried to explain that our bylaws from
the beginning had stressed our commitment to gender parity, substantial
racial and ethnic representation, and the inclusion of board members
who were independent scholars not affiliated with academic institutions.
To date we'd done pretty well on all counts, though we were hoping to
do better still. A frequent problem that kept coming up (this was the
mid-to-late '80s) was that the limited pool of openly gay, non-White
academics was mostly untenured (thus unprotected), and usually faced
the insistent demand on their limited free time to join overtly political
minority organizations.

Most of those who spoke in defense of our efforts to date were
themselves members of minority groups, and one would have thought
their words would carry weight. Not for Marion—and there would
be other Marions through the years (multiple Marions, it sometimes
seemed) who were eager to square off for a fight. The inaugural Marion
was incensed, not calmed, by what was said, and didn't seem to be listening very closely. Following the explanations offered by various committee members she simply repeated her initial speech, even using some
of the same words: "What's needed here," she reiterated, is "a *people's*
center that takes into account all segments of community viewpoints

and meets all expressed needs." (Again: that's a verbatim account.) Her aggressive tone—accusatory, not collegial—was again repeated, as well as her underlying premise that we were "academic elitists"—that is, morally deficient.

I tried making the point that to demand we do everything that needed doing in the gay community was tantamount to ensuring that we'd be able to do nothing—there were simply too many needs, not nearly enough hands or money to handle them, and too much entrenched homophobia for easy victories. One of the more daring souls on the committee chimed in to say that what Marion had described sounded like "a large coffeehouse, with a hospice attached for AIDS patients." That may have been clever, but it wasn't tactically wise; on the spot Marion gained several allies. I jumped back in to explain—aiming for a neutral tone—that the center had a *specific* mandate: to increase and disseminate reliable scholarship about gay people. That was the only "community need" our actual skills had prepared us to meet. Marion scowled but didn't reply. Soon after, she resigned in a huff. It was a scenario that, give or take a few details, would reoccur a disheartening number of times in the years ahead.

At around this same time, I got a call from Larry Kramer. We were by this point no more than nodding acquaintances; earlier, when I wrote a pan of his 1978 novel, *Faggots*, in the *New Republic* ("throbbingly self-righteous"), I hadn't known him at all. My review, understandably, had deeply angered him, as he later told me. He was now, in January 1987, calling to tell me that he'd just returned from attending a meeting at Yale convened by John Boswell to discuss forming a center for gay and lesbian studies. Boswell had told him, Larry said, that I'd been "extremely difficult," and he was proceeding independent of my efforts. Knowing that Larry was smiling out of both sides of his mouth, I sucked in my exasperation and told him, "The more centers the better," adding that although our group had *not* formally severed negotiations with Yale, we *were* exploring options at CUNY. Larry then asked me if I'd be open to a "reconciliation" with Boswell. I said I certainly would be—the gay community "doesn't need another destructive feud." But I didn't know, I added, whether the women on our committee would feel the same way, since they uniformly regarded Boswell as a male chauvinist of the worst sort. Larry said he'd "mull all this over."

I didn't hear again from either Larry or Boswell. I did hear, definitively, from Benno. He said he could not proceed further; with Boswell in opposition there was no chance of winning approval for a center at Yale. Nor did Boswell's own efforts ever get very far (a contributing factor, I later learned, had been his patronizing attitude toward female professors). Larry Kramer, in turn, would within a few years denounce our organizing committee in the *Advocate* as "second-rate academics [attached to] . . . third-rate educational institutions." His slavish allegiance to Yale, somewhat sadly, remained intact despite (or perhaps because) he'd felt mistreated there as an undergraduate. Still later, in 1997, Larry offered to endow a professorship in gay and lesbian studies at his alma mater, and to build as well a gay and lesbian student center. Yale turned him down—on the transparently homophobic grounds that the field was not yet "a legitimate academic institution."

At that point, furious, Larry denounced Yale's president, Richard Levin, as "spineless" and provost Alison Richard as "that termagant woman." But Larry's heart still belonged to Daddy, and in 2001 he donated his papers to Yale's Beinecke Library, and his brother Arthur gave $1 million to the university to fund the Larry Kramer Initiative for Lesbian and Gay Studies at Yale. Larry and I did subsequently have a personal reconciliation of sorts over dinner, but we never drew close. I think in a better world he and I would have been allies and friends; we did share much in common and I still have a soft spot for him—a good man does lie amid the braggadocio.

Yale having definitively turned us down, the Organizing Committee in the spring of 1987 turned to the CUNY Graduate School (where I held a distinguished professorship) as an alternative prospect. We sent a formal proposal to Harold Proshansky, president of the Graduate School, emphasizing that (to quote directly from the document) "lesbian and gay studies, almost unimaginable a decade ago, has emerged in the last five years as a dynamic field of scholarly inquiry. . . . In recognition of the growing importance of such work, lesbian and gay caucuses have been organized in all of the major scholarly associations and have sponsored panels at their annual conferences . . . [but] while gay scholarship has received increased recognition from the disciplines," our proposal went on, "it has still received scant support from individual academic institutions. It is time for such support to be mobilized."

In a personal letter to Proshansky that accompanied the proposal, I emphasized that "The City University of New York . . . seems to us the most appropriate possible institution to serve as sponsor for the scholarly center we envision, and as the primary institution for research in the CUNY system, the Graduate Center is a particularly attractive potential home for us." Accordingly, I requested, in the name of a four-person delegation we'd formed for the occasion, a meeting with him "to explore our proposal and to seek your advice on the best way to proceed in presenting it to the University."

Proshansky responded immediately, set a date for the meeting, and welcomed us to his office with open arms. He told us straight off that he was *for* the center, strenuously for it, and *he* actually thanked *us* for coming to him with the proposal; the time for such a center, he said, was overdue. That was a wondrous contrast to Benno's evasions and retreats—to a lifetime, for that matter, of having to justify our lives; we now had the legitimacy of who we were and what we were trying to do taken respectfully for granted. In a private note I sent Proshansky, I described the meeting as having been "an historic occasion—nothing less—the inauguration of gay and lesbian studies on the university level. For that reason alone," I wrote, "it was a moving moment. But more moving still, on a human level, was your own response to us. We did not have to *persuade* you of the worth of our lives and the legitimacy of what we are trying to do. My guess is that you're too nice a man to know how rare that attitude is. Our respect and affection for you is already enormous."

Proshansky had also given us some practical advice during the meeting, warning us that "a great deal of hard work lies ahead." To start with, he said, we had to set clear parameters. We would be a research center, not a department—not able to generate courses, hire faculty, or grant degrees. All or any part of that *might* come later. The most immediate hurdle to formal accreditation, he went on, was to prove to the CUNY Board of Trustees that we were financially "viable." The Graduate School would only be able to supply "in-kind" financial support: a small office with minimal furnishing, the use of the auditorium for public events—and printing facilities to publicize them. Not only was the strapped Graduate School unable to provide direct financial support, he said, but in the beginning we couldn't even expect to be assigned work-study graduate students or receive any reduction in teaching hours for board members who had a CUNY affiliation.

We soon learned—perhaps to shield us from the extent of administrative hostility—that Proshansky was *not* being entirely candid. One of our committee members investigated the Graduate School's contributions to its other centers and reported that it gave yearly grants of between $10,000 and $20,000 toward operating costs, including the hiring of a half-time administrative assistant. The school also granted the faculty member who headed every CUNY center one unit of release time from teaching. We got no money, no assistant, and no reduction in teaching—but who cared? We were still delirious!

"Proof of viability," Proshansky added, meant *cash in hand*. We had to prove, he told us, that we had the ability to raise enough money to fulfill the mission we'd outlined: providing fellowships to encourage young scholars to enter a risky field, organizing public colloquiums and conferences, and putting together a scholarly directory that would facilitate contact between academics, often working in isolation though eager to become part of creating a viable new field of study. Proshansky put our "viability" goal at a cool $50,000—a huge sum for a group of scholars whose constituency largely consisted of young, openly gay scholars, along with impecunious graduate students and low-salaried junior faculty. (In the mid-'80s very few older faculty members had come out.) Seeing our collective jaw drop at the $50,000 figure, Proshansky broke into a grin: "You academics know nothing about money! I know that. But don't worry: I'm going to help you raise it." He went on to tell us that he planned to go first to Joseph Murphy, the chancellor of CUNY, who was known as a champion of minority rights, and then to what he called "a select group" of presidents of the two dozen CUNY colleges and ask each of them to kick in $5,000 from their slush funds. Proshansky beamed: "I think you might be able to set up shop by January 1, 1988."

We were floored, amazed, grateful, celebratory—and premature. In the upshot, it wouldn't be until 1991 that the Center for Lesbian and Gay Studies ("CLAGS"—as it was by then being called) would win formal approval from the CUNY Board of Trustees. What happened? What went wrong? Why the long delay? Answer: the usual culprit—homophobia. Only a few days after our meeting, Proshansky phoned me with the gloomy news that Chancellor Murphy had not only turned him down but had also forbidden him to approach any of the campus presidents for money. Murphy claimed that the Graduate School budget was already tight and that no additional expenses could be entertained. Uh-huh. I'd been down that path too often to confuse the underlying reason with the one given out for public consumption. The real story was that "gay liberation" was, to put it mildly, *not* a popular cause, not even on the left. Ours was only the latest cause turned down by expected allies. In the '60s it was the men in SDS who mocked feminism, and earlier still, it was the White trade unionists who refused to enroll Black workers.

It was back to the drawing board. Back to passing the hat at the public events we'd begun to put together, back to applying to foundations that (with the exception of two small gay-oriented ones) turned us down out of hand, back to trying to organize house-party fundraisers and to wining and dining potential gay philanthropists, almost none of whom would come through. (Ellen "Pucky" Violett, who threw us a party, was one of the few exceptions.) Scholarship wasn't sexy or—in an epidemic—a pressing need. We quickly learned that we were a hard sell even among those wealthy gay people who considered themselves intellectuals. The community was, after all, rightly concentrating on the ever-deepening horror of the AIDS epidemic. "Gay studies" struck many as a removed, amorphous enterprise of little value to those struggling for survival and for basic rights like health care.

I often met with blank stares when I gave my pitch to potential donors about how scholarship was itself a crucial form of activism, a needed source of reliable information in combating and dismantling negative stereotypes about gay people. I often gave as an example Anita Bryant's homophobic crusade to Save Our Children. Thanks to recent scholarship, I pointed out, it was now clear that in the vast majority of cases involving the sexual abuse of children, the predator was a heterosexual male, often a family member or friend.

By January 1988—when Proshansky predicted we'd be up and running—we'd been turned down by five foundations (all of them left leaning) and after two and a half years of passing the hat and pressing the flesh, we had accumulated a grand total of $10,000. To make matters worse, the Organizing Committee had broken out into another round of acrimony, though what we were really in need of were some powerful hugs. During the first two years the committee had grown in size and diversity, but there had also been a fair amount of turnover, some of it ideological, most of it a variation of "I just don't have enough time to get involved." And among those who accepted election to the committee, several were by temperament malcontents: you name a position and they'll oppose it. One woman came and went in a flash, staying only long enough to denounce *all* scholarship as "male-dominated"—and ignoring the fact that from the first the committee had put gender parity at the top of its agenda. In regard to minority representation, one newcomer to the committee delivered a throbbingly righteous lecture on the subject without seeming to know that it had all along been a priority issue with us, or that our past efforts had met with considerable success, *even though* the pool of openly gay people of color in academia was small.

I was bothered most by the drop-ins, board members who occasionally showed up for a meeting but never hung around to, say, help get out a mailing. In general I held my tongue, but I did grow weary now and then of the growing parade of self-styled "stars" (i.e., contentious flakes) who marched in and out of our meetings: they didn't "do" scholarship, yet felt free to denounce its "relevance"; they'd been "activists" as of that year, yet couldn't possibly find time to sign up for one of the committees that did actual work. The relentless negativism would have been more digestible had it been accompanied, at least now and then, by a pat on the back. Warmth and generosity were sometimes in short supply.

I often felt puzzled at their lack. There were some wonderful people on the Organizing Committee—I think particularly of the sweet-tempered Ellen Zaltzberg, the ever-reliable David Kahn, the warmly supportive Vivien Ng. But during some periods they were overbalanced by the uncharitable naysayers. Surely some of that hard-hearted stoniness, as I've earlier argued, had to do with the fact that the early years of CLAGS coincided with the height of the AIDS epidemic. The prevailing emotions of grief, fear, and helplessness made many of us psychologically fragile, a state so constant we often weren't aware of it. Surrounded by the ravages of AIDS and the death of loved ones, grief was nearly ubiquitous in the gay community and made us susceptible to randomly dumping excess anger or despair on the nearest target.

Most of us, moreover—certainly me and other members of the older generation—had long been carrying around buried wounds from growing up at a time when homophobia was at its height and queers were mocked and humiliated as "sickos." It was the kind of anger that doesn't always land discriminatingly on a deserving head. Besides, it's generally safer to dump on your own kind than directly on your tormentors, some of whom have real power over your well-being. Many of us had been damaged: raised in a climate that constantly shamed, mocked, and silenced us, made to feel uncomfortable about our own desires, we were prone to maximal resentment at minimal slights.

It became clear to me early on that I'd been marked down as Big Daddy, the Old Man approaching sixty, the Credentialed One easily mistaken for the White Male Enemy who needed to be constantly monitored and put in his place. OK, I get it. I've had a privileged life (though not exactly a carefree one), and privilege helps to account for my string of publications and promotions. I'm also aware that my work drive can sometimes make me impatient with those less willing to match my pace: I *should* be working harder than anyone else at getting the center established—it was, after all, my baby. I tried my best to keep my head down and my expectations low, yet sometimes I *did* feel misunderstood and unappreciated. In that mood I was lucky to have a sympathetic ear in Eli, who over the years as executive director of Literacy Volunteers knew all about the frustration of constantly fielding complaints that are either misdirected or of scant substance—and delivered in a tone disproportionately mean-spirited.

But antagonism within our committee was child's play compared to the unswerving enemies of the center among a small group of conservative gay White men who held tenured faculty positions at CUNY. Two were especially dogged in trying to sabotage our plans, and would periodically write to Proshansky to warn him that we were left-wing fanatics. One was Jim Levin, professor of history at City College, who in the summer of 1988 expressed his outrage to Proshansky at having never been invited to become a member of our board. He inadvertently went on to reveal exactly why we'd steered clear of him: "I have noted," Levin wrote Proshansky, "that many persons without traditional academic credentials are involved in the planning and presentations of the proposed center. This reflects badly on the university . . . [and] will certainly not serve to help produce any meaningful contribution to the scholarship about lesbians and gay men."

An even more dedicated enemy of the center was Wayne Dynes, professor of art history at Hunter. The animosity of Wayne toward me went back some fifteen years to the Gay Academic Union,[1] when he and I had periodically clashed over feminism in general and, in particular, Charlotte Bunch (who I counted as a friend). Wayne regarded me as a confirmed Marxist (I was in fact far more drawn to Emma Goldman's brand of anarchism), an enemy at the gates, and through the years he regularly took up pen and paper to warn Proshansky of our pernicious plans. "Should CLAGS be granted official recognition without responding to well-founded criticisms," Wayne wrote Proshansky in one letter, "this could only be regarded as a serious breach of well-established academic norms, a breach that could engender serious extramural repercussions." The latter went unspecified, but to my mind conjured up some burlesque version of hot lava and the scaling of ramparts. Wayne, however, was deadly serious: "Please rest assured that this forecast . . . reflects adverse comments volunteered by a number of other CUNY scholars [unnamed] who share my dismay at the self-serving arrogance of the CLAGS group." Proshansky sent me copies of Levin's and Dynes's letters, but as grounds for amusement, not action.

All of us involved in the early years of CLAGS were novices at fundraising, and *nearly* all of us were intellectual snobs who considered "moneygrubbing" beneath our exalted calling. We couldn't afford to hire a full-time professional fundraiser, but a committee member who knew Eli's background suggested we hire *him* part-time. Currently completing his training as a psychoanalyst, Eli had for years headed up Literary Volunteers, building that organization into a powerhouse and in the process becoming comfortable with the world of foundations and wealthy donors. Initially, Eli and I agreed that the idea was a lousy one—it would look like a case of nepotism—and he rejected the offer. The committee, though, asked him to reconsider; they insisted, unanimously, that it would be a favor to *them*: he could provide the organization with the skills of a seasoned fundraiser that we couldn't otherwise afford, and at the same time it could provide *him* with some needed income as he shifted careers. The committee recognized it would be getting a very big bang for its buck. Eli and I did finally, uneasily, agree, knowing that he was a prodigious worker and would unquestionably invest much more time in helping to secure the center's future than he was being paid for.

He showed his stripes right off, single-handedly organizing the first of what would become an annual fundraising event for CLAGS. He formed a prestigious sixty-person host committee for the event with so many notables on it that we promptly got several aggrieved phone calls from people protesting their omission—a sure sign that we had "arrived." He also got the much-admired designer Chip Kidd to do the invitation—and pro bono, no less. His design was stunning, yet when I showed the mock-up at the next meeting of the committee, one member angrily denounced the images as "not sufficiently androgynous."

I could have cheerfully murdered her on the spot but remained tight-lipped; I simply told her that she was free to take on the chore of commissioning and raising the money for an alternate design, though I warned her that Chip Kidd's usual fee was $5,000. It angered me that no one offered Eli a word of praise or thanks—not only for corralling a brilliant host committee and producing an eye-catching invitation but for persuading Allen Ginsberg and Gloria Steinem to serve as the benefit's cochairs. The host committee was itself a knockout: it included Bella Abzug, Susan Brownmiller, Cheryl Clarke, Judy Collins, Jules Feiffer, Vivian Gornick, Allan Gurganus, Bertha Harris, David Levering Lewis, Stephen McCauley, Frances Fox Piven, Ned Rorem, Alix Kates Shulman, and Edmund White. Not bad—and several of them actually showed up for the event.

Eli had accomplished all that by juggling a thousand details and working far beyond the minimum number of hours he'd contracted for. I served on the margins as his "sous-chef," but not a single committee member ("I wish I could, but I'm *so* busy") lent a helping hand, not even in packing up some four hundred "gift bags" for attendees to take home with them. By any measure, the benefit was a huge success—we grossed what for us was the gigantic sum of $25,000. Yet at the committee meeting the following week, not one word—literally—was said about the benefit, nor was any offer of thanks made to Eli.

Instead, one of the few members Eli had asked to do a single task in helping to get ready for the event complained about being *pushed* to do more than her schedule allowed. In my view, this was beyond mean-spirited, but I didn't say so. The woman in question, an anthropologist, had simply been asked to get Eli a copy of the gay anthropologist mailing list. When it failed to arrive and Eli called her to inquire, she curtly told him that she had no time for addressing envelopes (which no one had asked her to do). He refrained from saying that he and I had already handwritten and sent out some fifteen hundred invitations; instead, he simply said that we'd be glad to do the addressing if she could get us the needed list. She never did.

This was the same woman, astonishingly, who turned to me for help some months later when it became clear that her tenure was in jeopardy. She taught at an upstate college and asked me to plead her case in person at the next meeting of her department. And I did. I spent the day upstate dutifully arguing that her one book had been "path-breaking" and her next would be likewise (I'd in fact rewritten her book proposal and found her an agent). When I arrived at her campus, it became immediately clear that her department was leaning against tenure. One of her colleagues in particular argued vociferously against her promotion, calling her not only unproductive but ill willed. "I know what you mean," I was tempted to say, but didn't. Lying through my teeth, I told him that I'd always found her amiable and cooperative. They call it "gay solidarity"—and it should be resisted. She got tenure.

Sometimes, when our meetings got overheated, I longed for a good old shout-out: "Hey! We have real enemies out there, and some of them are well-positioned professors and administrators right here at CUNY! Could we please put our squabbling aside and concentrate on what I *hope* is our common goal: the establishment of a center for lesbian and gay studies?" Probably no one will believe me, but I can honestly say that I wasn't interested in a one-man show and that temperamentally I *hated* being a full-time administrator.

I had the thought that maybe what was needed was a full-day retreat where we could talk out the personality conflicts that had—again—arisen and also rethink both our organizational structure and mission. The notion of a retreat was met with enthusiasm, and we quickly implemented it. We rented an out-of-town facility and hired a professional facilitator, Donna Jensen, to smooth the discussions. Several board members briefed her in advance about the heated climate of late, and at the start of the retreat Donna pointed out the need to put our recent bickering—she went so far as to use the word "trauma"—in perspective. We were, she said, moving from being a grassroots board that had nothing and did everything to becoming a working board that has something and does something. Short of being able to hire a staff and becoming a *corporate* board, we had to understand that a working board meant precisely that: everyone pitching in to do a modicum of chores.

She then invited us to review the committee's history to date and to try and pinpoint the areas of most disagreement. That proved helpful: we succeeded in reminding ourselves that our real antagonists were a cadre of conservative gay academics who *un*like us did *not* believe in addressing racial and gender issues and perspectives and who felt perfectly at home in a university world in which women and people of color were satisfyingly absent. With that reminder, tensions notably deflated. It was only at the end of the daylong retreat that a certain amount of anger resurfaced, though this time around it was at least straightforward. It began when I acknowledged that my own work ethic made me impatient with those who volunteered to do a particular job and then failed to.

More mea culpas followed. The art historian Jim Saslow said that most people feel threatened by somebody like me who knows how to get things done, "or seems to." Perhaps, Jim suggested, being "too busy" to follow through wasn't really the central mechanism at play but rather an entrenched, even unconscious, need to defy Big Daddy. Jim also suggested that I acknowledge more fully that the center was my baby, which fed my exasperation at those who shirked responsibility for its survival.

I had no trouble acknowledging my investment in the center's success, but thought that "it wasn't nearly as high as some people presumed." My ego had always been primarily tied, I added, "not to institutional prestige but to the success of my writing." In any case, I *did* feel that it would be a disservice if the center became known as "Marty's project." Even as I said the words, it suddenly dawned on me *to step down right then and there*—and I said as much. A spirited discussion followed. Bert Hansen, a historian of science and one of the more active committee members, predicted that the center wouldn't survive without me "at the helm." Others felt that after a period of transition, the ship would right itself and perhaps be stronger than before.

The historian Randy Trumbach, seconded by several others, jumped in to insist, adamantly, that it *was* imperative for me to remain the official director at least long enough to get CLAGS through the CUNY Board of Trustees—and to attend the various hearings and meetings that invariably precede a formal anointment. I agreed to stay on for that long, but at the same time felt strongly that the founder of an organization at some point *should* step aside—if, that is, it was to develop an independent identity and an ongoing life of its own. I had never wanted the center to be a one-man show; my hope had all along been to help set it on its feet and then leave it to others to carry into the future. I looked forward to the day when, a new director installed, I could be set free from the administrative functions I loathed and able to return to my writing.

Soon after the retreat we expanded the board, adding a number of members, including two gay students working toward degrees at the Graduate School. All the new people, unburdened by past grievances real or imagined, signed up to participate in one of the subcommittees (finance, programming, outreach, membership, etc.), which now started to meet more frequently. Since the committee work was self-selected, people could contribute ideas and energy to the group that dealt with matters closest to their own interests. Final decisions on subcommittee recommendations would be made by majority vote when the full committee convened for its monthly meeting. It soon became clear that clarifying the mission of each subcommittee and matching up interests and energy did improve the general mood. The dithering and accusations that had marred much of the past year began to recede.

Some of the old hands, of course, continued to play out their lifetime roles: "S" still simmered through meetings in silent petulance, grievances unknown; "B" still indulged his ornate theatricality; "F" still rambled on with his pretentiously irrelevant speeches; and "E" continued to regularly announce that "as always, the men are doing nothing and the women are doing all the shit work" (though at the retreat she'd confessed to feeling guilty that over the past six months she'd essentially done nothing). But at least the professional malcontents were now surrounded and neutralized by the "can we get on with it, please?" adultness of the newer members. The overall tone of our meetings became much more good-natured and efficient. I did sometimes wonder whether the new folks simply hadn't had time yet to flaunt their own peculiar tics—but I quickly buried what would, alas, become a premonition.

By 1990 we'd further broadened our outreach. We started on a regular basis to publish a hefty newsletter, and we held monthly colloquiums in which the still-small but growing band of academics who'd shifted their academic specialty to "gender and sexuality studies" could share their recent scholarship with others. To further facilitate the exchange of views, we compiled and published a Scholarly Directory that listed the names, locations, and research subjects of scholars who'd begun to enter the new field but were isolated at small colleges in the boondocks, disconnected from any network or community of like-minded researchers. I discovered many of their names by scouring scholarly journals, on the lookout for mention of a relevant article or doctoral dissertation. Almost invariably, they would turn out to be the work of a fledgling young scholar bravely unintimidated by warnings from their senior professors that entering such a "tainted" field would put their careers at risk.

––––––––

After Knopf had thoroughly vetted the manuscript of my Robeson biography, publication was set for 1988. In the interim, bound galley proofs went out to certain key people, including Revels Cayton, the prominent Black labor leader on the West Coast (and grandson of Hiram Revels, the first Black US senator). Revels had long been Robeson's closest male friend, and I'd interviewed him and his wife Lee several times. Another set of galleys went to Helen Rosen and—as a contractual obligation—to Paul Jr. Helen called me from her vacation home in Key West to tell me she'd stayed up all night reading and considered the book "a triumph—you've captured the man I knew." She called back again the next day to report an hour-long conversation with Paul Jr. after she'd phoned him to offer "congratulations." He told her the manuscript was too "pro-Essie" (his mother, Eslanda) and "ranted on at considerable length," according to Helen, about my "refusal to acknowledge" his father's "six *Black* lovers," claiming that he'd given me the list and I'd deliberately suppressed it.

In fact, I'd never seen any such list. The only Black lovers Paul had ever tried to persuade me were "significant" in his father's life were the actresses Nina Mae McKinney and Ethel Waters. On the basis of *one* reference in a letter of Essie's, I'd managed to squeeze Nina Mae into the book. In the absence of *any* evidence about Ethel Waters, even of a one-night stand, I was unable in conscience to include her. Neither, in any case, was remotely as significant in Robeson's life as his White lovers (Yolanda Jackson, Freda Diamond, Helen, Clara Rockmore, and Uta Hagen). As Helen said on the phone, "Big Paul himself told me he didn't like going to bed with Black women because they were too ladylike." She advised me, in regard to Paul Jr., to "try to stay cool and calm. You're dealing with an unstable man—and I'm so angry at his reaction that I'm now prepared to say *publicly* that he's unstable."

I also put in a call to Revels Cayton in California to tell him that Paul Jr. was on the warpath and asking for his advice. "Hell," Revels laughed. "I tried to warn you five years ago! At one point I thought maybe you should reconcile with him, but no—just leave him be."

Some weeks later, when I was having dinner with Helen in her apartment, Paul Jr. called—and Helen signaled me to get on the other end of the phone. What I heard was a twenty-minute (short for him) diatribe about what a "disaster" my book was. He told Helen that I was "a racist and a Red-baiter" and had a "hidden agenda" all along to destroy his father, but he "doesn't intend to let Duberman get away with it." Just the sound of Paul's ice-cold, singsong voice chilled me. He *is*, I thought, capable of anything—a lawsuit being the least of it. He was too agitated, I felt, to acknowledge his real grievances, even to himself: that he wasn't at the center of the book because he wasn't at the center of his father's life, as he'd long claimed; that I didn't buy his pet theories—for example, that his mother was a double agent—because she wasn't; that he denied his father's depressive disorder because he preferred to believe that "sinister forces" were responsible for his father's failing health (as well as his own); that I didn't describe him as his father's closest confidant because, as both Helen and Revels had confirmed, his father felt they had little in common and gave him, even as a child, very little attention.

In the weeks immediately preceding the official publication date of the book, Paul presented Knopf with a typed *seven-hundred-page* diatribe that he claimed irrefutably exposed the book's factual errors and distortions. He threatened to sue if Knopf went ahead with publication. Knopf immediately set its battery of lawyers to work evaluating the validity of Paul's complaints, and the lawyers in turn insisted that I provide documentary proof that Paul's contested interpretations were inaccurate. That required a hellish amount of digging on short notice through huge stacks of photocopies, but I wasn't about to let seven years of labor be buried by Paul's accusations. In the end, the lawyers declared themselves wholly convinced by the evidence I produced and told Knopf that Paul's charges were a compound of distortions, contradictions, and outright inventions—that *none* of his claims and assertions held up.

Knopf, with my consent, decided to offer Paul an olive branch: since he didn't accept the lawyers' judgment of his complaints, Knopf offered to submit galley proofs of the book to any expert *of Paul's choosing* to evaluate his charges against me. Paul agreed, and chose the left-wing editor Angus Cameron, who'd had a dazzling early career at Little, Brown (his authors included J. D. Salinger, Lillian Hellman, and Evelyn Waugh) until he was fired for refusing the company's request to "clear his outside political activities" with the firm. He had remained blacklisted until Knopf hired him as a senior editor in 1959. Cameron agreed to read the manuscript, and the report he turned in went beyond a press agent's dream: the biography is "spectacular," he wrote Knopf; he didn't know "how [I] managed to pull it off" and felt that I'd written a "marvelously balanced portrait of what is now for the first time clear was this country's greatest black figure." Cameron added that he would write a "careful" letter to Paul Jr. that he hoped "will bring him to his senses." He did, but it didn't. Paul Jr. decided he'd chosen the wrong mediator, someone unfamiliar with the *true* course of his father's life. I decided to exhale anyway.

Just before publication, Paul Jr., in a weirdly unpredictable twist, called both my agent Frances Goldin and my editor Bobbie Bristol with firm "instructions" about how best to promote the biography in the Black community! To say that we were startled understates the case, since Paul had fiercely denounced the book in his mendacious seven-hundred-page critique and had for months tied up Knopf's legal team with disproving his bizarre counternarrative. Having tried to stop the book, Paul was now stepping up to advise the publisher on how best to sell it! He even told Frances and Bobbie that it was essential that a Black press agent be hired if they hoped to push the book successfully in Black circles. He also gave them a message for me personally: "Martin should answer the 'Red-baiters' by telling them that the charge was a cover for Black-baiting." "Don't you think Martin knows that?" Frances replied.

Given that the Robeson archives had been previously closed and his remarkable life story largely untold, the biography in a real sense sold itself. Even before Knopf threw a party for the book in mid-February 1989, three laudatory front-page reviews had already appeared (within the week the tally would rise to eight out of eight), along with an inundation of requests for interviews. To my great relief, the critical reception from Black scholars was glowing. Henry Louis Gates Jr. called the book "brilliantly realized," Harvard professor Nathan Huggins hailed it as "magnificent," and Du Bois's biographer, David Levering Lewis, declared it "a marvel."

The nicest surprise came from Princeton's Nell Irvin Painter in her *Boston Globe* review. She and I had recently been on a panel together where she'd pointedly and sharply spoken out—staring directly at me—against *any* White person attempting to write the biography of a Black figure. Now, in the *Globe*, she did a magnanimous about-face, writing an undiluted rave and praising me for my understanding of Black people—*and* women. I felt the review in the *Washington Post* ("a marvelous story marvelously told") by Arnold Rampersad, the biographer of Langston Hughes, closely aligned with my own interpretation of Robeson's stance on the Soviet Union. Instead of crucifying him—as had so many during his lifetime—for not publicly denouncing Stalin's crimes, Rampersad underscored my view that the blame for Robeson's silence rested squarely on a racist American culture that limited and confined Black political options. Rampersad verified my argument that the generosity of Robeson's spirit got squeezed into an airtight container *because* he was unwilling to add evidence, to bestow his blessing, on the racist and reactionary right wing that dominated American politics in the 1950s; he refused to deepen its sway, refused to bend the knee. Since Rampersad had failed to Red-bait Robeson, the *Post* supplied an accompanying cartoon showing him with a leering, buffoonish grin on his face and a hammer-and-sickle medal pinned to his chest.

White conservatives, of course, had a field day. Barry Gewen in the *New Leader* accused me of being an "apologist" for Robeson's "Stalinism." Similarly, Harvey Klehr in *Commentary* dismissed my "strained" effort to excuse Robeson's support of Communism, and Eric Breindel in the *Wall Street Journal* claimed that I shared Robeson's "abject fealty to Stalinism as a virtue"—though he was unable to cite a drop of evidence in support of the assertion.

The award for Strangest Review went, hands down, to the all-important *New York Times*. The head of the book section, Michael Levitas, assigned the biography to John Patrick Diggins, author of *The Rise and Fall of the American Left* and a man who had declared Ronald Reagan "one of the two or three truly great presidents in history." In his front-page Sunday review in the *Times*, Diggins called the biography itself "superb," but devoted most of his lengthy review to denouncing Robeson himself, in language reminiscent of the Cold War, for his unflagging allegiance to the Soviet Union.

At a party some months after the review appeared, I was introduced to a staff member of the *New York Times Book Review*. He told me that both he and Rebecca Sinkler (who was second to Levitas and would herself become head of the *Review*) "think *Robeson* is a great book and were terribly upset" at the way the *Times* handled it. "Someday," he confided, "I'll tell you the full story." To which I said, "I think I know some of it—Michael Levitas." "Yes, that's right. I can't go into the details, but they're hair-raising." I assumed—though there may be more to the story—that he was referencing Levitas's background. His parents had fled Russia after the Bolshevik Revolution and he himself had in 1951 joined Voice of America, the government-funded broadcast begun in 1947 "to counter the more harmful instances of Soviet propaganda." Many on the left considered the Voice itself a forum for propaganda.

Knopf threw a gala party for the book, and the turnout was large and enthusiastic. Rose Rubin, who'd illegally produced Robeson recordings during the worst years of his ostracism and had eyed me suspiciously throughout the interview she'd reluctantly granted, passed through the crowd like a tour director loudly proclaiming the book "perfect! definitive!" Leonard Boudin, an equally confirmed leftie who'd spent years fighting to get Robeson's passport returned, was also warm in his praise. But nothing surprised me more than the appearance at the party of my old buddy Lew Lehrman, with whom I'd had an intense friendship back in the '60s. Standing in a group of people, I felt a tap on my back and turned around to find myself staring into Lew's face—I hadn't seen him in years—creased with his trademark devilish grin. The two of us dissolved into a hug. When I'd known him, he'd been a fierce left-wing radical and was working toward a PhD in history. Later, after we'd lost touch, he moved further and further to the right, converting to Catholicism and becoming a wealthy pillar of the establishment. Just a few years earlier he'd narrowly lost the race for governor of New York to Mario Cuomo. Three or four people came up to me after Lew had gone home and asked, their tone censorious, "What is Lewis Lehrman doing at *this* party?!" "He's an old friend," I replied, "and I couldn't be happier that he came."

As any writer can testify, the appeal of a book tour, initially flattering, rapidly deflates in the face of the banal questions most interviewers pose, plus the sound of one's own voice repeating nearly word for word the "insights" delivered during the previous interview two hours earlier. When, as a kickoff to the tour, I was invited on the *TODAY* show, my initial pleasure quickly faded during the "preproduction" interview when, bizarrely, I was asked, "Can you explain why, in some of the photos of him, Robeson looks sad?" Waiting in the wings to go on the show, I resolved to forget the absurdities and hype and use the opportunity to deliver a worthwhile political message. As the bored-looking host, Bryant Gumbel, started to read off *his* prepackaged questions, I talked *through* them (as a friend had advised) and delivered my own prepackaged statement denouncing single-issue critics who would rather harp on Robeson's purported "Stalinism" than grapple with the totality of his life—in particular his indictment of capitalism and his militant insistence on *full* freedom for Black people. Gumbel looked startled, then pleased. Afterward he asked me to sign his copy of the book.

As I learned early on in the tour, fatuous questions and formulaic responses were par for the course. One radio show host memorably introduced me by announcing, "My guest today is Martin Duberman, the author of a novel on the life of Paul Robeson." Another host—with Robeson's face staring up at him from the press packet—opened the interview by saying, "I'm a little confused, Mr. Duberman. Have you written a biography or an autobiography?"

When I reached San Francisco on the tour, I again dropped in to see Revels and Lee Cayton. Revels was guarded by nature, but not this time around. He threw his arms around me in a bear hug, beaming with pleasure. When I told him that Paul Jr. had called the book "prurient," Revels chuckled in disbelief at what he called my "*restrained*" version of Paul Sr.'s sex life.

In Los Angeles, I had a prearranged "power lunch" with Sidney Poitier's close associates Tom Mount and Terry Nelson. Earlier, when the book was still in galley proofs, Poitier had contacted Frances, my agent, to say he was interested in making a movie based on the biography. The "power lunch" was supposed to iron out details, and the offer Tom and Terry laid out was stunningly good, with my own package coming to about three-quarters of a million dollars. Plus there was much earnest, believable talk about making a film that "told the truth." Poitier himself later phoned me to underscore his determination to tell Robeson's story in all its "radical richness."

There was one hurdle only that needed to be cleared. Back in 1981, when my contract with Paul had been drawn up and with all my terms met, Frances had suggested that "as a gesture of goodwill" I voluntarily offer to give Paul veto power over all future deals regarding secondary rights. Knowing nothing of such matters, and trusting Frances fully, I agreed to the clause without hesitation. It proved a bad mistake.

When Frances made Poitier aware of the contract clause he straightaway got on the phone to Paul, whom he'd known most of his life. When he hung up an hour later, he described the conversation as "nuts." According to Poitier, Paul had spent the first half hour insisting on final approval of the movie's contents, and spent the second "detailing" (as Poitier recounted the call) "his own hitherto unrecognized 'genius'"—announcing that he would probably make the movie himself. Poitier felt certain Paul could never put together the needed funding, nor get agreement to the absurd terms he outlined: control over the script, plus the right to choose director and cast. Poitier's prediction would prove accurate: Paul never did make his movie. But he also managed, despite dozens of inquiries over the years, to prevent anyone else from doing so.

Following the phone call with Paul, Poitier, understandably, withdrew. He told us he wasn't willing to try "cajoling" Paul, because even if that proved possible, working with him would be a nightmare. On the same day that we got word of Poitier's withdrawal, Frances told me that Paul had delayed so long in considering an offer from the Book-of-the-Month Club that the deadline had passed and the offer was withdrawn.

And so it would go, over and over, through the years. It's no exaggeration to say that over time a multiplicity of offers came in to make a movie based on my biography. Among the more glamorous close calls was a bid from Lorimar; they wanted to do a feature film—the "full treatment à la *Gandhi*"—and dangled vast sums. Paul, exercising the veto right we'd gratuitously given him, refused to proceed: having given a White man control over the biography, he announced that he intended to refuse all offers from Whites and would himself raise the needed $20 million—and would maintain control over the final cut. Lorimar threw in the towel, and so, eventually, did a number of other successful producers eager to make a movie or a miniseries. For a time, Frances continued to take the most promising offers to Paul in the hope he'd have a change of heart, but he never budged—nor did he himself ever find a producer who'd accept his exorbitant demands. After a while Frances, too, gave up; anyone inquiring about the movie rights was simply told they "were not available." Paul died in 2014, Frances in 2019. As for me, at ninety, I'm better off not thinking about it.

By the time of Stonewall's twentieth-anniversary event in 1989, Eli and I had already consolidated households and pledged eternal troth. I was even busier than usual, what with the turmoil surrounding the publication of the Robeson biography, and Eli was in an uneasy state as he shifted careers from running Literacy Volunteers to becoming a psychoanalyst. The result was a pretty steep roller coaster of adjustments during our first two years together. Fortunately, we both did know for certain that we wanted the relationship, and we worked hard, in therapy and out, to get through the rough spots. Over time—this year marks our thirty-fifth together—we've learned how to cope with them. Like most long-term couples, "smooth sailing" never becomes a given (not if the relationship is still alive), though you do get better at accepting imperfection and compromising differences. That is, if you're lucky and willing to work at it.

The Robeson biography behind me, I decided to write my next book about growing up gay during the '40s and '50s, a time when homophobia was at its virulent height and many of us had internalized the need to seek a "cure" for our affliction through psychotherapy. When embarking on a new book, and even more when writing it, I almost never talk about the process, not even with Eli. I sit, rather, with the nervous aplomb of a mother hen shielding her unhatched egg. But in regard to the new book (ultimately titled *Cures*) I was more communicative than usual, mostly because I needed feedback about whether revealing so much intimate and painful material was in fact necessary. And so I sent off portions of the manuscript to a few close friends.

The response was mostly encouraging, to a degree even enthusiastic. One friend, though, a prominent feminist, was, somewhat to my surprise, rather sharply negative. She felt I'd needlessly opened up my personal life for crass inspection—and likely dismissal—and didn't see why on earth I had decided to. I had trouble myself with the "why." The urge to open for scrutiny some of the more excruciating, even humiliating episodes in my life didn't *feel* either self-destructive or exhibitionistic. I expected the dominant reaction to run along the lines of "How could a smart—or at least accomplished—guy fall for such a load of shit about the 'pathology' of homosexuality for so long?"

In the upshot, that *would* be a common response and, I felt, a legitimate one. "Why all that guilt?" "Where did it come from?" "Why did it maintain its iron grip for so long?" "How had someone like [me], known to widely challenge authority in areas ranging from traditional education to organized religion to knee-jerk 'patriotism,' allow [myself] to be so thoroughly brainwashed by the unearned authority of psychotherapy?"

Good questions all. And pretty much the same ones that had led me to undertake the book in the first place. I was convinced that my story was essentially a generational one, and not unique. In laying out my own psychic trauma during the pre-Stonewall years, I felt I was usefully revealing the tale of how several generations of gay people had profoundly internalized a negative view of their humanity. I'd anticipated that reliving and writing up the story wouldn't be easy, and I realized, too, that the depth of self-doubt endemic in my generation might well be impossible for younger gay people, who grew up in a more tolerant climate, to understand, let alone regard with compassion.

It came as a considerable surprise when *Cures* was published that it got mostly favorable reviews that typically hailed it as "a book of admirable affirmation." The large batch of private letters redressed the balance by pointing to the considerable residue of self-distrust that did, and does, persist. Even now, after the psychiatric climate has dramatically shifted and charges of "perversion" and "sin" have weakened, an irreducible amount of internalized homophobia remains, along with the ongoing, deeply imprinted conviction that we are "lesser" beings. Remarkably, the Book-of-the-Month Club back in 1991 chose *Cures* as its first-ever gay-themed book, and it became one of the company's leading sellers. Expecting brickbats and getting instead widespread praise could be taken as a sign of the country's pronounced change of heart about homosexuality. I doubted it then, and I still do. More likely, I think, the applause *Cures* received was symptomatic of the country's indelible habit of embracing stories of "affirmation" while burying the darker side of reality.

By 1990 CLAGS had begun to hold ambitious one- to three-day conferences on such central matters as "AIDS and Public Policy," "Feminism and Lesbianism," and "Black Nations/Queer Nations?" Probably the most notorious among them was the combustible two-day event in December 1991, "The Brain and Homosexuality." It featured the recent article in *Science* by Simon LeVay, the British neuroscientist, claiming discovery that the INAH3 (the interstitial nucleus of the anterior hypothalamus) in gay men was smaller in size than that of straight men and women. Lesbians, as is often the case, weren't discussed. The article caused a considerable stir, with the *New York Times* summarizing its contents on the front page. That alone gave enormous currency to LeVay's contention that the INAH3 differential *proved* that the root cause of male homosexuality was biological, not cultural. Supporters of the view that homosexuality was innate were delighted. The long-standing, much debated question of the origin of sexual orientation appeared to have been solved.

Few gay scholars agreed—no more than did most feminists to the parallel claim that men and women are from "different planets" (in the case of gender the purported determinant was again the brain—not LeVay's INAH3 but rather the corpus callosum tissue that connects the brain's left and right hemispheres). In regard both to sexual orientation and to gender, those who hail biological explanations usually have an unexamined agenda: believing that "different" automatically equates to "lesser" leaves the usual suspects, exclusively heterosexual men, in the saddle. Add in the comparable arguments long used about the "innate" differences between "analytic" Whites and "emotional" Blacks, and the profile of those "destined" to rule is once again familiar: heterosexual White men.

The CLAGS conference on LeVay's findings constituted one of the earliest sustained attacks on the inadequacy of both his science and his logic—and he himself was present throughout, smiling puckishly under the avalanche of academic blows. As the conferees pointed out, nearly all the gay men whose brains LeVay studied had died of AIDS, and the HIV virus, as was well known by 1990, did affect the brain's structural functions. His sample of a mere forty-one brains, moreover, was too small to warrant the broad conclusions he drew—especially since the INAH3 structure was tiny and difficult to measure precisely. Besides, it turned out that the size of the INAH3 structure *did* vary among both gay and straight men. And finally, it was generally accepted (if not by LeVay) that the environment *does* influence the brain's structure and function—a fact LeVay had wholly ignored.

Speaker after speaker at the conference pointed out that conservatives generally choose to believe that homosexuality is a biological phenomenon for the same reason they want to believe that women and Black people are innately deficient in their capacity for rational analysis—thus confirming the *rightness* of their own entitlement to hold on to privilege and power. A side "benefit" to viewing homosexuality as biological in origin is that it assigns the phenomenon wholly to a small group of Others, thus implicitly denying that the impulse and capacity for same-gender erotic arousal is widespread rather than confined to a limited (and despised) few.

Throughout the conference, LeVay seemed unruffled, which—given the sharpness of the criticisms being leveled at him—astonished me. But then again, I hadn't taken to him personally from the start. At the lunch the two of us had preceding the first day of the conference, I'd found him insufferably smug and unappealingly fey. He was constantly "on"—a forty-eight-year-old imp poured into skintight T-shirt and jeans who talked "electrically," nonstop, and with a steely overlay of arrogance about his favorite topic: himself. Ours was not a meeting of hearts and minds.

The year 1990 also marked a turnaround in my personal reconnection to the Graduate School. The background tale, which I briefly mentioned earlier, is a bit of a saga. Back in 1971, when I accepted CUNY's offer, I'd been asked to teach at the Graduate School as well as at Lehman, one of CUNY's undergraduate campuses. I begged off at the time, having become weary during my years at Princeton at the dutiful way graduate students wrote down and parroted back—instead of challenging and modifying—my every word. For the preceding five years I'd been experimenting at Princeton with my *undergraduate* seminars on ways to demilitarize the learning process, shucking off the authoritarian apparatus that had long inhibited any authentic search for meaning. I'd had a fair amount of success with undergraduates, but the graduate students had mostly proven immune to innovation. After a few years I stopped offering graduate seminars but did continue to advise doctoral theses and to serve on PhD orals.[2]

That pattern held for a decade. By the early '80s, having gotten increasingly involved in researching the history of sexuality and gender, I changed my mind. I thought graduate students, with their greater life experience and information, might welcome a plainspoken, nonjudgmental dialogue on controversial material if presented in an unthreatening way. That was not a view shared by the Graduate School History Department. Its notoriously conservative chair, Gertrude Himmelfarb (wife of Irving Kristol, the "godfather" of neoconservatism), had already informed me that there was no such thing as the "history of sexuality," that the subject was an offshoot of a political agenda and not a legitimate subject for intellectual discourse.

That made me bristle; it was all too reminiscent of an incident back in 1971 when a member of the History Department at Lehman had unsuccessfully tried to block my elevation to a distinguished professorship by announcing to the Committee on Appointments that I was "a *known* homosexual." That memory still lingered, and I pulled no punches with Himmelfarb: OK, I told her, you're clearly telling me that my current scholarship is ersatz, perhaps even borderline obscene. Since in your eyes I'm "contaminated," you certainly won't want graduate students coming into contact with me. Ergo, I will no longer advise PhD theses or sit on doctoral exams. Exit Duberman, to no fanfare at all.

That stalemate had held until 1990. By then the Graduate School History Department had *somewhat* changed in both personnel and attitude. Besides, the news was already out that CLAGS was in the pipeline awaiting accreditation—which meant, like it or not, that LGBTQ studies was about to be certified as a legitimate field of scholarly study. I duly resubmitted my earlier proposal to the History Department to teach a course called Lesbian and Gay History, Politics, and Culture, and this time around it was immediately accepted, no strings attached. I was warned, though, in a tone meant to sound predictive, that it was standard policy to cancel any seminar that enrolled too few students.

To the shock of everyone, me included, some forty students registered for the seminar. They included two faculty members and students from three other universities, and represented a wide range of academic disciplines, including Japanese literature. Tellingly, not a single student from the History Department enrolled, and a sympathetic colleague told me why: "The department is still so conservative that students are afraid that signing up will damage their careers."

The large enrollment confirmed the existence of widespread interest in the study of gender and sexuality, underscoring its legitimacy, even necessity. When enrollment climbed to forty-two—too large to allow the kind of free-flowing exchange I aimed for—I divided the group into two.

Already overextended, I knew that scheduling an extra seminar would complicate my life, but I couldn't in good conscience do otherwise. The presence of CLAGS at the Graduate School had led to a proliferation of gay graduate students, and I could hardly send them away.

What followed for the rest of the term was a raucous, at times rancorous give-and-take that thoroughly shook *me* up, as it did many of the students, and that highlighted the seismic split—and not a particularly cordial one—between gay generations. In one of the two seminars the no-holds-barred climate became so clamorous that I often felt overwhelmed. Having taught only undergraduates for some fifteen years, I'd unwittingly lost touch with the latest wave of academic fashion—with what, in shorthand, I'll call "poststructuralism." I'd never read Jacques Derrida, and although one of his subtlest critics, Richard Rorty, had been a good friend of mine at Princeton, I'd never read him either!

Forced by the seminar's demands, I put myself through a rapid tutorial on "deconstruction" and found—to my surprise—that I'd long since been advocating some of its central principles, even if I lacked the fashionable vocabulary of its practitioners. For thirty years I'd been delivering my own set of warnings to historians that they needed to more carefully examine the subjective assumptions that underlay their glib reference to "facts," their certitude about the fixity of "truth," their unawareness of the deception inherent in a binary perspective, and the subtle way the "accidental" features of a text can subvert its intended meaning. I'd long thought historians were remarkably uninterested in the ambiguities inherent in their own enterprise.

The more cantankerous seminar of the two was dominated by what I thought of—though never said out loud—as the Triumvirate: "Alice," "Jean," and "Liz." They made it clear early on that they regarded me as some sort of antique—a creature of grossly outmoded habits of thought and perspective. And they were dazzlingly, gleefully adept at patronizing and openly denouncing me (along with some of the other members of the seminar). Two of the Triumvirate were in addition proud enthusiasts of sadomasochism, and even the most respectful question, the barest hint of disagreement, brought down an avalanche of sarcasm and patronizing mockery. At this distance it's hard to recapture, let alone convey, the very real and prolonged pain of being the chief target of their belittlement. Having long prided myself on being a nonauthoritarian teacher wide open to challenge and controversy, keen to encourage contradictory views, I now had many a sleepless night agonizing over my inadequacy, blaming myself for being inexcusably out of step with the avant-garde.

Alice led the pack, and she was relentless in scorning what she called my "knee-jerk humanism," my naive elevation of "contradictory impulses" over the unvarying, fixed desire of, say, a confirmed "top" or a single-minded "bottom." All three stingingly patronized my "primitive" views as barely worthy of combat; I wasn't conversant enough with the new vocabulary to bother with, to deserve their respect, to warrant their attention. As I say, it was *painful*. Occasionally they'd deign to challenge me, as when they dared me to define what I meant by the term *intimacy*, suggesting that it referred to absolutely nothing—other than an unexamined cliché. Before meeting Eli I might well have been on their side of the argument, but now I knew about the special comfort that comes from dailiness and from being loved *after* one's secret self is known—though I wasn't about to reveal any of *that* to the Alice clique, lest they further level the dreaded accusation of "sentimentality."

During our discussion of sadomasochism, Alice harrumphed over what she labeled my "negative" view. I thought she'd misunderstood certain comments of mine, and made the mistake of trying to explain myself. Every person, I said, should have the right to do what they want with their body, and I rejected their presumption that I felt otherwise. But, I added, I *did* have mixed feelings about sadomasochism when it became a way of life, locking the individual into an airtight, unvarying role. I'd hoped, I went on, that in the safety of the seminar we could give expression to those hidden, often semiconscious feelings. "Nonsense!" Liz interrupted. "We believe in *texts*, not in 'judgments,' not in emotion. *Texts* should be the channels and intermediaries of discussion!" She chuckled over my "lame" concern that a focus on texts valorized a kind of dehumanized impersonality.

And so it went. I was alternately angry at their patronizing manner and chagrined at my own feelings of inadequacy in struggling with a new vocabulary and set of perspectives. Much of the time I sat in nervous anticipation of attack—which I told myself was good for me: I'd gotten too comfortable with students behaving like adoring fans. This bunch, who treated me as an obsolete "old-style gay," might in the long run (if I survived) serve me better. But easy it was *not*. It helped to think that a lot of their own hurtful history—which they dismissed as irrelevant—was being dumped onto a conveniently penitent target. I found a sort of dubious comfort in a colleague's derisive remark that "a whole generation of doctoral theses will in ten more years seem hilariously archaic."

All I knew for certain was that for a long time after the seminar ended I remained in a mixed state of resentment and bewilderment, of wounded anger alternating with glimmers of enlightenment. I kept thinking about why—unlike so many of the students I'd interacted with in the past—they saw an invitation to speak openly about their lives as an unwelcome threat; why they insistently rejected personal feelings in favor of abstract paradigms; why they heard "nonjudgmental acceptance" as a malignant cover for denunciation; why they viewed "honesty" as a threat to safety—and why safety had become prioritized. Why was the mere mention of "values" derided as ersatz, and the attempt to examine them hooted down as some sort of feeble moralizing? Why was personal narrative regarded as an evasion and dilutant, rather than a complication of purportedly "neutral" analysis? Why was the notion of neutral analysis thought *possible*, let alone superior? Had my own eager advocacy for what I'd (perhaps too early on?) called a "no-holds-barred" discussion of difficult subject matter established a climate of guarded alarm, the opposite of what I intended? Why did the members of the *second* seminar welcome my invitation and proceed week after week to have lively and trusting conversations—to the point that one woman (herself a teacher) came by my office at the end of the term to tell me she "had never seen a class run more according to feminist principles"? Over time, the questions tortured me less and less—though I never found satisfying answers to them.

Having made a dent in the curriculum (and in my psyche), I refocused my energy on the Center for Lesbian and Gay Studies (now widely called CLAGS). We were finally at the point in 1990 where we'd managed to stitch together the needed $50,000 to formally place us before the CUNY Board of Trustees. We'd accumulated a good chunk of the bankroll from the fundraising events Eli organized, and a lesser sum from enrollment fees and passing the hat at our conferences. During the first few years our biggest hit (a standing-room-only crowd of some five hundred) had been a panel discussion on whether or not "butch/femme" roles remained relevant; the LeVay conference was the stand-out event of the early '90s; and "Black Nations/Queer Nations?"—the indisputable triumph of the mid-1990s.

We also raised some money from the occasional donor lunch or house party, as well as a $10,000 grant several years running from the gay-oriented Paul Rapoport Foundation. (Rapoport, a founder of the Gay Men's Health Crisis—for a time the largest volunteer AIDS organization in the world—had himself died of AIDS in 1987.) What put us over the top, though, was a totally unexpected $20,000 bequest in 1990 from David Clarke, a gay man unknown to any of us, who'd died of AIDS.

In addition, an old friend of mine, the psychiatrist David Kessler, agreed in 1992 (*after* our formal establishment) to provide a $110,000 endowment that enabled us to offer an annual $2,500 award to a scholar for his or her outstanding contribution to lesbian and gay (later broadened to LGBTQ+) studies. Each year the awardee would give a public lecture in the Graduate School auditorium, followed by a celebratory post-lecture party. Inaugurated in 1992, the first ten Kessler Lectures were in 2003 published as a book, *Queer Ideas*, edited by Alisa Solomon and me. The Kessler Lecture has continued down to the present day and become a widely anticipated event in gay academic circles, something of a festive gathering of the tribe.

We chose Joan Nestle, cofounder of the Lesbian Herstory Archives, to give the first Kessler Lecture, which she titled "I Lift My Eyes to the Hill: The Life of Mabel Hampton as Told by a White Woman." Hampton, a lifelong lesbian, had danced during the Harlem Renaissance in all-Black productions, but had then fallen on hard times and spent most of the rest of her life as a cleaning woman for White families (including Joan's). The lecture was powerful, the auditorium packed (mostly women), with people sitting in the aisles and standing in the back. And the rapport between Joan and the audience was palpably affectionate. She did a marvelous job of re-creating Mabel Hampton's life out of bare fragments of evidence, showing how our lost voices *can* be reclaimed, and with deep respect. Many were in tears at the end, including me (and also Frances Degen Horowitz, the new and very supportive president of the Graduate School).

By the spring of 1990, with our $50,000 in hand, I started in on the string of calls and meetings needed to put CLAGS on the CUNY Board of Trustees agenda. As I made the rounds, I rarely ran into outright hostility; polite patronization—the unspoken "*we're* doing *you* a great favor"—was the more characteristic response. President Horowitz and Dean Alan Gartner were themselves entirely cordial and helpful. But even our allies in the administration warned me that following board approval—which they estimated would take about a year—the overcrowded Graduate School had no available office space and the temporary solution would have to be to let my own office (cramped quarters shared with two other professors) double as the CLAGS office. In the upshot, it would be ten months *after* our accreditation, and following my angry confrontation with a hostile vice president, before we got the semblance of an office—and still longer before we could make it habitable. No matter: we were finally on the map.

By 1990 the death toll from AIDS in the United States had risen to more than fifty thousand. None of the drugs that had been serially heralded as lifesaving had proved worth a damn, and none of those in the pipeline appeared more promising. The Reaganites continued to play deaf, dumb, and blind, and religious leaders continued to gloat with sick glee over "God's righteous punishment of sinners." By 1990, fortunately, ACT UP had become a national force, and its militant, daring tactics were making it impossible for the bigots to hold the national stage unchallenged. By persistently refusing to take no for an answer or to "go quietly into that good night," ACT UP's tenacity did lead to accelerated research and efficacy trials, though effective treatments for AIDS were no more available in the early '90s than they'd been a decade earlier.

Given the initial mix of hostility and apathy that had characterized both the public and governmental response to AIDS, those afflicted with HIV in New York City had banded together as early as 1981— preceding the 1987 advent of ACT UP—to create the Gay Men's Health Crisis (GMHC); a comparable group (which later morphed into the San Francisco AIDS Foundation) also formed on the West Coast. By early 1983 GMHC had put together a hotline, crisis counseling, and a volunteer buddy system to visit and run errands for those housebound with the virus. Admirable as these efforts were, GMHC's advocacy of less sex with fewer partners (and only "healthy" ones) alienated those "sex-positive liberationists"—preeminently Michael Callen and Richard Berkowitz—who rejected GMHC's effort to downplay gay male sexual promiscuity and to convince the general public that AIDS was about to cross over into the straight world. Callen and Berkowitz worked to set up "safe-sex" guidelines that stressed the dangers of anal sex but did so within a context that continued to affirm and celebrate sexual liberation.

My own sympathies were with Callen and Berkowitz (I would later tell their story in my 2014 book, *Hold Tight Gently*), and when the two men joined with others in 1983 to form the People with AIDS Coalition (PWA), I volunteered for a number of years to answer the office phone one afternoon a week. During those years I often felt stunned at the nonchalant bravery of those on staff and of clients in compromised health who passed through the office. Most of my own friends had, like me, tested negative for the virus: having grown up in a climate of sexual repression, we weren't fully able (some were entirely unable) to shed the view imprinted on us that sexual "adventuring" was a symptom of pathology. In the liberatory post-Stonewall period many of us elders—in 1990 I turned sixty—had learned to mouth celebratory words about the wonders of promiscuity, and even (mostly) to believe them, but we found it much more difficult to comfortably or fully participate in the new orgiastic rites, not that our sagging tits and unreliable erections were much in demand. It was no credit to us, but our truncated joie de vivre proved a safety net.

I did have some friends younger than me, and a number of them did come down with AIDS. They, like the people I was meeting at PWA, gave bravery a whole new dimension. I think here especially of Tom Stoddard, Ken Dawson, and Vito Russo. Like AIDS sufferers everywhere, all three, being human, had periods of panic and hysteria—I was in fact witness to a few such agonizing occasions—but they were not the rule. Overriding the frightened, grief-stricken moments was an astonishing gallantry that accepted the lousy odds and insisted, animatedly, on playing out the hand.

I'd gotten to know Tom Stoddard during the mid-'80s when I served on the board of the New York Civil Liberties Union, of which he was a staff member. Tom was a charmer—dashing, articulate, impassioned (and now and then affectionately arrogant, too). When, in 1985, the office of executive director became open, I thought Tom would easily win out over the other finalist, Norman Siegel, who to me *obviously* lacked Tom's talent and charisma. I was wrong. As I've described earlier, in a marathon meeting of the board, Tom lost on the second ballot by a vote of 19–14. During that lengthy board meeting I'd been shocked to hear a number of coded homophobic remarks—Tom was variously described as "a whiner" and "a real risk."

After the vote went against him, Tom and I went out to dinner with two of his other supporters on the board to hash out the disappointing results. Tom had a strong sense of his own worth and was enraged, not crestfallen. Soon after he lost the NYCLU job, he got another offer: the Lambda Legal Defense and Education Fund invited him to become its executive director. Lambda was at the time a fledgling outfit, but its stated mission was an important one: to fight discrimination in employment, housing, health care, and the military. Hesitant about accepting, uncertain if Lambda was sturdy enough to accomplish its own goals—indeed, even to survive—Tom asked me for my opinion. I urged him to take the job, given its potential and the certainty I felt that Tom would make the organization into a real force. He did. In 1986 he wrote the landmark gay-rights legislation that—after many unsuccessful previous attempts—the New York City Council finally passed that same year. Tom also tirelessly built Lambda's reputation and stature before resigning in 1992.

He took on several other posts after that, and continued for the next five years to fight his own debilitation as vigorously as he had institutional discrimination. He maintained a rigorous diet and exercise regimen with the same consistency he'd brought to his legal career. And he tried nearly every promising new drug that came through the pipeline; most of them produced debilitating side effects, but none of them proved worth a damn. Yet Tom fought on. I remember one night in 1996 when Tom and a few other friends came to our place for dinner. Tom looked ghastly, devoid of the bright eagerness that had long been his trademark. I didn't think he'd make it through dinner—but in fact he was one of the last to leave. *Tom Tenacity*, I thought.

He was still alive when the breakthrough protease inhibitors finally arrived in 1996. Tom was skeptical: "My viruses," he said, "are too old and sophisticated" to suffer defeat. Alas, he was right. He died on February 12, 1997, at age forty-eight.

Ken Dawson, sweet souled, classically handsome, took the helm of SAGE (Senior Action in a Gay Environment) a decade after Stonewall and built it into a major organization that provided a wealth of services and social opportunities for the gay community's often-isolated elders.

He was one of those rare leaders—Ann Northrop and Tim Sweeney are two others—who go about their business with maximum efficiency and minimal theatrics, shrugging off personal praise as overblown or as needlessly distracting from the organizational mission. I'd met Ken through Eli, who Ken had asked to serve on the SAGE board (which Eli ultimately chaired).

Ken's forty-fifth birthday party illuminated his character. He was hospitalized at the time, so seven or eight of us gathered to celebrate the milestone in his hospital room. One friend brought a cake, Eli and I party favors, and the others assorted gifts, including Silly Putty that we gleefully threw against the walls. Throughout, Ken's spirits were good and he talked of going home "soon"; in fact he didn't have long to live. I wondered what he told himself, whether he was consistently able to allow himself the comfort of denial about his own condition. He took solace in religion, but his valor was grounded in *character* more than gospel. The homophobes, with no trace of irony, describe homosexuality as "a character disorder"—what they don't mean but should is that courage isn't an everyday human trait.

Three days later, when Eli and I went back to visit him, Ken suddenly couldn't hold back the tears and in strangulated words told us that he couldn't hang on much longer. For the next few months he was in and out of the hospital. At home Ken was still living with his ex-lover Todd, who became his devoted primary caretaker. When some of Ken's support team failed to show up as often as promised, Eli pitched in to make sure that he had at least one visitor a day. By the fall of 1991, Ken was clearly failing. He developed an undiagnosed infection, complete with fever, diarrhea, rectal CMV, and then, more seriously still, a collapsed lung already severely damaged from pneumonia. Ken focused on the "treatability" of the CMV and even talked about how "lucky" he felt. When let out of the hospital, he started doing psychotherapy with the openly gay Father John McNeill (whose 1976 book, *The Church and the Homosexual*, had led to his expulsion in 1987). The therapy, in Ken's words, helped him "to deal with issues relating to spirituality and dying."

As Ken awaited lung surgery at 7:00 AM one day in mid-November 1991, the brutality of the hospital system kicked in and he was kept waiting—no explanation offered—until midday. The surgery revealed extensive damage, and when I visited that night, Ken lay immobile in his bed, his few words coherent but muted. I got him to take a little tea and accept a gentle massage, but I felt anguished and inadequate. Two days later—the doctors "suspected brain involvement"—we had to help maneuver him through the ordeal of a CAT scan. By now Ken was terrified, afraid to be alone, and Eli had to scamper to keep a more or less steady flow of people in and out of his room. "Ken's such a dear man," I wrote later that night, "but there's so little anyone can do . . . and they talk about Magic Johnson's courage!"

Soon after, Ken passed away. At his packed memorial service, several of those who spoke did so movingly, capturing Ken's character—a decent, dignified, cautious, gentle, lonely man. John D'Emilio effectively summarized what Ken had stood for in the movement: the insistence that "we stop trashing each other and look for the *good* within our fellow activists." That seemed to capture the decency, the essence of Ken's character.

Though I knew Vito less well than Ken and Tom, I became part of the "support" team that his closest friend, Arnie Kantrowitz, and Arnie's partner, Larry Mass, put together during Vito's last few years. Vito had long been a well-known figure in the movement as both activist and film critic. In 1981 he'd published *The Celluloid Closet*, a classic work on homosexuality in the US film industry, and in 1985 he'd cofounded GLAAD (Gay and Lesbian Alliance Against Defamation), a watchdog group devoted to monitoring antigay slurs in the media.

On a June day in 1990, Vito had been scheduled to introduce to a New York audience the pathbreaking 1986 film *Parting Glances*, which dealt frankly with the subject of AIDS. To fulfill the engagement he'd managed to get himself checked out of the hospital where for a week he'd been suffering from AIDS-related pneumonia. Just before he went onstage he told me that he felt so weak he wasn't sure he'd be able to make it through. But he did—and in style. His voice was a little thick at times, and his trademark exuberance was missing, yet he was just as articulate as he'd always been—and possibly *more* moving than ever.

In fact, Vito had only a few months to live. When he was out of the hospital, I'd run occasional errands for him and we'd sometimes sit and talk. There were days when he was fiercely sealed off—*not* complaining, *not* self-pitying, but simply not interested in idle conversation. By July he was still more frequently in and out of the hospital in order to get chemo treatments, but by September it had become clear that the chemo had done what little it could. When I arrived at his apartment one day to accompany him yet again to the hospital, it was obvious that he was gulping down his fear, though he never verbalized it, focusing instead on the tasks at hand ("Do you think I should pack a sweater?") and speculating on whether he would be able to sneak out of the hospital to see the movie *Postcards from the Edge*.

Toward the end of his life he was subjected to assorted medical interventions that seemed to do little more than heighten his suffering. Entering his hospital room one day I found him shivering under a pile of blankets, yet resolutely insisting to the doctor that he felt "definitely improved." Denial? No, more like determined affirmation. He died on November 7, 1990.

At his memorial service, with Vito himself omnipresent through film clips and posters, the vitality of his image contrasted sadly with the purpose of the day. It was immensely touching to see many faces in the crowd—including Ken Dawson's—who were themselves known to be weak and endangered. Their haunting bravery in sitting through what must have felt, devastatingly, like a rehearsal for their own services brought tears to my eyes.

I spoke last, after five others, with their assorted styles and agendas, had paid their tributes. All, I thought, had been moving in their own ways, though Larry Kramer, running true to form, marred his fierce and fearless message with his own brand of indignant self-righteousness. "This is what it comes down to for all of us, Vito," I wrote that night, "others performing on the subject of your life while *incidentally* celebrating it."

Keeping super busy had long been my time-tested remedy for assuaging anxiety. But mounting sorrow (and terror) over AIDS in combination with several unexpected and overlapping additions to my calendar tipped the balance and I abruptly shifted into reverse. I took a three-part oath: to take a two-week vacation from CLAGS, to completely put aside the book I'd been working on during occasional free intervals, and to stop answering the phone.

That interregnum lasted exactly two days—interrupted in the nick of time by an invitation to resume a hectic schedule much more suited to my temperament than idleness. A consortium of the city's major cultural institutions—the New-York Historical Society, the Brooklyn Historical Society, the Museum of the City of New York, and the New York Public Library—contacted me to ask if CLAGS would be interested in participating in the planning of a joint celebration in 1994 for the twenty-fifth anniversary of the Stonewall riots. I of course jumped at the opportunity but didn't want to bypass the CLAGS board and make a decision on my own. Three of the institutions offered to send staff members to our next board meeting to discuss incipient plans and to solicit our participation.

To my amazement, the meeting did *not* go well. The ghost of Scrooge—doubtless in training for the upcoming Christmas season—shrouded the evening. After the three visitors had outlined their institutions' tentative plans—I, for one, thought the presentations warmly welcoming—our board members, puzzlingly, sat on their hands and neither query nor comment followed. I was dumbfounded, and to this day can't account for the curmudgeonly spirit. *After* the museum representatives left, the questions—or rather, objections—came tumbling out: "How can we trust their mainstream agenda?" "Since they have paid staff and we don't, can we count on them doing most of the work?" Weirdest of all the questions, in my view, came from the male student rep on the board who grumpily wanted to know, "Why should we want to celebrate a bunch of apolitical drag queens anyway?" Sylvia Rivera and Marsha P. Johnson—apolitical? The student badly needed a course in gay history.

"Because," I stonily responded, struggling not to sound as annoyed as I felt, "a lot of people feel that drag queens were instrumental in *starting* the Stonewall riots." I added, in as neutral a tone as I could manage, that in my opinion a twenty-fifth-anniversary citywide celebration of Stonewall, in combination with the Gay Olympic Games also planned for New York in June 1994, could mark a major milestone. Besides, I added, CLAGS's prominent role in organizing the event "would be a huge boost to our own credibility, to putting us on the institutional map. And it wouldn't cost us a dime!" By the end of the evening I finally got a begrudging go-ahead to participate in at least the next round of discussions with the museums.

When I notified David Kahn, head of the Brooklyn Historical Society, who was openly gay (and a sturdy CLAGS board member), to say that our subcommittee was "eager" to proceed, he opened up to me about some of the politics involved, revealing a considerable range of attitudes potentially wide enough to hamper any combined institutional effort. According to David, a leading figure at the Museum of the City of New York was a confirmed homophobe and no sooner had CLAGS been added to the group of sponsoring organizations than he'd begun to back away from his commitment to participate. Still, David thought there was a fair chance the other institutions would remain in partnership. Seizing on that, I argued at the next meeting of institutional representatives (stretching the case a bit) that CLAGS was "uniquely" well equipped to serve as a kind of "think tank" for the event, that it could be, as it were, a sort of authoritative scholarly resource, able to pinpoint knowledgeable experts to consult and necessary historical subjects to include. In follow-up discussions with the other institutions on CLAGS's role in planning Stonewall's twenty-fifth, I got pretty much everything I asked for: equal billing as cosponsor with the other cultural institutions, and no required financial contribution toward producing the event.

After the CUNY Board of Trustees in 1991 certified CLAGS as an official center at the Graduate School, we did done some internal restructuring. Board membership was further broadened and committee agendas more tightly defined. Also, to lessen my own workload, we elected Cheryl Clarke and Esther Katz as board cochairs.

Some of the structural changes were contested and led to an intriguing—and needed—dialogue about the nature of our mission. Given how few openly gay non-Whites were enrolled for advanced degrees in the Graduate School or held faculty positions, someone suggested that the ongoing issue of how to make our board more diverse could only be resolved by adding more *nonacademic* community activists to the available pool. We decided to devote a special board meeting to discussing the whole question of representation. It proved a contentious yet illuminating one. The historian Randy Trumbach spoke incisively for one faction when he heatedly declared that he, for one, felt no need "to apologize for being a full-time intellectual"; scholarship itself, he insisted, *could* be socially transformative. I agreed with his view that scholarship was inherently "activist," but not with his follow-up: though appearing to be White, Randy archly invited us to count *him*—due to a mixed racial background none of us had previously known about—as a "minority" member of the board. The revelation hung in the air, no one knowing quite what to say in response.

Jim Saslow adopted a more directly belligerent tone. He pronounced himself "delighted" to have recently received tenure—to be, as he put it, "on the 'inside,' where nobody could 'touch' me." He "would never again be 'mau-maued,'" he pugnaciously added, for not being radical enough. "It's not our fault at all," he rather cogently added, "that we haven't had more diverse representation—it's society's fault." I braced for a full-blown clash, but Cheryl Clarke aborted it with her calm suggestion to Jim that he think a bit more about his "unfortunate" use of the term "mau-maued." Jim looked still angrier, but said nothing.

Cheryl went on—impressively, I thought—to ask all of us to acknowledge that there are "many ways of knowing and to stretch our definition of what scholarship can and does consist of." She even seconded Randy's earlier point that "we shouldn't be 'guilt-tripped' for not being in the streets" (though the streets had made us possible). It was true, Cheryl went on, that "our movement *is*, due to AIDS, in an activist phase, but we need some people to be doing other things too." Alisa Solomon sensibly added that to become more inclusive didn't necessarily mean that we were opting for anti-intellectualism, as both Randy and Jim seemed to fear.

At that point, I deliberately shifted us away from what loomed as a potential conflagration by soliciting concrete proposals for expanding our outreach. In the upshot, we were able to agree on issuing invitations to six non-White people to join our board. As backup we put together a list of another twenty names—fourteen of them non-White. We then went on to deal with a different complaint about board diversity: insufficient graduate student representation. A growing number of LGBTQ+ graduate school students had been drawn to enroll at CUNY because of CLAGS's existence, and they wanted more of a voice in our deliberations. That seemed wholly warranted, and the board acknowledged that there was room for improvement. We fixed a date to meet with the gay student organization that had formed at the Graduate School in order, we hoped, to establish a mutually agreed-on plan.

With CLAGS now firmly established, I again thought of stepping away. I wanted to finish the book on Stonewall that I'd been working on intermittently, and I also wanted to pursue a few feelers I'd been getting for possible productions of several of my plays. I was ambivalent, though. The prospect of participating in a consortium to plan a citywide celebration of Stonewall was exciting, and I wanted to be part of it. In addition, the Graduate School had finally come through with a work-study student to help out with the daily minutiae of running CLAGS, freeing me up from much of the drudgery of recent years. There was also the problem of finding a replacement: the CUNY trustees *had* set one condition when accrediting us: the director of CLAGS had to be a member of the Graduate School faculty.

Besides me there was only one other board member—one of our newest—who had a Graduate School appointment. "Brian" was my age, a full professor and a department chair who knew the political ins and outs of the Graduate School and seemed to enjoy its machinations, which I did not. But Brian's patronizing (and devious) ways, his tendency to explode when thwarted, and his attachment to tie-and-jacket old-school niceties had quickly made him unpopular. He was constantly blowing up at committee meetings, walking out in a rage, and threatening to resign. Worse, he began to take it upon himself to make unilateral decisions unauthorized by the board.

The most bizarre episode involved "Eric," that same male graduate student member of the board who'd earlier announced (in regard to Stonewall's twenty-fifth) that he was against "celebrating a bunch of apolitical drag queens." Eric had been put in charge of the CLAGS mailing list (which we'd laboriously built to 2,500 names; two years later it reached 6,500), and he insisted that the board buy a $5,000 computer to do "proper honor" to his elaborate database. CLAGS didn't have that kind of loose change lying about, nor did it think such elaborate equipment necessary. When I asked Eric why he was being so insistent, he replied, "Read *The Fountainhead* and you'll understand my reasons." In other words, his genius lay beyond the comprehension of mere mortals.

Brian sided with Eric, insisting that a recent $10,000 grant from the Irene Diamond Fund could hardly be better spent. "Not even on research grants for graduate students?" I asked. Instantly furious, Brian did another of his walkouts—and without further consultation unilaterally promised Eric his $5,000 computer. When the board voted against the expenditure, Brian resigned—and Eric upped the ante by refusing to release the CLAGS mailing list. Cochair Esther Katz was so enraged at his antics that she seriously suggested we bring criminal proceedings.

Another new board member, Marcellus Blount, humorously suggested that we should "hire a few friends to deal with the brat."

We laughed, but the damage to CLAGS's reputation threatened to be real. The finely muscled Eric, it seemed, had some well-placed and wealthy admirers. One of them promptly wrote to Alan Gartner, the dean of the Graduate School, suggesting that he and other "important" contributors would refuse further contributions unless Eric's complaints were taken seriously. Gartner, a CLAGS ally, cleverly did just that—he listened to Eric's lengthy spiel about his grievances, calmed him down, and persuaded him to return the mailing list. Within months Eric put on thirty pounds, lost his admirers, and resigned from the board. I didn't consider that a happy ending but *was* relieved that the incident was closed.

Relieved—and depressed. Lord! Unexpectedly, we seemed to have gone back to where we'd been five years earlier, bogged down in bickering and resentment. Eli, with his nonprofit background, told me that the real problem was that I was still a novice about the daily shenanigans, the tempests in a teapot, that take place in the nightmare world of nonprofits. He reminded me that when he'd been Literacy's director, two of his social-climbing board members, Parker Ladd and Sonny Sloan, had launched a generalized assault on him (no reason was assigned, but a "lack of pedigree" was implied) that had hurt him deeply. "When you try to make things happen," he counseled, "crazies will always come at you—especially if you appear to be successful." I decided to believe him.

Anyway, with Eric and Brian both gone, the temperature on the board soon cooled. Unfortunately, though, with Brian gone I remained the sole board member with a Graduate School affiliation—and thereby was stuck for now with continuing to serve as director. Still, I rarely felt as resentful as I sometimes had in the past. With a work-study student now available on whom I could fob off many of my errand boy/secretarial functions, I was able to cut down my hours in the office and use the salvaged time to do more writing.

I've long seen the wisdom in the definition of insanity as "repeating the same behavior and expecting it to produce different results." Alas, the aphorism sometimes applied all too accurately to my own expectations in regard to playwriting; in that area, hope *did* spring eternal. I'd been spoiled by the success of my very first effort back in 1963 with *In White America*, and thereafter could never entirely shake off the conviction that I was *meant* to have a second, and successful, career in the theater. That callow attitude had been further enhanced by a brief run of good fortune in the decade following *In White America*. In 1968 I'd been included with ten other "most talented playwrights of the new American theater" (Terrence McNally, Rosalyn Drexler, Jules Feiffer, Israel Horovitz, etc.) to contribute a one-acter to *Collision Course*, an evening of short plays that was well received, with Clive Barnes of the *New York Times* singling out my piece as "razor sharp." Random House even published the plays as a book.

It had also been in 1968 that Elaine May invited me to join up with Terrence McNally and the novelist Bruce Jay Friedman in writing a trio of one-acters (*Three from Column A*), which she would direct. During an extended rehearsal period Elaine proceeded to lay in broad burlesque elements that were directly at odds with my oblique, cerebral script—masking as well its homoerotic overtones. I not only protested but, when Elaine refused to budge, demanded the return of my play. The producer refused—preview audiences had been laughing uproariously at Elaine's version, and besides, contractually the producer "owned" my play. Wonderful, sez I, but my play is *not* a comedy. If Elaine refuses to return to the script and the producer refuses to insist on it, then I'll stand up in the audience on opening night and publicly disavow the play as Elaine's misguided, mangled version. The threat worked, probably because they realized I meant it. I got my script back, Elaine substituted a play of her own—and the evening became the toast of the town.

The road to glory had hit a major bump. It hurt like hell, and recovery was prolonged, but eventually I managed to convince myself that the fall from grace had been circumstantial, and in the summer of 1969, I began work on a full-length play about gay male prostitution,

Payments (still my own favorite). The following year a pair of my one-acters, *The Memory Bank*, was produced, and though Clive Barnes of the *Times* called them "exquisitely wrought," overall the critical reaction was lukewarm. The gay subtext of both plays didn't, to put it mildly, appeal to everyone. The disgusted *New York Post* critic declared me "obsessed with homosexuality," and Harold Clurman, the prestigious critic at the *Nation*, disdained an evening devoted to "sexual anomalies." Up to then I'd been coming out, as it were, through a side door. *Payments* was a full-frontal assault.

Frances (my agent) was high on the script and began sending it out to potential producers. The reception was not what we'd hoped. The well-known and well-meaning producers Herman Shumlin and his wife Diana, who had a long track record of hits (*The Children's Hour, Inherit the Wind, The Little Foxes, Watch on the Rhine*) read *Payments* and—unlike the brusque team at Lincoln Center—kindly took me to dinner at the Plaza to explain their concern in the most kindhearted possible way: "We love your writing but do regret the subject matter you've chosen to write about. We feel you're killing your own chances of being produced, and do hope that you'll find other subjects of interest to you." Grateful for their gentle, gracious concern, I promised to take their advice to heart.

I couldn't, of course. I could only continue to write about what came most naturally to me, and at the moment that meant *Payments*. I put it into workshop at New Dramatists (where I'd been elected a member), and in the spring of 1971, we did five performances before invited audiences. Even had the cast been more talented and the rehearsal time longer, I doubt the reception would have been notably different. The limited praise, such as it was, was confined to the closeted coterie that took care to whisper their encouragement in my ear. ("What did you do—swallow a brave pill?" actor Jimmy Coco asked sotto voce.)

No commercial producer was willing to touch *Payments*, and that remains true down to the present day. Yet that same summer of 1972, Edward Albee and Richard Barr did produce an evening of my one-acters that, in a more muted way, featured gay characters. The *East Hampton*

Star summed up community reaction: "The Duberman evening is an insult. . . . There is no room in a good society for that which tends to drag it in the mud."

Given my dimming track record, I was stunned when the United States' bicentennial celebration rolled around and the Kennedy Center chose *me* as one of three playwrights commissioned to write a new play "on any theme of your choosing" to commemorate the bicentennial. Once more visions of glory swam before my eyes; I *was* destined for a major career as a playwright. I deliberated long and hard before settling on the subject of the Beats, being primarily drawn—uh-oh—to the homoerotic relationship between Jack Kerouac and Neal Cassady. Yes, you might call me stupidly stubborn—but I'd never been easy to deter. I spent a fair chunk of 1975 working on the play and sent it off—entitled *Visions of Kerouac*—with high hopes.

What then followed was an extended, agonizing period of many months during which Roger Stevens, who headed up the Kennedy Center's theater wing, remained resolutely silent. It finally dawned on me that Stevens, who'd publicly pronounced the language in *One Flew Over the Cuckoo's Nest* "disgusting" and had also been "offended" by "the four-letter language and nudity" in the Broadway hit *Equus* wasn't likely to be enthralled with the Beats' multiple expletives (not to mention their mix-and-match sexuality). The Kennedy Center played hide-and-seek for a full year, refusing to return my calls or to offer comments on my script. Finally tired of the demeaning evasions—and blatant homophobia—I withdrew in an angry, and explicit, letter.

Not the least disheartening aspect of the incident was learning somewhat later that my agent at the time, Sterling Lord, had played a major role in sabotaging some potential production opportunities for my plays—and in particular *Visions of Kerouac*. I should immediately add that it had been thanks to Sterling that I'd been able to write the play in the first place. When Kerouac was alive, Sterling had been his agent, and after his death had remained in control of his work. Once I'd settled on the Beats as the topic of my play, Sterling had seen to it that I got legal rights to weave bits of Kerouac's own words in and out of the script.

But after I'd completed the play, an agent in Sterling's office let me know, sub rosa, that Sterling was "upset" about the script and thought I'd skewed "the sex thing" out of all proportion. I have no knowledge of whether he and Roger Stevens ever conferred about *Kerouac* and together agreed not to let it see the light, but I do know that after I withdrew the script and made suggestions to Sterling about where else it might find a home, he ignored me. When a few producers initiated discussion with the agency about the play, it never went very far. I learned that the legendary producer Zelda Fichandler, head of the prestigious Arena Stage, told the agency that her staff was "uniformly excited" about *Kerouac*—and then inexplicably fell silent. I heard that Wynn Handman, head of New York's American Place Theater, had also expressed interest in a workshop—but Sterling never followed up. Ditto CalArts. The pattern seemed clear: the agency was in fact *suppressing* any signs of interest in *Kerouac*. Convinced, finally, that I was being badly served, I severed ties with Sterling Lord.

In the years since, *Visions of Kerouac* has had a number of low budget productions, the most notable being a monthlong run at the Lion Theater Company in New York. Though most of the reviews were terrific (the *Village Voice*: "That rare thing in today's theater—it's alive. In its gut and its head"; *New York* magazine: the play "succeeds in capturing honestly and powerfully, a fascinating moment in this country's literary and social history"), there was one all-important—and transparently homophobic—dissent: Mel Gussow in the *New York Times*. His review claimed the play had "a single-edged" theme: "If Kerouac had admitted to a preference for homosexuality, he would have been healthier, perhaps even a better writer." Several producers who'd expressed interest in moving the play to a larger house and for a longer run quietly disappeared. *Kerouac* did have a substantial run at the Odyssey Theatre in Los Angeles—that is, until the review of yet another homophobic critic, Walter Goodman of the *New York Times*, again killed off interest.

Two other commissions later came my way. The City of Philadelphia hired me to write a film—the choice of subject mine—for the bicentennial. I chose to tell the story of how the Quakers refused to wage war against the Delaware Indians; it was rejected out of hand. New York's PBS station was next up on the firing line. When they commissioned me to write a play of my choosing, I settled on my longtime hero, the anarchist Emma Goldman. After reading the completed script, *Mother Earth*, PBS suddenly remembered that federal budget cuts loomed, and since my script was the most "radical" of those not yet in rehearsal, they canceled it. As recently as 2001, the prestigious New York Theatre Workshop came within a hair—or so it seemed—of doing a full-scale production of *Mother Earth*, but after several workshops and much hemming and hawing, finally passed. With that, I retired from the field.

I did complete two more full-length plays in the '80s, one on Roy Cohn, and another (*Posing Naked*) on the Newton Arvin gay scandal at Smith College. I didn't bother to peddle either, nor did I any longer have a theater agent to do it for me. I started a third play, centered on my 1979 heart attack, but it never amounted to more than a few dozen scattered pages.

Scorecard: much drama, no star on the Walk of Fame.

In much the way that the homoerotic and radical themes of my plays proved unpalatable for mainstream critics and sent most producers scurrying for the woods, my books—now mostly devoted to gay-themed history and politics—no longer received the wide attention they once had. As my politics (radical and gay) remained adamant, outlets and invitations significantly decreased over time. The straight left has never regarded gay rights as a significant matter, and the gay movement itself has mostly lost its radical edge. The enthusiastic invitations I used to regularly get to participate in a symposium, attend a conference, give a talk, sit for an interview, or review a book have over time all but evaporated. An aging, politically radical queer no longer appeals to (merely) liberal straights, and is regarded as something of an anomaly in what is now a mainstream gay movement.

The *New York Times'* shift in attitude toward me became pronounced—and emblematic. Upon the publication of my 1991 memoir, *Cures*, a nonfiction work quintessentially in the American confessional mode, the *Times* assigned it to an English fiction writer to review; he was less than enthusiastic. I had to remind myself that for two years I'd been blasting the *Times* in public for the subtle ways it "managed" the news, and I shouldn't have been surprised when it seemed to go out of its way to choose reviewers likely to be unsympathetic. I couldn't reasonably have it both ways—and I had trouble getting this through my head. I couldn't attack the mainstream and at the same time expect its applause. If I'd become a determined outsider, I had to get a grip on my simultaneous desire to become a household name.   .

Early in 1992, CLAGS hit the jackpot. I got a call from Tomás Ybarra-Frausto, an officer at the Rockefeller Foundation, to tell me that its scholarship panel had recommended CLAGS for the prestigious Humanities Fellowship. I was stunned! No gay organization had ever succeeded in breaking into the mainstream foundation world. (We would subsequently turn the same trick with the Ford Foundation.) The Rockefeller Humanities Fellowship represented a quite different stratosphere of acknowledgment. The three-year grant was for an astonishing $250,000. It allowed us to award two $35,000 grants to researchers in the field of lesbian and gay studies each year for three years, with the remaining $40,000 going to CLAGS itself. To our subsequent amazement, at the end of the grant period, the fellowship was renewed for *another* three years—which, so I was told, Rockefeller had never done before.

A colleague who sat on the foundation's scholarship panel let me know that the committee's sole doubt about making the initial grant had concerned "the degree of institutional support for CLAGS"—meaning the Graduate School itself. Its president, Frances Degen Horowitz, was a wholehearted supporter, yet ten months after being approved by the CUNY Board of Trustees, we *still* didn't have an office—making us the only Graduate School center without one. I don't know who twisted whose arm, but a mere four days after the higher-ups got word of the Rockefeller imprimatur, my own office ceased to double as CLAGS's home and we suddenly found ourselves in our own space. It was hardly glamorous. A dark, shabby basement hole in the wall, devoid of furniture, filing cabinets, typewriter, or computer, it had electric wires hanging from the ceiling, a torn rug, and one (filthy) window that faced a brick wall. It was hardly a serviceable office, but it *was* a home—and within weeks we made it into a real one.

With this new symbol of permanence, and to ensure that gay studies remained solidly on the map, I started to do more traveling than I had in years. I'd earlier learned from book tours how little I enjoyed flying, meeting a bevy of strangers, or sleeping in unfamiliar quarters. Even when I was vacationing, the pleasures of seeing the Ishtar Gate in Berlin or the stark, whitewashed houses on Mykonos were for me more than offset by the anxiety of travel. Severed from the daily rituals and physical comfort of home triggered my alarm system. I was never able to write when in strange places; I needed a neutral environment, needed my surroundings to go dead, to *not* bid for my active attention.

But to spread the word about CLAGS, I almost never said no to an invitation: I went, inwardly anxious, outwardly smiling. Those listening to me lecture were often "amazed" (so they would tell me) at how relaxed and articulate I seemed, and at "the pointed, witty way" (said one report) I responded to questions. Sometimes I even spoke without notes, showing off a little. The chameleon's talent for disguise comes fairly easily to those who have spent decades in the closet.

Though usually treated well and received enthusiastically, I never enjoyed my campus proselytizing. Back from a trip to Hobart and William Smith Colleges in Geneva, New York, I scribbled this note: "Even at their best I'll never enjoy these gigs. The flights—especially without Eli to grab on to—are never less than nerve-wracking." But several impulses kept me going: missionary zeal to spread the word and swell the CLAGS membership list, the applause and attention, and the fees. Ironically, I was getting considerably more invitations to speak on "Reclaiming the Gay and Lesbian Past" than I had on *Paul Robeson.*

Only in a few instances did I run into overt hostility, and it surfaced in predictable places. During one call-in show in Phoenix, so many vile things were shouted at me over the phone—a dismal mix of arrogance and ignorance—that at one point I momentarily lost it: "I feel like a Jew trying to talk sense to Hitler," I shouted back at one caller. The show's host chuckled—at what he called *my* "outrageousness." I strongly suspected that the relative absence of hostility at my talks was a case of "bringing coals to Newcastle"—of preaching to the already converted. Still, I told myself that even if an audience was already gay affirmative, few knew about the advent of lesbian and gay studies and the existence of an academic center devoted to scholarship on the subject.

In limited circles, CLAGS was becoming well known. In a piece in the *Village Voice* titled "Gay Studies Spawns a Radical Theory of Desire," Richard Goldstein suggested that if CLAGS added "chamber music, it might be the gay equivalent of the 92nd Street Y" (famed for its wide variety of offerings). One gauge was the increasing tide of mail, a fair amount of it from would-be students inquiring about whether we were offering courses with gay content that could be applied toward an advanced degree. By 1992 my own course was on the books, but for a while longer it was the only gay-themed one. Gradually, though, a number of CUNY faculty (mostly gay) began either to include gay content in their standard courses or to offer new courses entirely centered on queer material. Jumping ahead, the CUNY Graduate School today offers an interdisciplinary concentration in LGBTQ+ studies as well as an LGBTQ+ track within the women's and gender studies MA program. In addition—to take the spring 2017 catalogue as an example—the Graduate School now offers ten relevant gender/sexuality courses in fields as diverse as anthropology, art history, film, sociology—and, yes, history!

The frequent one-to-three-day conferences that CLAGS began to organize in 1990 soon came to include scholars from around the country and did much to expand the growth of interest in the field. "Crossing

Identifications," to give but one example, made a particular splash in the fall of 1992. The multicultural nature of the event—the first three speakers were all Black women—was itself deeply gratifying, and Wahneema Lubiano's brilliant presentation proved particularly remarkable. The two days were in fact filled with outstanding plenary speakers and panelists. In her commentary, Biddy Martin, who later became president of Amherst College, even dared us to ponder the question of why couples of the same gender require partner differentiation—and why in the forms of sadomasochism and butch/femme in particular.

Also at "Crossing Identifications," Michael Moon of Emory University offered an offbeat effort "to rescue Oklahoma from disparagement," and Yukiko Hanawa of NYU cast doubt on the validity of the category "Asian American." Judith Roof of Rice University, for her part, presented a very funny and smart account of her encounter with a lesbian student who she knew she was supposed to like and identify with but who she in fact intensely *dis*liked. Kendall Thomas, professor of law at Columbia, took on the Supreme Court's notorious 1986 *Hardwick* ruling, which had upheld the constitutionality of a Georgia sodomy law criminalizing homosexual oral and anal sex, and provocatively dissected Justice Blackmun's landmark dissent arguing that the decision at base perpetuated the closet. Summarizing the conference on the last day, Judith Butler played the role of "respondent" with stunning authority—even if I myself remained uneasy about a set of linguistic conventions wildly out of touch with and inaccessible to vernacular expression.

The excitement and success of CLAGS's first formal year of existence in 1991–92 made me much less resentful of the time spent in its toils, even if on occasion I felt stupefyingly busy (which, to be forthright, is probably my preferred state). I'd never before let phone calls go unanswered for two to three days or mail unattended for two weeks, but both were coming in at an inundating rate. For my sins in avoiding administrative duties all my life, I was now reconfigured as that low-totem object of scorn, the bureaucrat, and—so sayeth the new linguistics—not encouraged to "theorize ambivalence." I was simultaneously commuting one day a week as a visiting professor in gay studies at Vassar, completing my book on Stonewall, attending donor lunches, putting together two Chelsea House gay young adult series, helping to plan a proliferating number of CLAGS conferences, and representing CLAGS at multiple meetings connected to the possibility of creating a new doctoral program at the Graduate School on the "interdisciplinary study of subaltern cultures" (which over time erratically shifted to "studies in multiculturalism"). Yes, too busy even for me. I had become the Energizer Bunny.

Initially, it did my heart good to have lesbian and gay studies included as a natural ally and equal partner in a proposed new doctoral program devoted to multiculturalism and centered on marginalized people. But as it turned out, our inclusion was *not* a given. The more meetings we had, the more contentious they became, and I soon realized that there was a considerable amount of not-so-polite opposition to including gay studies on an equal footing. The chairs of Black and Latino studies kept insisting that the curriculum for the new PhD should focus primarily on African American, Afro-Caribbean, and Latin American subjects.

One of the arguments used *against* our equal participation was that the "easy" way in which CLAGS had gotten accredited demonstrated our "privileged" position. In response, I invited them to visit our wretched little office and its nonexistent staff to see just how privileged we in fact were. The Black and Latino chairs then shifted the argument to emphasizing the old chestnut that the gay community, unlike their own constituencies, had gobs of wealthy people with endless amounts of discretionary money. Yes, I acknowledged, there were some wealthy people who were gay or lesbian, but most of them tended *not* to be political and the few who were had consistently turned down my pleas for support on the grounds that scholarship had little or nothing to do with achieving our rights.

Three months into discussions we'd still made little progress in negotiating the contours of a new multicultural PhD; the same arguments kept surfacing, the same underground swell of contempt for gay inclusion—which when pointed out would be denied. Then suddenly, at the end of February 1993, matters came to a head: Ed Gordon from the Black studies program announced that he'd spoken to the CUNY chancellor, Ann Reynolds, and she had agreed that the focus of the new PhD *would* be on African American and Latin American studies. Others in the room that day nodded in satisfaction. But Stanley Aronowitz (an old friend but comparatively new to the meetings) leaned over and whispered in my ear, "I don't believe the homophobia that's going around."

I challenged Gordon on several grounds, arguing that what might seem "safe" to the chancellor or the Board of Trustees would in fact entail the sacrifice of what I *thought* we'd agreed were our collective principles. Gordon huffily snapped back that *his* dominant concern was to ensure that African American studies not be relegated yet again to "a backseat." I reminded Gordon that the Graduate School had recently offered Manning Marable (the noted Black scholar) a center of his own, $100,000 a year toward its budget, and *three* work-study graduate students. Would that gay studies, I unwisely added, be "left behind" in such opulent circumstances! I further emphasized the importance of seizing this rare opportunity to combine our "subaltern" strengths for the common good. Gordon seemed to acquiesce, and proposed a resolution "to include all minority identities"—yet I had to lean over and remind him to add the words "as equal partners." He scowled but assented.

Though we'd decided to meet every two weeks, two and a half months went by before Gordon scheduled another session. He arrived at the meeting half an hour late and exited forty-five minutes early. In the brief period between, a tight rein was kept on avoiding a rehash of the "equal partners" issue. It seemed obvious that during the ten-week interval since our last meeting, jockeying had continued behind the scenes. According to Aronowitz, Gordon had been using the interval to solidify with the Graduate School administration his insistence that lesbian and gay studies *would* be shunted to the side.

What Gordon didn't know was that I was friendly with Alison Bernstein, a vice president at the Ford Foundation—which had provided the money to put together the new doctoral program. I still had a few weapons up my sleeve, Alison being the most potent, and I intended to use them.

———————

On the home front, meanwhile, the CLAGS board had a brief relapse, with frequent bickering again erupting—*not* about newly emergent issues but restating disagreements that had supposedly been laid to rest. "T," the board's self-designated traditionalist, continued to lecture the other members on the absurdity of aiming for the unattainable goal of "diversity." "The demands of multicultural representation," he'd periodically announce, "necessarily dilute the intellectual content of our enterprise." His phrasing was patently offensive, yet some of us felt he had an underlying and genuinely troubling point that did need ongoing attention: if we continued to insist on enlarging board membership to encompass every "subaltern" group, we would have to recruit outside academia for the multitude of minorities underrepresented within it. In fact we *had* fairly often over the years extended invitations to community activists who were not academics, and in some cases not even notably interested in lesbian and gay studies. Unfortunately, "T" phrased the dilemma in inflammatory rhetoric, equating multicultural representation with mediocrity at just the point in time when we were inducting two Black female activists onto the board—which was tantamount to telling them that they'd been chosen as a desperation measure only.

One (White) female board member was so angered at "T's" position that she left the meeting in tears and phoned me that night to underline her distress. I told her that I shared her dismay and suggested that speaking out when "T" was actually making an offensive remark was more likely to embarrass him than a belated, behind-the-scenes chiding. She did try, but "T" was the kind of person who when chastised got angry, not repentant. And so the offensive remarks continued and a strategy for ending them—short of kicking "T" off the board—continued to elude us. The cochairs and I both did what we could to soothe hurt feelings, but consolation wasn't always effective; it simply wasn't possible to compensate for the wounds all of us in our own circumstances had accumulated over time and which we (often unconsciously) brought to our CLAGS interactions. (In fact I sometimes felt that as Big Daddy, blame would land on my head precisely because I failed to make everyone feel magically restored to wholeness, free of the damage inflicted by a lifetime of homophobic abuse.)

At the same time that internal arguments continued to erupt at board meetings, CLAGS's right to exist was still under fire from segments of the gay community itself. During one CLAGS-sponsored panel on the future of queer (the new terminology) studies, two prominent activists, both of whom I liked and respected, made surprisingly hurtful comments. One of them challenged academics to "surrender their place of safety" and make their work "relevant" to the community's needs. But what did those shopworn words *mean*? Was she saying that scholarship and activism were opposing enterprises? How then would she account for Thurgood Marshall's reliance on scholarly evidence to prove the detrimental effect of segregation when arguing the *Brown v. Board* case before the Supreme Court? Nor did the other activist's comments provide much clarification. She called for queer studies to adopt "a coherent political framework" but failed to tell us what the content of such a framework would or should be.

In the meantime, the twenty-fifth anniversary of the Stonewall uprising was drawing near. The consortium of representatives from the city's major institutions—the New York Public Library, the Museum of the City of New York, the Brooklyn Historical Society, and the New-York Historical Society—had continued to meet and draw up plans to celebrate Stonewall's anniversary. The enthusiasm that marked the initial meetings had begun to dissipate in the face of unexpected difficulty in raising money for the event (the foundation world had proved indifferent to the project), as well as knee-jerk and ongoing distrust in sections of the gay community of institutional "elitism." At one point the consortium seemed about to break apart, but thanks largely to the efforts of David

Kahn, director of the Brooklyn Historical Society, it held together. The New York Public Library, under the guidance of its chief archivist, Mimi Bowling, had from the beginning spearheaded the search for historical collections and had succeeded in gathering an impressive amount of archival material on LGBTQ+ life. Mimi made it clear that whether or not the other institutions went forward, NYPL would definitely mount a major exhibit.

The weakest link in the coalition was the Museum of the City of New York, which was undergoing a considerable financial crisis; its head, Robert Macdonald, began making noises that certainly sounded like retreat, though he denied it. David urged me to sound him out on his intentions, which I reluctantly proceeded to do. Aiming for a diplomatic tone—not always my strong point—I suggested to Macdonald that if MCNY backed out, the consortium itself would appear infirm and confused of purpose, and MCNY itself would be denounced "in some quarters" as homophobic. Macdonald squirmed but did agree to proceed—that is, if the museum was ultimately allowed to contribute something *other than* an actual exhibition—a lecture series, say, or a video presentation.

Since I felt that resistance would hasten his exit, I told him that lectures and video sounded fine, since none of the other institutions had as yet decided on the specific nature of their in-house events. As it would turn out, MCNY would produce a photographic display on the history of gay life that included a significant number of misdated and wrongly identified captions—and placed it in a narrow corridor where the soundtrack from an adjourning exhibit blared out, making concentration difficult.

Over time, the complaints against CLAGS changed somewhat in content, though intermittent griping seemed part of our DNA—a deeply appealing outlet for discharging frustrations more encompassing than could be named. One gay graduate student protested CLAGS's "elitism" (*that* again); another announced himself angry that we were paying too *much* attention to women and people of color (who themselves felt otherwise). The complainers, I noted, tended to fall into the category of those who rarely volunteered to do any of the shit work—perhaps viewing complaining itself as their contribution. (I managed not to say that out loud.) When we began to publish a monthly newsletter, no board member would agree to serve as its editor, and so my sister Lucile, already a CLAGS volunteer, took on the job. An outraged response promptly followed: my sister "wasn't even lesbian!" Besides, why was she being *paid* to do the job? She wasn't. Not needing the grief, Lucile resigned.

I swore, yet again, to reign in my *reactive* temperament. It helped when the Canadian scholar Kathleen Martindale (*Un/Popular Culture: Lesbian Writing After the Sex Wars*) dropped by the office one day and got me laughing over her report that the feeling was "widespread" that CLAGS was "loaded with money and staff—after all, how else could they be doing so much so stylishly?" She also buoyed me up a bit with her view that the internal squabbling on the board was much like what had gone on earlier in the fields of women's studies and Black studies; they, too, had been rent with class, gender, and racial tension—and the massacre of innocents. Still, it hurt to have people constantly taking potshots—heightened by my inability to let *anything* slide off my back. Instead, I kept busy puzzling over why I (or my role) attracted so much negativity, and decided I should take more time stroking people, however irrational I thought their psychodramas.

I learned pretty quickly that appeasement wasn't always possible. My chief antagonist throughout 1993 was a female graduate student I'll call—aiming for a light touch—"Cassandra" (Cassie for short). She was a pal of Eric's (the computer maven and Ayn Rand fan who'd earlier threatened to abscond with our membership list), who'd recently returned to graduate school. Together Cassie and Eric sent a letter to President Horowitz accusing CLAGS of "under-representing" gay graduate students on the board. In fact, one of our cochairs and I had some months back set up a meeting with the gay student group to express our eagerness for better communication. Though we did publicize the event, only three or four students had shown up. Chagrined, they asked for more time to consult together as a group in order to "get their priorities straight," and promised to get back to us with a concrete plan for student representation. That was the last we heard from them.

Instead, we heard from Cassie (who *hadn't* shown up for the meeting), joined by "Jonathan," yet another student malcontent, who together had taken up the anti-CLAGS cause. Fortunately, I got a call at that point from Sarah Schulman. She'd heard that Cassie was trashing CLAGS and asked, "How much do you know about Cassie's history?" Not much, I said. "The *best* I can say for her," Sarah went on, "is that she is absolutely psychotic. For the past six years she's tried to destroy every gay organization that she's been a part of. She's ripped apart Lesbian Avengers [of which Sarah had been one of the founders] and had even launched an attack on the Irish gay group, ILGA. Beware of her, Marty; she's dangerous. Larry Kramer calls her the single most destructive person in ACT UP."

Soon after that, Matt Foreman—who at various points in his activist career headed up the Gay and Lesbian Anti-Violence Project, the Empire State Pride Agenda, and the National Gay and Lesbian Task Force—and I were catching up over lunch and I brought up CLAGS's difficulties with several students at the Graduate School, mentioning Cassie by name. Matt raised his eyebrows in horror, then went on to describe her as "a real sickie." He said her negative reputation was by now widespread; he even repeated what he called "a common rumor" that she wasn't even lesbian, but rather simply enjoyed provocation—whether "paid or not" wasn't clear. The warnings from Matt and Sarah were a great relief. Perhaps I could finally stop worrying about what *I* might be doing wrong.

It so happened that I'd already scheduled—in an effort to "talk things out"—a coffee date with Cassie for the very next day. Weirdly, the meeting went better than I would have predicted. Cassie inadvertently helped me better understand why some of the lesbian and gay students at the Graduate School still felt aggrieved: they're angry, she said, because CLAGS is "powerful," yet isn't pushing for more gay-centered courses. I tried to explain that for the past few years—with no staff and needing to get a foothold—we had to stick strictly to our agreed-upon mission of encouraging research.

Students, I said, may see CLAGS as powerful, but it's in fact been a daily struggle just to keep the organization afloat. Moreover, as a research center, not a department, we had zero control over curriculum: we weren't allowed to generate courses or to hire faculty. All we could hope for was that our presence at the Graduate School, along with pressure from the mounting number of openly lesbian and gay students, would inspire some of the professors to offer courses with gay content—and there was evidence that was beginning to happen. CLAGS itself, even on an informal basis, didn't have enough clout to persuade various department chairs to add gay-centered seminars. That initiative finally had to come from faculty members within each department. I sensed, though I didn't say this to Cassie, that the single issue of "more courses" wouldn't satisfy a larger, inchoate need for validation—a lifetime paucity we all shared.

I suggested that she and I have a follow-up meeting a month hence, this time with additional members of the CLAGS board and all interested students; the agenda would be the two items Cassie herself had brought up: curriculum and board representation. That meeting came off as scheduled, but only eight or nine students and four board members showed up. Cassie herself proved a model of restraint, at least when compared to the newcomer, "Jonathan," who charged CLAGS, among other crimes, with failing to provide grant-writing seminars, for not finding enough ways to ease students' financial burdens, *and* for not telling them how, as openly gay people, to *ensure* their academic futures. Would that we could, I wanted to say (but didn't)—would that we had the power to create such a desired utopia. The four board members at the meeting did, I thought, clearly demonstrate our goodwill and our understanding of the students' plight. We also pressed them to hold an election as soon as possible to select additional representatives to the board and invited them to come to our next meeting to get a feel for how we operated and to join the newly inaugurated Curriculum Committee as well.

One board member—a bit too sardonic, in my view—predicted that the disgruntled students didn't really want to be deprived of their grievances *or* to put in the hard work of board membership; they would rather continue to use CLAGS as a scapegoat for the indignities that society as a whole had heaped on them for being "different." In his opinion, the students misconstrued who was the enemy and who the friend; CLAGS, tangible and near at hand, was a satisfying target for grievances that in fact originated with mainstream America's profound homophobia.

He predicted, tongue in cheek, that should we take the two steps to the left on offer, the students would promptly express outrage that we hadn't taken two to the right—which was what they had *really* meant and which we should have realized had we not been so closed off to student needs. Maybe so, I said, but we still needed to go the extra mile. On the curriculum issue, I set in motion a survey to locate gay-centered courses beginning to be offered by other colleges within commuting distance—but, predictably, turned up only a minuscule number. To my knowledge no gay CUNY graduate student sought out the listings. Then, further feeding the cynicism of some of our board members, neither Cassie nor Jonathan showed up for the next board meeting, though they had been specifically reminded of the date. Well, at least we were clearly on record as having been responsive to their grievances.

But the disgruntled Jonathan turned out to be unappeasable. Another graduate student reported to me a conversation he'd overheard in which Jonathan—this was a new arrow in his quiver—said that he'd decided not to apply for one of our two Rockefeller fellowships because "Duberman would secretly destroy my application before the jury could consider it." He then went on, reportedly, to denounce the research project that *had* won one of our fellowships—"AIDS and Africa"—as having "nothing to do with race and class." That seemed even to me too bizarre to warrant a response.

Early in 1994 I sent out two letters to our mailing list (which had now reached 7,300) outlining the plight of gay graduate students unable to find funding for their lesbian and gay research projects, and pleading for help. To my delight, the letters brought in $4,500 in donations.

I then scheduled a meeting with the graduate students on our board (the number was now up to four) to discuss how best to distribute the money. None of the four showed up—and none even bothered to call with an explanation.

Jumping through hoops seemed to lead nowhere—except to more hoops. The CLAGS Executive Committee, in the upshot, decided to earmark the money as an emergency fund for students pursuing LGBTQ+ research—for travel, books, photocopying, whatever. Would creation of the fund help smooth our relationship with the small posse of malcontents? I'd by now been through the wringer too many times to feel less than cynical.

Yet I couldn't entirely let go of my need to somehow win the approval both of Jonathan and Cassie—chalk it up to ingrained people-pleasing. Given the number of times they'd rebuffed me, I was puzzled at my tenacity. Throughout my academic life I'd been perfectly willing, in pursuit of what I considered a worthy cause, to earn the enmity of some of my colleagues—be it antiwar activism, renouncing "authoritarian" teaching, or coming out publicly as gay. Did I have to gain *everyone's* approval? Why in the hell was I still knocking myself out trying to win over Cassie and Jonathan? Somehow, I couldn't bear the notion that all my efforts to build an organization and a field likely to make their own lives easier had failed to win their allegiance. Doubtless I'd made mistakes, but as I should have known from my own study of social justice movements, strategic errors are inevitable—as are malcontents to point them out, some of whom are honorably motivated, others who are fighting internal demons of which they're unaware or unable to acknowledge.

At this point, my new book *Stonewall* appeared. The early signs weren't encouraging. Mark Thompson, the senior editor of the *Advocate*, the leading gay magazine (in terms of subscribers, not content), told me that they'd recently run into serious trouble following the owner's string of disastrous financial decisions. A group of wealthy gay men had been called in and had stopped the hemorrhaging through "huge cutbacks."

Among the casualties, Mark told me, was a thousand-word rave review of *Stonewall* along with a two-page photographic spread. The photos had been deleted and the review confined to a single—and garbled—paragraph.

Along the same lines, I learned from the journalist Andy Kopkind that the *Nation* viewed its reviewer's favorable piece on *Stonewall* as "a young man's self-puffery"—and had killed it. Ditto the *Village Voice*; Richard Goldstein, a frequent contributor, told me that he'd requested the book but had given up when M. Mark, a senior editor at the *Voice*, insisted he could only review it if coupled with a book by a lesbian (even though of the six people featured in *Stonewall*, two were lesbians and a third a male-to-female trans person). Paul Berman, for his part, turned in an eighty-page essay-review to the *New Yorker* on *Stonewall* and other books relating to '60s radicalism, and it had been rejected. Berman subsequently included the review in full in his 1996 book, *A Tale of Two Utopias*; it praised *Stonewall* highly for its "perfect focus," for having "tenderly brought to life" the '60s rebellion, and for its "narrative glory." The much-appreciated praise, alas, saw the light three years after *Stonewall*'s publication—a bit late in helping to sell books.

And then there was my nemesis, the *New York Times*—again. *Stonewall* had gotten a raft of good reviews in various outlets, but the all-powerful *Sunday Book Review* did its usual number on me, stopping the book's momentum in its tracks. The *Times* chose as its reviewer Sara M. Evans, a feminist historian who complained in her review about my lack of contextualization, though I'd gone out of my way to embed gay history in the broader cultural frame of the '60s. Still more bizarre, she objected to the street language in the book—the "fuck yous," and so on, used in particular by one of the book's central characters, Sylvia Rivera, who used to hustle in Times Square and assuredly did not speak the King's English. I'd taken Sylvia's words directly from our taped interviews, but Evans found them so offensive that she had scant space left over for assessing the rest of the book (which is probably just as well). I didn't know that a feminist with "moral standards" reminiscent of Anthony Comstock existed—but the *Times* managed to find her.

I've never been given to conspiracy theories, but I *was* puzzled at how often—the pattern would continue into the future—the *Times* would assign my books, especially my gay-themed ones, to inappropriate or uninformed reviewers.

I did learn that the *Times* received a raft of letters protesting Evans's screwball review, and when none of them were printed, Frances, my agent, phoned Rebecca Sinkler, then head of the *Sunday Book Review*, to politely ask why. According to Frances, Sinkler told her that "the *Times* does not print letters that rewrite the original review—unless they're by prominent people. We only print letters that correct factual errors." That was absolute rot. I saw some of the letters and by several definitions they *did* correct "factual" errors and *were* written by "prominent" professionals. It was hard to shake the sense that the *Book Review* was operating out of deliberate bias. Herbert Mitgang—a longtime daily reviewer for the *Times*—had warned me some time earlier that I couldn't continue to level criticism at the *Times* for its political views and at the same time expect them to praise me. It was advice I couldn't afford to take—not, that is, without revamping my politics.

The book party, which was held at the original Stonewall Inn, helped to lighten my mood. The large, supportive crowd included Ruth Messinger (she would lose the 1997 mayoral race to the incumbent, Rudy Giuliani), Quentin Crisp (*The Naked Civil Servant*)—and, in a much-appreciated gesture of affirmation, Frances Degen Horowitz, president of the CUNY Graduate School. Five of the six people whose stories I featured in the book were also present and much applauded. (The sixth, Craig Rodwell, was in the last stages of liver cancer.) Sylvia Rivera arrived in drag ("I wanted to come as a whore," she whispered to me), was good-naturedly voluble throughout, and stayed till the very end, by which time a forlorn look had settled in around her eyes.

Throughout this period I'd continued, as I had for the past four years, to answer the phones one afternoon a week at the People with AIDS

Coalition (PWA). On May 28, 1993, arriving for my regular shift, I heard the startling news that some of the staff had been let go and in short order the entire office would shut down. I'd come to view PWA as something like a family, and news of its imminent demise saddened me. There was some talk of reconstituting if bankruptcy proceedings proved able to rescue PWA from its albatross lease; it did manage to struggle on a while longer, but then had to close its doors. Simultaneously the 1993 International AIDS conference in Berlin concluded with the upsetting news that no promising new drugs were in the pipelines and that the epidemic was spreading dramatically in developing nations, with women increasingly infected. At the moment, the conference glumly concluded, salvation lay not in science but in increasing prevention—in "safe sex."

In the meantime, the first three manuscripts arrived for the Chelsea House young adult series of lesbian and gay biographies I'd agreed to oversee and edit. Two of the first three gave me an unwelcome jolt: they were decidedly subpar. I'd gone to the leading lesbian and gay writers, activists, and scholars rather than to standard young adult writers and had told them to envision hip, smart, mid-to-late teenagers as their target audience; I'd strongly urged them *not* to write down. The real shocker among the first three manuscripts was the biography of James Baldwin by a gifted young Black fiction writer who I knew and admired. I'd been delighted when he said yes to taking on the Baldwin book—and envisioned it as the ideal send-off for the series.

It wasn't. The banality of the manuscript mystified me. One simple declarative sentence followed relentlessly on the other, the prose devoid of imagination and political insight. Since the writers were being paid a pittance, I didn't feel I could ask for major rewrites; in general I did them myself and then forwarded them to the authors for approval. I worked hard on the Baldwin manuscript but still wasn't satisfied that it passed muster. At that point, Sean Dolan, the in-house editor, took over, though I doubted how much he could do to salvage the book. In fact he did a first-class rewrite—so much for academia's condescension toward the "lesser folk" who till the young adult field. Among much else, Sean corrected a slew of historical inaccuracies in the manuscript—everything from wrong dates to wrong names. I couldn't explain it; perhaps, I thought, the author, desperate for money and protective of his time, had farmed out the assignment to some hack. But why he would then have been willing to put his name on the pedestrian product baffled me.

The very next manuscript to arrive, a biography of John Maynard Keynes, did little to lift my spirits. The author, Jeff Escoffier, did lucidly analyze Keynes's economic theories, but in labored prose. I again had to do a considerable rewrite, which was much more work than I'd bargained for. I had the sinking feeling that few of my "star" authors were taking their assignments seriously; either that, or they were throwing themselves a curveball by insisting, despite what I'd said, that they were writing for fifteen-year-old dumbbells unable to deal with more than short, declarative sentences.

A third possibility also began to dawn: Philip, the head of Chelsea House, who I liked personally, thought of writers as short-order cooks, interchangeable, deservedly impoverished; the fact that some of them had agents, he considered an affront; that even more of them expected him to promptly send contracts and advances, preposterous. Nor could Philip understand that I myself had a number of other commitments and couldn't spend endless hours doing rewrites or debating with him who was luminous enough to qualify for a biography (even though our original agreement empowered me to make all final decisions about subjects and authors). Martina Navratilova and Oscar Wilde got Philip's swift OK; Alan Turing, Elizabeth Bishop, and André Gide his unmovable veto. ("Whoever heard of these people?!") The battle over Willa Cather and T. E. Lawrence was prolonged, but they did, barely, make it through.

Philip didn't believe that bisexuality was anything more than a "cover" and kept insisting that rumors alone about Leontyne Price and Judy Garland qualified them for biographies. ("They'll sell, they'll sell!") I refused to agree and argued that if he wanted to include certain celebrities, he needed first of all to provide proof that they "crossed over" and second had to add bisexuals to the overall title of the series, *Lives of Notable Gay Men and Lesbians*. Philip refused. I stood my ground, but he never believed it was firm; he kept insisting over and over again that we add Judy Garland et al. to the list. I continued to resist, and Philip, in turn, remained scornful of the gifted writers and scholars I'd managed to sign up, having heard of none of them.

From the beginning, moreover, he'd been miserly with the authors' fees and even, sometimes, uncivil to them. I got an increasing number of calls from disgruntled writers protesting Chelsea House's "ugly treatment" and high-handed ways. Philip thought gay people should be kissing his ring—or his feet—even as he kicked them in the head. Goodwill toward the series in the lesbian and gay intellectual community gradually evaporated.

I hung in there through fourteen books. By then Philip had decided, weirdly, that the books were "so good" that they should be marketed for *everyone*. I failed to convince him that the shift of target audience was a mistake, that excitement about the series had specifically centered on the urgent need it met to fill the yawning gap in the young adult market for books that included serious discussion of the subjects' sexuality *and* the role it played in their life and work (which in fact I had made a contractual condition of taking on the job). Philip's shift in target audience destroyed the special mission I'd signed on for and soured our personal relationship. After all the work invested, I might have hung in there longer had Philip shown any sign of mending his ways, but his tenacity was more than a match for my own. Not even shouting could produce the slightest shift in attitude or policy. Ultimately, we made the mutual decision to part company. It was particularly infuriating because the fourteen books published up to that point had been mostly of high quality, and some remarkably so.

In the biography series my own favorites were Jane McIntosh Snyder's *Sappho* and Sharon O'Brien's *Willa Cather*. In the foreshortened second series (Issues in Lesbian and Gay Life), I thought two of the books were flat-out brilliant: Ruthann Robson's *Gay Men, Lesbians, and the Law* and Jan Clausen's *Beyond Gay or Straight: Understanding Sexual Orientation*. Ah, well . . .

CLAGS meanwhile was on all fronts less fraught with tension than had recently been the case. It was still eating up more of my time than I liked, but the rewards had become commensurate with the effort—and the time invested was mostly enjoyable. The monthly colloquiums, where a given scholar presented work in progress, continued to be well attended and stimulating, even if my eyes did glaze over during the one on "the linguistic body." The most brilliant colloquium of the year was for me Suzanne Kessler's analysis of "corrective" surgery on intersexed children, along with her analysis of the medical world's view of the "permissible" size of a penis or a clitoris.

The subcommittees were also functioning well, and attending their meetings had become my preferred substitute for a social life. In addition, after several years of work we were able to publish our Scholarly Directory of those working in the field of lesbian and gay studies. We also published a substantial monthly newsletter that went out to nearly eight thousand members. And when the time came around for our second Kessler Lecture, Ed White spoke with subtlety and grace to an overflow crowd—leading Ruth Messinger, the Manhattan borough president, to top off the evening with an eloquent tribute to CLAGS's "importance."

I continued to go on the road now and then, and it constantly reawakened me to the fact that the infighting at CLAGS would be an inconceivable luxury in most of the country, where gay people were still deeply uneasy about coming out—let alone arguing publicly with each other. One of the starker reminders came during a visit to the University of Charleston in West Virginia. A gay student there confided to me that the only "semi-out" faculty member on campus was himself so conservative that he refused to sanction any effort to form a gay group on campus, lest it "offend" the campus authorities. A financial officer at nearby Marshall University took me aside to tell me about a recent attempt by some forty people to have a gay pride march that had been set upon by a mob of two hundred, injuring some of the marchers. His story provided a needed reminder of how fortunate we New Yorkers were—and how easily we forgot that much of the country remained fearful of any challenge to traditional gender and sexuality norms, and would angrily resist the threat to their understanding of how the world did, or should, work.

By a different measure, on the other hand, we New Yorkers in 1995 *exceeded* the misery of most gay Americans: nationally the number of AIDS cases had passed the half-million mark, and New York led the country in a mortality toll nearing fifty thousand. Plus, the mood was grim, with previous drugs having failed to prove efficacious and with no new medical breakthrough on the horizon. It was even decided not to hold the yearly International AIDS Conference. We were, it seemed, in a losing battle, with little hope of a turnaround.

In comparison, the worst that had happened in the small world of CLAGS was that several of our recent conferences—on "Aging," "Great Dykes," and "Sissies and Tomboys"—had been less than thrilling (though the philosopher Naomi Scheman had stood out for her brilliance and self-scrutinizing wit). The temporary decline in the quality of our conferences set a new round of brickbats flying our way: we'd been "overly ambitious," we'd deservedly "fallen on our face," we were, as privileged academics, immune to the suffering of those less fortunate. There was some truth to the accusations; even some of our own board members felt that we were taking on more than we could successfully handle.

The complaints evaporated, at least temporarily, in the face of the knockout event Eli put together for CLAGS's third annual benefit. Not only did we clear a cool $20,000 from the event but the packed house was treated to a spectacular set of readings as well. Eli had somehow managed to enlist a stunning group of readers: Stephen Sondheim, Terrence McNally, Grace Paley, Gloria Naylor (*The Women of Brewster Place*), and Danitra Vance (an Obie winner and the first Black actress in the *Saturday Night Live* cast, Vance died tragically young at forty of breast cancer). Each of the readers performed wonderfully and Sondheim, who performed last, twice broke into tears while reading lyrics from his theater hits. It was a miraculous evening, charged with excitement. The only person who didn't perform well was *me*. During the backstage chatter preceding the event I felt wholly relaxed, but once onstage—despite years of speaking in public—I barely got the stilted words out of my cottony mouth. Oh well, it happens. . . .

We'd arrived—even I could confidently admit it. I thought again, as I often had in the past, that maybe now I could comfortably resign. Yet the ruling still held that the director of any research center had to have a Graduate School appointment. Besides me, there was still only one other person available—the infamous "Brian." (In case you've forgotten: we'd elected Brian to the CLAGS board but he'd proved to be a dictatorial hysteric who stormed out of meetings when he failed to get his way, and had finally resigned in a huff.)

I was willing to hang in there for one more year. I wasn't in the middle of writing a book or rehearsing a play, and after eight years of ups and downs, some of them frantic, I was content to enjoy—however foreign to my nature—a while longer the fact that CLAGS and gay studies were finally on solid ground. But one more year, I made clear, was definitely *it*: moving into the future I thought it best for CLAGS to have a younger director, one who could represent the shifting interests of a new generation of gay scholars.

———

The new multicultural PhD program came suddenly back to life. The prior marathon of meetings had been so devious and contentious that I only half welcomed the news. Stanley Aronowitz confided that the long silence had in fact been filled with behind-the-scenes maneuvering designed to solidify African American and Latin American studies control of the new program. What Stanley didn't know was that (as I mentioned earlier) I'd made my friend Alison Bernstein at the Ford Foundation, sponsors of the new doctorate, aware of Ed Gordon's maneuvering. Alison was the openly lesbian vice president of the foundation and had been instrumental in getting Ford to fork over $115,000 as start-up money for setting the new multicultural PhD in motion—and she'd done so, Alison told me, *because* she'd been led to believe that lesbian and gay studies would be integral to the program. When I told Alison that Gordon, with an assist from Frank Bonilla (director of CUNY's Center for Puerto Rican Studies), had in fact been doing his best to ease us *out* of the coalition, she was furious and told me that she'd "see about that." I don't know for sure, but I suspect Alison's intervention had *something*—perhaps a lot—to do with the sudden reconvening of our committee.

Yet when the meetings started up again, discussions moved quickly away from curriculum—the heart of the matter—into gaseous abstractions that had me champing at the bit. "Epistemic forms of knowledge as intersected by discursive acknowledgment of how meaning is produced" (that's a literal transcription) wasn't my idea of how to move with clarity and dispatch toward a consideration of core curricula.

Gordon and Bonilla were now joined on the committee by Colin Palmer, a historian of the African diaspora, who spoke out more plainly: our "structural" premise, he announced, was "incoherent." Women's studies, cultural studies, and gay and lesbian studies, he acknowledged, *did* form a distinctive grouping—but not one relevant to ethnic studies. That angered Stanley Aronowitz, who said flat out that the stance of the African American and Latin American members of the committee should now be considered, "without question," as "deliberately obstructionist."

Five of us from CLAGS were present at that meeting and joined Stanley in holding the feet of the Gordon-Bonilla-Palmer group to the fire—or rather, the embers. We did still hope for renewed collegiality, feeling strongly that the new PhD would mark a giant step toward firmly embedding in university curricula lesbian and gay studies (or "queer," nonnormative studies, as the recent—and necessary—shift in language has it). Yet everyone present knew full well that we were dangerously close to formally and permanently disbanding. Some noises were made about a cooling-off period, to be followed some months later with another effort at cohesion. But it was not to be. The cooling-off period extended indefinitely—and the multicultural PhD finally bit the dust.

Alison and I had also been consulting together about how CLAGS might itself get a grant from Ford, knowing that if successful it would be a land-mark—the first time a stand-alone gay organization had broken through the barrier at Ford. Following Alison's suggestion, I focused my campaign on Sheila Biddle, one of the foundation's grant officers. After multiple rebuffs, she finally agreed to a meeting—humorously referring to me as "M. Tenacious." I brought along Jacqui Alexander of the New School, one of our recent board members and part of the subcommittee that was putting together the future conference "Black Nations/Queer Nations?" Jacqui was brilliant, fierce—and imperious. She fixed her eye on Sheila and held her spellbound while delivering a mesmerizing argument for why the "Black Nations/Queer Nations?" conference would prove *the* intersecting event for women's studies, Black studies, and lesbian and gay—or LGBTQ+—studies. (The plus sign was increasingly being used about this time, to avoid unending proliferations; among the young in particular the term "queer" was also becoming common usage, especially for its in-your-face connotations—a preference I myself shared.)

In the upshot, Sheila was impressed enough to help us figure out a proposal to which she could comfortably say yes—since Ford didn't fund conferences per se. We fastened on a grant that would allow us to *document* the conference—via video, pamphlet, or book—and got a near promise from Sheila of a $50,000 grant. Before we submit-ted the reworked proposal, though, she required various items from us (like a detailed budget), and over the next few months that led—for a change!—to some harrowing discussions and a near explosion within the "Black Nations/Queer Nations?" committee itself.

That eight-person committee was made up entirely of African Americans, most of whom were CLAGS board members, past and present. Since I'd all along felt obligated to attend all committee meetings, I'd also taken part in the first "Black Nations/Queer Nations?" meeting late in 1993. But I suggested early on that my presence might be taken as an unwanted intrusion, and my own feeling was that I should not continue to attend. I was assured by one and all that I was very welcome. And initially it not only felt that way but I admired the group's insistence from the first that the conference had to represent and attract a variety of African American communities, not just the academic one. I was equally impressed with the group's refusal to regard the medium of print as the exclusive conduit of wisdom and truth, or to automatically assume (as scholars are wont) that it's the only or even the best way to reach people. Above all I marveled—in comparison with the scorching disagreements that had marred many of our board meetings—at the warmth and high spirits of the BN/QN discussions and the sensitive way disagreements were modulated.

Over the next few months, though, I grew somewhat uneasy at the random, inconsistent attendance—for one meeting only three of us showed up. It got to the point by March 1994 that both Jacqui Alexander and Kendall Thomas (a professor at Columbia Law School) expressed doubt that enough time remained to pull off the ambitious conference agenda we had in mind; they suggested at least a postponement of the date and possibly—given how much everyone had on their plates—even canceling the conference for the time being. I argued strongly against either postponement or cancellation. All the work we'd already done, I said, warranted some payoff, and I felt we could still pull off the event as scheduled—and in style. After much discussion, that view somewhat uncomfortably carried the day.

Yet I too began to worry after Sheila Biddle of the Ford Foundation let me know that in the six weeks since she'd met with Jacqui and me, she hadn't received any of the material—like a detailed budget—that she'd made clear was necessary before she could move the grant forward.

Not wanting to push myself to the front, I passed on Sheila's message to Kendall and Jacqui, striving for a neutral tone. Neither returned my calls. One White member of the board let me know that he'd heard someone on the BN/QN committee say that their group could not "afford to be sponsored by a White-dominated organization"—meaning CLAGS. That view was underscored when the first flyers for the conference were released: CLAGS was nowhere mentioned, not even as a *cosponsor*. In truth, the idea for the conference and the first written proposal were mostly my own work, as had been all the fundraising to date. Kendall had early on rather breezily told us that he'd have no trouble coming up with the needed financial backing, but he'd left for Europe with no further word.

I was well aware by now that a potential disaster loomed. If given the choice, I'd much prefer to lose the Ford grant and cancel the conference rather than risk having the African American members of the board resign in a huff. The very thought made me shudder, and I immediately backed off from any mention of Sheila Biddle; I refrained from even making a phone call to any member of the committee. A month later Kendall invited me—to my relief—to help whip the Ford proposal into final shape, an invitation I of course accepted.

Unfortunately, the May 1 meeting of the full CLAGS board put a damper on the incipient reconciliation. Kirk, one of our more difficult White members, checked in advance with me if he could ask for clarification at the upcoming meeting about why CLAGS was no longer being credited with sponsorship of the BN/QN conference. I told him he could—but only if he swore to do so in the most subdued, cordial way possible. Kirk agreed—and promptly did the opposite. In a tone both peremptory and patronizing, he all but insisted on an accounting from those involved in planning the BN/QN event. Other White board members instantly jumped in to reprimand Kirk for his implied insult and to apologize for his acting like a "White overseer."

Additionally, the CLAGS Executive Committee immediately set up a meeting with the BN/QN committee, expressing the hope that any differences between the committee and the CLAGS board could and should be quickly ironed out. Only Kendall showed up, but he made it clear that he spoke for the others—and that they all felt deeply aggrieved. Far from welcoming any attempt at reconciliation, he brought a stern, "nonnegotiable" (Kendall's word) message from the BN/QN committee: "We demand absolute autonomy in planning the conference and in arranging for publication of its proceedings." Kendall and I had talked at length the day before and, as we'd preplanned it, at that point I quickly jumped in to say that I found the BN/QN position "completely understandable—and necessary."

One board member, "Joan," came perilously close to rocking the boat: she started to ask—before I interrupted her—for additional reassurance that CLAGS would receive appropriate billing for its investment of time, energy, and money (CLAGS had itself contributed $7,500 to the event). The rest of the board, fortunately, followed my lead. Kendall declared himself "satisfied" and left the meeting. I then explained to Joan that I felt it "better that CLAGS ends up at the bottom of a list of fifty sponsors—or not on the list at all—rather than risk a rupture with the African American members of the board"—*that* would be a disastrous blow to our reputation for being seriously committed to racial justice and multiculturalism.

Soon after that, I was invited to return to BN/QN meetings, and of course did so. Under Jacqui Alexander's ice-cold glare, I stayed mostly mute, meekly trying to avoid charges of either interference or indifference. It all made me very unhappy, given the high state of camaraderie with which we'd started out some eight months earlier. But such was the current state of racial politics, even among supposedly "enlightened" queer academics—which was sadder still. In the upshot, the BN/QN three-day conference did come off on March 9–11, 1995—and in splendid fashion. Literally hundreds of people were turned away. All three plenary sessions were first rate, though they were of course followed, when the mics were opened up to audience participation, to the usual litany of complaints and non sequiturs ("Why was no session scheduled on youth issues?" etc.). But none of that detracted from the energizing, even inspirational nature of the conference. It exemplified what I'd all along hoped CLAGS would be: a site for antiracist, antisexist work.

Meanwhile, the Stonewall 25 celebrations had begun. My book, *Stonewall*, had recently appeared, and I'd already been doing a mind-numbing round of interviews and speeches. CLAGS itself organized a panel, "Twenty-Five Years After Stonewall," in the Graduate School auditorium so jammed that the overflow crowd had to be diverted to a screening in the third-floor studio. It wasn't long before I was once again questioning my own motives, suspecting that I was aiming for the laurels of a Stakhanovite worker-hero—he who did more (and better) than anyone else.

The two major municipal events that dominated all the others were the New York Public Library's magnificent exhibit, *Becoming Visible*, and the Gay Olympic Games held in Columbia's Wien Stadium. I had no connection to the Gay Games, though I attended them and thought they were gloriously offbeat; unlike the parent games, where perfectly toned bodies and competitive vigor were de rigueur, the Gay Games welcomed all comers, and the contestants appeared in wondrously sloppy, out-of-shape—and intoxicating—disarray.

I had a good deal more to do with the NYPL's exhilarating exhibit. Thanks to Mimi Bowling, NYPL's chief archivist, the library had amassed one of the world's largest manuscript collections of material relating to queer history. As I'd learned to expect, the triumphant exhibit that went on display at the library was preceded by a predictable amount of jockeying for position. In the months leading up to the exhibit's opening, Mimi, who I'd come to know well, would fill me in on some of the omnipresent bickering. An unnamed member of NYPL's prestigious board expressed open displeasure at the library's association with an event as "far-fetched" as a celebration of LGBTQ+ life. I wasn't privy to the details, but judging from the changes made, the protester must have been a donor with considerable clout. A brochure planned to accompany the exhibit was scotched, the panel texts (which I'd been asked to review and found fine) were withdrawn, and the wording on the photo captions was put on hold.

A gay historian (I'll call him "Robert"), an authority on New York City history, was hired to review all the written material connected to the exhibit, and an internal committee was appointed to review the reviewer. Mimi characterized the historian as "a high-priced fall guy" and expressed her anger to me over his "willingness to take credit for work he didn't do." Despite her disgruntlement, Robert not only remained in place but Paul LeClerc, then head of the library, decreed that *Robert's* voice—not that of Mimi and her staff (Molly McGarry and Fred Wasserman)—was for now the only acceptable one, even though Mimi described his new text panels to me as "not very good and overwhelmingly male, despite our efforts at gender balance and multiculturalism . . . and in several instances they say misleading things."

Despite the behind-the-scenes ruckus, opening night of *Becoming Visible* was nothing short of spectacular. A large banner—BECOMING VISIBLE—spanned the main entry to the library, along with the symbolic pink triangle. The sight was a heart-stopper, even if at the last minute the subtitle, AN EXHIBITION ON THE HISTORY OF NEW YORK'S LESBIAN AND GAY COMMUNITY, was dropped from the banner—due, rumor had it, to opposition from a disgruntled board member. Eli and my aunt Tedda went with me, and all three of us found the exhibit visually stunning and the content fascinating—not that my excitement allowed me to linger long over any one item. Yet even at a glance, it was immediately obvious that Mimi had won the battle and gotten last-minute concessions about gender parity and multiculturalism. The overall impact of the exhibit was enormous: Who could have dreamed twenty-five years earlier that we would see the pink triangle floating over what many consider the city's premier cultural institution?

The one unhappy surprise was a sign at the exhibit entrance: THIS EXHIBIT MAY NOT BE APPROPRIATE FOR ALL VIEWERS. Though I didn't want to rain on a glorious parade, I felt I *had* to say something to Paul LeClerc. Taking him aside, I told him that the sign, not the exhibition, was "inappropriate." He nervously said something about "concern for visitors from Peoria." "But those are precisely the people who need to see the exhibit!" I replied. "Well," Paul conceded, "the sign is certainly inappropriate *tonight*"—and to my surprise he went over right then and there and turned it to the wall. I realized that it might reappear the next day, though a number of people told me that they were prepared to write letters of complaint.

I felt this was a perfect time to step away from CLAGS and turn it over to the new generation of scholar-activists who, quite appropriately, would reconfigure its structure and mission in a way that best accommodated its own evolving perspectives. CLAGS, I felt, was on solid footing—and I myself badly needed a change of pace. Several other Graduate School faculty members had recently come out, and one of them, if available, could take over as director. I made only one recommendation: that I not be replaced by another White man.

I assured the board that I remained wholly committed to CLAGS and that I wouldn't abruptly step away but would stay in place until a replacement was found—though I hoped it could be soon. Eager at this point for release, I felt a little uneasy when a full two months passed before the board formed a search committee in July 1995. I reiterated my hope that the end of the year would see my replacement installed.

Part of my eagerness to be free lay in the fact that in the interstices between events, I'd been at work on a new book (which I would call *Midlife Queer*), and I wanted to devote myself full-time to its completion. The book's contents were pretty raw, and as it would turn out, I wouldn't easily find a publisher; it centered on a difficult period in my life during the '70s—my mother's death, an extended involvement with drugs and hustlers, aborted productions of my plays, and an incapacitating heart attack. Neither Frances, my agent, nor Arnold Dolin, my editor at Dutton, reacted favorably to the first draft of *Midlife Queer*, acknowledging that they were put off by the nature of the material. Frances was rather sniffy about it and urged me to write instead "a straightforward history of the '70s." But she wanted to keep me as a client, and reluctantly agreed to send out the finished manuscript to the few editors she thought might be sympathetic.

Unexpectedly, her very first submission—to Don Fehr, an editor at Addison-Wesley—got an enthusiastic response, and Fehr said he was prepared to make an offer. But he soon ran into opposition; as he told it, the president of Addison-Wesley vetoed the recommendation of the editorial board to proceed. Don ascribed the rejection to "homophobia and inter-publishing paranoia" (meaning, it turned out, that Addison-Wesley, like Dutton, was part of the Penguin empire and it was thought "unsuitable" for one branch of the empire to publish a book rejected by another). Fehr claimed he was so angry that he intended to look for another job.

Frances decided that the next stop should be Crown, since (according to Frances) they'd "long coveted you." The manuscript cured them in record time: within ten days they turned it down, claiming that it was "three different books in one." Worse, though refraining from saying "I told you so," Frances said she was reluctant to send it out again. Still, she did pride herself on loyalty to her clients. (And besides, she'd long credited my Robeson biography with having put her agency on the map.) She ultimately decided to give it "one last try," but her truculent tone, alas, was a foretaste of what would become a rupture between us that would be deeply saddening.

Luckily, she chose Bill Goldstein, a senior editor at Scribner, for her "final" submission. Goldstein not only liked the manuscript but had some smart comments on it (like not burying my wit in parenthetical clauses). Unfortunately, he was in the midst of a career shift to the *New York Times* online. Scribner, happily, decided to proceed anyway, and Leigh Haber became my new editor. She thought the manuscript was "essentially there, needing only some tightening."

Midlife Queer came out in 1996, and the initial reception was, surprisingly, near rapturous. A starred prepub review in *Publishers Weekly* was quickly followed by Ed White's rave in the *Village Voice*. Just as I was beginning to have hopes for the book, up popped my old antagonist, the *New York Times*. For their hatchet job this time around they chose the fail-safe Walter Kendrick, whose own book, *The Secret Museum*, I'd earlier reviewed negatively. Kendrick paid me back in kind—and then some. His review was positively aflame with venom; he managed all at once to disparage my productivity, my political activism, and my self-exposure. The book's momentum screeched to a halt. A few weeks later the *Times'* Sam Roberts had me on his TV show, *The New York Times Close Up*, and during the few minutes before taping, he sympathetically said, "The *Times* really has it in for you, doesn't it. Do you want to talk about it on air?" I was tempted but said no. "In the book you do attack both Mel Gussow and Walter Goodman, two *Times* reporters, which wasn't wise," Sam said with a twinkle. "I didn't attack them," I said, "I told the truth about their homophobia."

At this point I was still officially the director of CLAGS, my replacement not yet selected, and that meant now and then interrupting my giddy new freedom with a few ongoing chores—like an all-day board retreat, and several round-the-clock days getting out the newsletter and membership renewal notices. Also, after skipping a year, I was again giving a graduate student seminar. I stuck to the formula I'd developed through experiments that dated back to the mid-to-late '60s: a collaborative study group in which people with like-minded interests gather to exchange views on a set of issues *they* choose as being of vital concern to *them*. To help create a climate of trust, I did away—as before—with exams, papers, and grades, and instituted shifting leadership within the group that paralleled changes in areas of experience and expertise. This time around there was a minimum of angst and a maximal sense of camaraderie. It was a relief to be in a setting where—unlike the jolts of recent CLAGS board meetings—I felt appreciated and comfortable, not on guard against an attack from right field, ersatz accusations, guilt-inducing glares.

As the months passed and I gained more distance from CLAGS's squabble-filled history, I was able to see that together over the years and against the odds, we'd accomplished a great deal. The many milestones of the past decade, I felt, needed some form of remembrance. I hit on the idea of putting together a CLAGS reader. I hoped it would make available to the expanding audience for reliable scholarship on queer subjects the material that had been presented over the prior decade both in our monthly colloquiums and in our one-to-three-day conferences. In the past, people unable to make the trek to New York had often expressed regret at "how much I wish I could have been there." Perhaps it might be possible, I thought, to reverse the process: to gather the cutting-edge and controversial material that had been presented at CLAGS over the years into book form—thereby making it accessible to a much wider audience than had been able to attend the original events.

I took the idea to Niko Pfund, then head of NYU Press, and he was immediately enthusiastic. He agreed that gathering the material would be a formidable undertaking, but he encouraged me to take it on—and to help steady my nerves offered a contract. And so the hunt for lost treasures began. I started to track down the (literally) hundreds of scholars, activists, and culture workers who'd taken part in our events. In the early years CLAGS hadn't taped its presentations, and only in the early '90s did we start to do so with any regularity. Extracting, polishing, and negotiating edits with dozens of authors would, predictably, prove a challenge.

Adding to the difficulty of creating a readable text, some speakers at CLAGS events had talked with only limited notes, and others—including several of the most eloquent—used no notes at all. Would they be willing to reconstruct and update their remarks? Would they be open to incorporating the scholarship that had accumulated in the years since their presentation? Happily, many of them did prove willing, and over a period of many months and several drafts, they created serviceable essays. What that inescapably meant, in some instances, was that the new piece bore only a tangential relationship to the material that had originally been presented at CLAGS. In the upshot, I opted for sacrificing absolute historical accuracy (in some instances impossible anyway) in the name of producing essays that represented whatever additional insights and data had accumulated since the original presentation. A good number of the pieces, however—especially the section I titled "Genes, Hormones, and the Brain"—had not only been recorded and transcribed but required little change.

As the stack of essays grew higher, choices had to be made and the survivors then grouped into coherent units. To give one example: fourteen people had presented papers at CLAGS's 1994 conference "Homo/ Economics," but only half of them appear in the final anthology. The papers not printed were excluded on various grounds: they existed only as sketchy notes, there was no tape of the original remarks to expand upon, the authors had already published the material elsewhere. As the anthology reached completion and the pile of essays grew cumbersome, Niko and I decided to divide the anthology into two separate volumes: *A Queer World* and *Queer Representations*. The combined set included the work of more than a hundred scholars. Both volumes were published in 1997, and the total number of pages came to 1,165. I finally had to admit that CLAGS had done *a lot*!

I steered clear of any involvement in choosing my successor, but I heard a fair amount about the behind-the-scenes jockeying of the four candidates and their supporters. Though I kept it to myself, my own choice of a replacement was, by a wide margin, Jill Dolan, a professor of theater in the Graduate School and a person of tact and efficiency. The final decision was in the hands of Frances Degen Horowitz, president of the Graduate School, and I was relieved to get a call from her in mid-June 1996 to let me know that she was appointing Jill. I told her I was delighted, that I thought Jill ideally qualified. Along with relief came a rush of sadness. CLAGS really was behind me now, and despite all my complaining through the years about how it had taken over my life, I suddenly and irrationally felt cut adrift. For a time, the void loomed large.

It helped to know that I was leaving CLAGS in good shape. Two months before Jill's appointment, news arrived that we had again won the Rockefeller Humanities Fellowship—which was apparently unprecedented (not to mention that the precedent-breaking nod had gone for a second time to a gay organization). In addition, the two CLAGS readers that I'd been working on were nearing publication and our directory of scholars working in the field was already serving as an important networking tool. Along with the prominent Kessler Lecture we'd also over time established a number of other awards and fellowships, and we had a solid network of contacts with gay-friendly foundations and individual supporters. We even had a comfortable sum in the bank.

With every passing year, moreover, our reputation had continued to spread abroad, and requests for information and assistance had steadily mounted. We became something of an international clearinghouse for information and, when possible, even books and bibliographies to make up for what one correspondent from Buenos Aires called the "utter lack of relevant material" available locally. For scholars from abroad, we arranged for formal status as visiting research scholars to allow them to secure needed funds from their own countries. Upon arrival some of them would drop by the CLAGS office, and they invariably expressed astonishment that in our small, ill-equipped space, and with only a single part-time intern, we'd produced a scholarly directory, a regular newsletter, and a steady flow of colloquiums and conferences. Some of the letters were deeply touching, and I tried to answer each one personally.

By the mid-'90s the board conflagrations of earlier years had been resolved, at least for now, through the resignation of the two most consistently antagonistic members (one of whom later let me know that in retrospect she regretted the "inflammatory excess" of the assault on me). Simultaneously, the number of openly gay graduate students at CUNY had grown considerably, attracted by CLAGS's existence and—*mirabile dictu*!—they were largely appreciative rather than antagonistic. A significant number of them committed to writing their doctoral theses on LGBTQ+ topics and envisioned careers focused on gender and sexuality studies. It was definitely the right time to pass the torch.

Though I'd turned sixty-five, I wasn't one for retirement—either from teaching or from writing. I still didn't feel close to my chronological age, yet my body was beginning to take note: a degenerative disc in the neck, a rising cholesterol level, chest pains, and three days of hospital tests ending with the diagnosis that "something is definitely wrong and there's a fifty-fifty chance you're having a second heart attack." I wasn't; a subsequent battery of tests resulted in a default diagnosis of "unstable angina," which my cardiologist dismissed as "jargon for 'I don't know.'" The old saw is true: aging is not for sissies. The trouble is that I am one; it's part of my cultural heritage. A *tough* sissy, of course. Is there another kind?

Matt, the graduate assistant who'd been helping out in the office, let me know that "plans are well along for a farewell party for you." When I learned that he and Eli had originated the idea, I firmly squashed it: I could hear it now—"Marty is giving himself a party and using Matt as the conduit for self-congratulation." Thanks a lot, but no thanks. I told Matt to bring all plans to a halt. He countered with, "How about a 'Changing the Guard' party to toast both you and Jill, the outgoing and incoming directors?" *That* I could agree to—but only, I told Matt, if *no* speeches were given about me (it turned out three had been planned) and that my role be limited to giving a brief summation of CLAGS's history that would segue into introducing Jill. Which is not exactly what happened. Ignoring our agreement, the committee planning the party went against my wishes and turned the event into a veritable tribute. I was greatly surprised—and touched. Half a dozen wounds healed on the spot.

For a while I was kept busy with getting the two CLAGS readers ready for the press, as well as with teaching. Nearing completion of the readers, I started mulling over new projects—not all of them scholarly. Having grown up with dogs and adoring them, I'd long missed having one, and Eli and I decided this was the ideal time. We located a reliable kennel in Sag Harbor, chose one of the seven-week-old yellow lab puppies, named her Emma (for Emma Goldman), and headed back home. True to her namesake she produced instant upheaval, throwing up all over the car. Unable to take her outside until she was immunized, and unwilling to put her in a crate at night, the nonstop assault on our cozy routines had us running in circles. As she barked us awake every morning at five o'clock I wondered how, under the guise of introducing more comfort into my life, I'd unerringly introduced more turmoil instead.

During the day Eli was away in his office and for the first few weeks, as I alternated between mopping up piss and shit, and washing the blood off my hands from her teething offensive, I had evil thoughts of shipping her off to the pound. Half the apartment was barricaded, and the other half in chaos. I, who was wedded to routine and isolation, decided that it had been madness at age sixty-six to be doing the equivalent of diapers and feedings. Before long, of course, the periods of calm and cuddling lengthened, and within weeks we'd become utterly smitten. There was something humbling and centering about having an animal around: no feigned emotions, no claims but the present, no strategic withholdings, indirections, apologies, and a whole new understanding that the tone, not the words, is what finally matters.

As Emma gradually became more integrated into our lives and decidedly less disruptive, I was able to explore in a more sustained way some of the *other* percolating discontents I'd been holding in abeyance. I knew I wasn't done with gay-related activism, yet I'd been feeling a deepening sense of disaffection from what I viewed as the increasing narrowness of the gay agenda. Linked to that was a growing urge to write about other matters and from a perspective less tightly bound to "rational discourse." I remained political but felt somewhat trapped: the (male) left in general remained essentially blind to the new impulses and insights represented by the feminist and gay movements and, conversely, the national gay political movement, dominated by the concerns of prosperous White men, remained essentially disengaged from deprivations relating to race and class.

For the previous fifteen years the gay movement had been centrally concerned, understandably, with the devastation wrought by AIDS. The number of cases worldwide had risen above a million, and many had lost all hope of a viable treatment emerging anytime soon—or, possibly, ever. But then suddenly, in December 1995, the FDA announced the release of saquinavir, soon followed by two other drugs, all three known as protease inhibitors. Having lived through so many false hopes, it was hard to take in the news. Yet reports of the effectiveness of the new medications were undeniable: HIV levels in most infected individuals treated with protease inhibitors rapidly declined, and in many cases became undetectable.

Though the news seemed miraculous, AIDS hadn't simply disappeared, and especially not in developing countries. The new drugs didn't work for everyone, and for others worked only briefly. Besides, the drugs initially cost $15,000 for a year's supply, which put them (like so much else) out of reach for most people. Drug-assistance programs existed in only about half the states, and most of those didn't cover protease inhibitors. Over time the situation greatly improved, but during the interim hundreds if not thousands of additional lives were needlessly lost. And so many of those lives were Black or Latino that AIDS became increasingly known as a disease of color: as late as 2007, Black Americans, just 13 percent of the population, were still accounting for more than 50 percent of new HIV diagnoses.

Still, for most sufferers AIDS now became a "manageable disease." Paralleling the surge of optimism was a growing conviction in *prosperous* gay circles that we should discard the role of pariahs and stress instead that we (i.e., White folks) shared mainstream values and wanted nothing more than the right to kill in battle and then to settle down to a lifetime of contented domesticity—monogamous, of course. The largest and wealthiest national gay organization, the Human Rights Campaign, waving the white flag of surrender, spearheaded the drive to assimilate, to make ourselves over into an acceptable version of middle-class respectability.

This centrist turn was not one I welcomed—indeed I would eventually, after a tendency had turned into a tidal wave, write an entire book (*Has the Gay Movement Failed?*) arguing against it. Back in 1996, I drew in my horns and searched the horizon for other avenues of involvement.

As a kind of holding action, jogging in place as it were, I plowed through my essays and articles of the last thirty-five years and selected for publication those I thought more durable. Basic Books published the collection (*Left Out: The Politics of Exclusion*) in 1999, and it got a positive, though limited, reception; still, some of the people I most admired—Jonathan Kozol, Doug Ireland, and Frances Fox Piven—wrote glowingly about it.

PART III

2000–2007

Having cleared a space, I was hoping for the swift arrival of a tenant. What descended instead was a series of misfortunes, mostly family related, that culminated in what I would never have predicted: a return to psychotherapy.

The rough patch lasted the better part of a year. It was triggered when Emma developed a bruised shoulder tendon and the vet ordered her "strictly confined" for up to two months—with no guarantee that she'd heal properly or that the condition wouldn't reoccur. Already a high-strung, hyperactive little girl, her energy barely containable through constant trips to the dog run, Emma now became housebound and unmanageable. The upheaval that followed uncorked some unrelated issues that we'd been stuffing down.

Even before Emma's injury, Eli and I had both been feeling over-extended, with no room in our tight schedules for dealing with some incidental complaints about each other that had been accumulating. Eli was juggling the completion of psychoanalytic training with starting up a therapy practice, and was often running on empty and less available emotionally. For my part, tending to a frantic puppy had been preventing me from making headway with several overdue writing projects—and I was increasingly irritable about it. Neither of us questioned the essential "rightness" of our relationship, but after more than ten years together we'd been neither counting our blessings nor opening up about our discontents.

They were manageable, but first had to be acknowledged, and for the moment neither of us felt up for professional counseling; what we both wanted was to plow ahead and be left in peace. Emma, not our own shortcomings, became a convenient substitute for discontents best sidestepped for now. I even returned to a question we thought long since settled: should we, after all, try to find another home for her? The answer was obvious: we'd never forgive ourselves—or each other—if we gave her away. Yes, she was a handful, but primarily because of the issues that caretaking, intimacy, and "home" raised in *us*. Before the year was out, we'd bitten the bullet and were back in couples therapy.

In the midst of all of this my ninety-two-year-old aunt Tedda became seriously ill. The middle sister (my mother was the eldest), Tedda had never married or had an alluring career; she'd worked as a modest-salaried secretary her whole life—and still was in 1997. She lived alone in a studio apartment in Manhattan, and movie and dinner outings with Eli and me constituted, along with regular visits to her younger sister Flo, the core of her social life. Though (lamentably) we never spoke in such terms, Tedda and I had an unvoiced but deep attachment, and Eli, too, grew very fond of her. Tedda was always included in holiday gatherings of our small family and always regarded affectionately, perhaps because she never burdened anyone with details, past or present, about her own life. Flo told me that Tedda had never had a boyfriend, had never in fact been interested in men; she thought that Tedda was probably lesbian, though she'd almost certainly have denied it—even, possibly, to herself.

Exacting and fastidious, Tedda never complained, ate little and cooked less, was thrifty to a fault, and never indulged in any other "extravagance"—like a vacation. She could be willful and stubborn, but didn't harbor grievances. If she had moods, she rarely displayed them; if she had secrets, she possibly confided them to Flo, but to no one else. She adored Flo, her outgoing, life-affirming sister—and Flo's death the year before Tedda herself took ill had devastated her. When she developed edema Tedda told me, "I want to die. I wish it would happen tonight." Her tone was matter-of-fact, not the least bit melodramatic.

As the edema worsened and she was diagnosed with pancreatic cancer, she continued to take the crosstown bus and go to work—though no one understood how she managed it. When home in her apartment she was listless, barely functioning, silently grieving Flo. I thought up a project for her, which I called "Tedda's Story." I told her that through talk, jottings, tapes, and transcripts, we would re-create her life story as a gift to the family. She shyly agreed to the project, and I positioned a writing pad next to her armchair for her to jot down a memory or thought between our visits. Almost the first thing she told me was that she "wasn't meant to be born." What did *that* mean? "I was a breech baby. The doctor told my father that he had to choose between saving his wife or his unborn child." Her father decided that since they already had Josie (my mother), he would choose his wife over Tedda. Unexpectedly, both mother and child survived.

I took Tedda to many of her doctor appointments, and on one of them he injected her with Gemzar, a touted new substitute for chemotherapy (which he didn't feel, at ninety-two, she could tolerate). He also recommended twelve-hour daily home care. In between, feeling vaguely nuts, I walked and fed Emma and did only essential errands. I've always been a natural caretaker, but of a special kind: one with an invasion problem; I can be on duty for only so long before I begin to crave isolation. Denied that for any length of time, I start to feel sorry for myself—start thinking I need someone to take care of *me*, though I couldn't specify what needed taking care of. Knowing the mechanism is irrational does nothing to reduce its force, but it does inhibit its expression.

By June Tedda was bedridden and weak, though blessedly free of pain. Her doctor told me that Gemzar helps only one out of five patients, and he wasn't willing to discuss whether "helps" meant anything close to a restoration of ordinary living or merely an added six months in bed. One family member impatiently advocated discontinuing the treatments, insisting that Tedda was simply waiting for me and Ron (Flo's son, with whom she and I were both close) to urge her in that direction. We couldn't. Tedda was an atheist, and to learn that death was imminent seemed to us the equivalent of pushing her through the door that fell off into a pitch-dark hole.

She finally took the decision out of our hands, telling us firmly that she'd decided to stop treatment. She repeated what she'd said some months earlier: "I don't want to live any longer, I want to die." Over the next few days, she gave no sign of wavering or regret over her decision. Coming out of a sleep at one point she abruptly said, her lifelong thrift to the fore, "Coffins are expensive." "Would you like a coffin just like Flo's?" Ron asked—which I thought shockingly direct, but it was just what Tedda wanted to hear. "Oh, yes!" she said, smiling radiantly. Symbolically, I guess, that was as close to a reunion with her beloved Flo as a total nonbeliever can get. Tedda also insisted there be no funeral—just a few words at the gravesite. No ritual, no self-dramatizing, no extravagance, financial or emotional—an end consistent with the life. She died at 4:30 AM on June 7, 1997.

It hit me hard. At the gravesite I was flooded with tears but finally managed to get out some words: she'd gotten so little attention all her life that I was determined to say *something*. I started by recounting the first thing Tedda had told me when we began "Tedda's Story," and her piercing words about being a "breech birth": "I wasn't supposed to be born." In large measure, I said between tears, she'd lived her life accordingly, kept her expectations low, settled for being a loving addition to other people's lives. Like so many women of her generation, like far too many still, she was trained in self-denial, trained to be (or act) selfless, the message subliminally conveyed that her assertiveness would be appropriate only in regard to matters of small importance. And so the strong-willed, opinionated, fiercely independent woman Tedda had actually been could emerge mostly in regard to the petty issues of train timetables or the choice of a restaurant—trifling matters that were transformed by Tedda's innate dignity, her strenuous character.

Tedda's parsimonious life hadn't even earned her a peaceable decline; Flo's death the year before had robbed her of the limited joy in her life. If there was such a thing as cosmic recompense for a restricted, uncomplaining life, the timing of the two sisters' deaths would have been reversed. Can the word "noble" be better used, I said at the gravesite, than to describe a ninety-two-year-old woman who ten days before her death had still insisted on taking the bus and hobbling to work on legs swollen with weeping edema, anchoring in concrete her desperately thin, eighty-pound body? She left few possessions, no progeny, the barest imprint of having been here. But for those who would read it, hers was a powerful legacy: Against Great Odds, and Without Complaint . . .

Grieving and exhausted, Eli and I kept close to home over the next few weeks. What finally injected minimal energy was a call from the Rattlestick Theater offering a reading of my newest full-length play, *Posing Naked*, a re-creation of the homophobic scandal at Smith College involving the well-known literary critic Newton Arvin. I gratefully accepted the offer but was in fact still seriously depleted. The last eight or nine months had shaken the defenses I'd built up as a youngster to ward off an invasive mother even as I tried to gain the attention of a withdrawn father, and revealed how much my early years continued to affect the way I reacted when threatened with any prolonged disruption of my routines. I wasn't very happy about the circumventions entailed and decided it was "now or never" to dig deeper into the fortress of "busyness" and "accomplishment" that I'd erected over the years, allowing me to function well—though weighed down by the needed armor. It was time to give therapy one more shot.

Thanks to the recommendation of a friend, I went to see Sue Grand, who had an office in Greenwich Village. I felt a near-instant connection much more powerful than any I'd felt during my earlier therapy-hopping. During our very first session I found myself—to my amazement—breaking down in sobs. I'd been sitting on more pain than I knew. Being for months in close touch with Tedda's wretchedness had opened a Pandora's box of unreliable family alliances, a history of mishandled grievances and misplaced or defective trust, of unread messages in a tightly sealed bottle, of muddled, joyless affection.

I was extremely lucky to have found Sue—after all, in a real sense I'd been searching for her in the therapeutic thicket for decades. I felt from the beginning that I'd finally found a genuine ally. Unlike the string of therapists I'd seen over the years, she wasn't a self-anointed sage, wasn't interested in debating politics or being my "buddy," wasn't at all defensive. She was quick to see that the surface annoyances I kept reporting were a strategy for avoiding my underlying fear that nobody had ever or would ever see beyond my accomplished veneer, be able to understand the cost of attaining it, and help me find trustworthy connection and comfort. Sue knew Eli professionally and helped me to see that despite our wasted year of periodic bickering, he and I had finally found in each other someone able to own up to *his* piece of the problem when the relationship got into trouble.

Much of the early months with Sue were peppered with crying jags and self-recrimination. Early on she let me know that she saw me as a sensible and reliable person, well grounded and levelheaded—a description that produced in me a storm of tears. I managed to say that when she got to know me better, she'd be disappointed, would learn the nasty truth. After six months or so she came up with what to me was the jarring insight that more profound than my need to be seen as an accomplished person was the far less acknowledged need to be seen as a *good* one. It felt to me—had long felt, but most recently during the harsh clashes at CLAGS—that I got plenty of credit professionally, but little understanding humanly, and that attacks on my *character* produced far more pain in me than challenges to my competence.

What were the qualities I felt so desperate to have others recognize? Over many months I was gradually able to itemize at least some of them: that I've never been a butt-kisser or a control freak—or even a careerist, in the sense of pursuing contacts or sabotaging rivals rather than simply doing my work. That I was good at listening to other points of view (even if I'd rather win them over to mine) and at understanding what someone else was feeling, or trying to say. That I tried hard to make people different from me feel comfortable. That I attempted to use my privilege to open up paths for others (even while keeping my own well paved). That I avoided flaunting my ability and didn't encourage others to distrust theirs—even though I could sometimes be an impulsive, effusive overreactor.

These propositions, which still needed testing, had opened up with remarkable speed. I suppose it would have been shameful at my age and given my accumulated years of therapy if they hadn't—except that so much of the therapy in the past had made me feel badly about myself and so many of my years, before Eli, had been heavily invested in the pursuit of sensation (coke, gorgeous young men), self-coddling, and becoming "friends" with difficult people who managed to confirm the same deprecating message that therapy did. Over time the primary evidence I'd cite to prove I was "not a good person" shifted. When younger it had been my "sick" sexuality, my "fear of intimacy," my "self-absorption." These gave way to more recent self-indictments: my membership in the "overprivileged, overachieving White male club," my "thin skin," my "tenacity" (the last three underscored, though not minted, during the CLAGS years).

For some powerful reason deeply embedded in my youth—probably my father's lack of interest in me—I'd internalized subsequent public attacks on my character, nurtured the sense that I was somehow constructed "wrong," had failed someone or something, was incapable of sustained connectedness or pleasure. Yet internalized only in part; if more than that, I would have been immobilized rather than driven to prove my worth. As for the charge that I lacked the capacity for intimacy, I'd in fact never given up the search and struggle for close connection, though accumulated disappointments over the years had made me unduly scrutinize and prematurely seize on signs that the ships would yet again pass in the night—thus helping to ensure that they did. Still, neither accumulated disappointments nor age had halted my persistent search for intimacy, even though the search had been shadowed by mounting skepticism and a need for solitude.

Where did that need originate? Surely my mother's anxious attentiveness, which could be intrusive, played a role: I'd early on learned to link closeness with invasion. But my father's role—or lack of one—was surely greater. He died of a heart attack in 1962 when I was thirty-two, yet he'd been such a cipher in my life that at the time I felt little sense of loss. That he'd played almost no role in my growing up made his passing, in a sense, sometimes feel more rather than less painful—it put beyond possibility the chance of my ever getting to know him. The man was a stranger to me, always had been, and always would be. I deeply wish it had been otherwise, but wishing has never yet turned an orange into a pear.

That lost cause made me sad, but also angry—that I didn't have a single memory of a day's companionship with him, a private talk, a display of affection. I grieved for the lack, but didn't grieve for the man—or for any other stranger. About his earlier life I had only the barest information; the family stereotype handed down was that he'd been a "quiet, nice, distant man who'd rather work alone in his vegetable garden than join the family circle." From his own lips I recall nothing, literally nothing—not a single conversation, not one direct exchange between us of any length or resonance.

Yet what a story he must have had to tell, and could have passed on—and how much I wish he had. How did he *do* it—a twenty-year-old Russian Jewish peasant with no English, embarking alone for the New World, somehow surviving, somehow ending up with a Tudor house in Westchester and a membership in Fenway Golf Club! No mere "nice" man had passed this way. Yet he chose to share nothing with me of his remarkable story. Now and then—almost entirely through photographs of him—I catch a glimpse of his sadness, more often of his buried anger, but get no sense of their context or cause other than the vague awareness that my parents' marriage wasn't good and that he would mostly go alone to see his Orthodox Jewish relatives in Brooklyn, most of whom he'd scrimped and saved to bring over from Russia.

He himself told me not a word about his history. I somehow learned that upon arrival in New York he'd lived in a one-room tenement, the subway rumbling by his window every few minutes. Where else did he live when still a single young man? Who gave him his first job? How did he end up working in the garment industry? How was he able to start his own business? Did he have friends? Had any of his family members preceded him to this country? Did he go to shul? Was he ever "political"—did he join the Workmen's Circle, take part in a strike? Did he go to the Yiddish Art Theatre? Did he have any fun? How did he meet my mother? Was there a courtship? Was he more smitten than she was? Did he want to have children?

Questions in a void, no particulars to curl my heart around. Therapy brought out my buried anger. How could he have left me so bereft of a history, of *connection*? During one session I became racked with grief over my blank memory, over how little he'd given me emotionally. I mourned the lack of even a semblance of generational continuity; I had no recoverable roots from the past, nor progeny to carry forward my own story. I lived in a void. I was an empty barrel rolling down somebody else's hill. . . .

And yet, as the months with Sue lengthened, and often through spasms of tears, I dug deeper, discovered ways to empathize with, not merely berate, my father (though much of the criticism held firm). Previously I'd been centered on *my* story of loss—ignoring the obliteration of *his*. Yes, he was closed off and unavailable to me, but what of his own annihilated past? When he left Russia he had to say goodbye, in all likelihood forever, to all that had been familiar, and perhaps even beloved. What a desperate, brave, wrenching away; no wonder he could never look back, or ever again fully attach. Some part of him did manage (for a time) to stay emotionally alive in this strange new country: family lore has it that in the early years of their marriage, he "adored" my mother. If so, it dissipated early; I never saw it. All I saw was the frustrated dynamo of a mother coupled to an uncommunicative, withdrawn father; they stayed together, but were miles apart.

My arrival—a blue-eyed, blond, Germanic-looking child—probably hastened my father's retreat. His surroundings suddenly became still more exotic. My "blondness" contradicted his family's prototype; I called up no associations or connections to the Semitic clan he'd left behind, no binding visual link of past to present. Later, the more educated I became, the wider the chasm between us, the further he withdrew.

He died before "the gay issue" emerged; during the years he was alive my consistent persona was that of an athlete-scholar. Yet I do recall one Halloween when, as a prepubescent child, I tricked and treated in our neighborhood wearing my mother's glamorous furs. What did my parents make of *that*? What, for that matter, did *I*? Had *I* chosen to deck myself out, or had my mother? Though I went on to play assorted female roles in high school, I never thought of myself as a girl. I wasn't *trans*—incipiently or otherwise. I was a star of the tennis team; I was a member in good standing of the "in" crowd; I knew I was a *boy*—and was glad of it.

A nonparticipant, my father failed me as a parent. My strengths, such as they are, derive wholly from my energetic, lively mother. The big plus in my childhood had, in general, been strong women—predominantly my mother but also her mother, Lily, and my two aunts, Tedda and Flo. Yet with Sue's help I was at least able to see that my withdrawn father was no mere nebbish: not only did he build a successful business but less than five years after the shock of his arrival in the United States, he was shipped back to Europe to serve in World War I, where he survived the frontline trenches at Verdun. Is it possible that one result was literal shell shock (today called PTSD)? Does his experience in the war help to account for his subsequent withdrawal? Or was he blessed with remarkable survival skills—with a resilient reservoir of strength, however passive the surface?

"What he doesn't seem to have modeled for you," Sue speculated, "and deserves no credit for, is that you've grown up to be a thoughtful, kind, compassionate person."

I gulped, then scoffed: "Therapists, as we know, are *supposed* to be on their patient's side."

In regard to my relationship with Eli, Sue helped me to see how much floating anxiety we *both* carried around, and how we tended to concretize and project it onto petty matters ("You're twenty minutes late!" "You haven't asked me if my tummy is still upset!") that evaded broader issues and had kept us stalemated for a year on symptomatic ones. After a time, we did couples counseling with Sue, and she helped us to see that our relationship was intrinsically sound and well worth the hard work we were willing to invest in salvaging and deepening it—a big relief to both of us given the turmoil and doubts we'd been experiencing over the past months. We *had* created a solid foundation and shared a candid awareness of what each of us could realistically, reasonably expect from the other.

———————

As if to certify our renewed commitment, Eli and I made the rather abrupt decision to shift apartments in our Chelsea brownstone from the top floor to the more spacious parlor one. I'd first moved into the brownstone back in 1980, when Chelsea was much more affordable and hadn't yet become the high-priced, tony address it is today. In 1980 my fourth-floor walk-up had been the least expensive apartment in the building, which stood across the street from a park that back then functioned as a drug drop and gay sex emporium. Yet by the time Eli moved in with me in 1987, an elegant fence girded the park, and it was locked up tight at night. Chelsea was well on its way to being gentrified.

It was Eli who excitedly rushed in one day in 1998 with the news that the parlor floor in our brownstone was about to go on the market. I didn't instantly jump for joy—not even when the bank told us they *would* approve a substantial mortgage. (Eli had only recently opened his private practice, which meant the bulk of the financial responsibility at that point was mine.) What was I doing? How had this happened? Just the week before, in my seminar, The History of Radical Protest in the US, I'd argued that the growing disparity of wealth and privilege was rapidly transforming the country into an oligarchy and as a corrective we should, for starters, cap personal incomes at $100,000 and guarantee a minimal annual income of $25,000 for every individual of voting age.

Yet here I was, at age sixty-eight, about to take out a pricey mortgage that would have led my students to laugh me out of the room.

It's not your fault, my inner ear falteringly tried to reassure me. *You never focused on maximizing your income. Just a few years ago you were still borrowing money now and then from Aunt Tedda to pay off your bills. Is it my fault that my university retirement fund has abruptly risen, that the fund's long-standing, long-ignored (that is, by me) investments in real estate and stocks had soared? I'd never focused on making money, yet it happened anyway. . . . But even if I didn't set the goal, I was happily going along with having "accidently" achieved it. I was no better than a capitalist pig—which made a mockery of my radical head.*

When I repeated that inner monologue to Eli, he snorted, "Nonsense! You've worked hard all your life, earned your money honorably, used your privilege to help others."

"As if that leaves me uncontaminated."

"As if that's even possible, given the structural unfairness of the system," Eli countered.

I sighed. "Thanks for the kind words"—and signed the mortgage.

All the rest followed in turn, a veritable rampage of acquisitions paralleled by a host of retaliatory bodily symptoms: dizziness, loss of balance, and a veritable flood tide of diarrhea. "A possible blood clot," my doctor declared. "Or, more unlikely, a stroke. We'll have to send you for tests." The CT scan was clear, the Doppler and colonoscopy likewise; parasites not present, nor spastic colitis. A neurologist cleared me for stroke. The diarrhea continued. "I've just moved," I sheepishly told the GI specialist: "I don't do well with change." (To put it mildly.)

The painters had been unable to complete the job before we moved in—they claimed my choice of "dawn red" (*oy vey*) for the bedroom had presented special problems—and for the first week all our belongings (the result of the spree of acquisitions) remained under canvas in the center of each room. With no habitable space to retreat to from the onslaught of noisy workmen and UPS deliveries, my "invasion problem" kicked in. Plus an acute sense of loss: my mother and her sisters had frequently been to our old place; they'd never see this one. It felt like an abrupt, painful separation from my own past. I longed for the cozy nest we'd abandoned. I bemoaned the "cavernous echo" of the sparsely furnished rooms. Deciding we needed more furniture, we made yet another raid on Bloomingdale's, buying the one sofa that could be delivered *today*.

By mid-October my deep sense of dislocation had eased. I also felt better physically, give or take occasional back spasms. I thought it conceivable that I might write again, but not yet. A week after that, I realized I was no longer obsessing about whether the orange pillow conflicted with the red couch or whether to stack the firewood outside or inside the apartment. In November 1998 I made two trips out of town to give talks at Ramapo College and Rider University. Back home Eli and I went to see the latest theatrical sensation, *The Beauty Queen of Leenane*. (We thought it a semi-intelligible melodrama.)

And then, after starting to teach again and to swim on a regular basis, I finally turned back to writing, the only activity that has ever made me feel reasonably at peace, even at times content. Just as equanimity threatened, an early copy of Paul Robinson's *Gay Lives* arrived. As an undergraduate, Paul had been in a long-ago seminar of mine when I was teaching at Yale. A bright student and more than a bit arrogant about it, he too had gone on to become a professor of history, later crediting me (so he writes in *Becoming Historians*) as "the teacher who, more than any other, provided an example I identified with . . . he seemed remarkably self-assured, yet also modest and candid." Paul and I had stayed in tenuous contact through the years but were too dissimilar (he was a Catholic centrist) to become friends. He seemed entirely comfortable with the smug formalities of academia, didn't feel "the need" to come out (or to join a political movement), and wrote critically about Foucault—that last *not* a cardinal sin. Paul married at twenty-four and at twenty-seven divorced his wife, having fallen in love with a man he met at Sporter's, a Boston gay bar. He remained a cultural conservative who kept aloof from activist involvement.[1]

In *Gay Lives*, his study of the autobiographies of gay men, Paul lavished considerable attention on my 1991 book *Cures*. He had some admiring words for it but the overall tone of his discussion struck me as markedly ungenerous (and in part seriously inaccurate). He reduced

Cures, my painful account of growing up gay during the most homo-phobic decades of the twentieth century, to a wounding phrase: "Apparently . . . [Duberman] was bound and determined to suffer." He also quoted "some critics"—never named (and I suspect, having seen a great many of the reviews, all carrying the same last name: Robinson)—who'd found *Cures* "insufferably arrogant and self-promoting." Several reviewers of *Gay Lives* in fact echoed my shock at Paul's malign description of *Cures* and in general his suspiciously mean-spirited personal attack—like dismissing me as a man "very much in need of psychiatric help." Since Paul had unconscionably distorted some of my views, I decided to write and tell him so. I aimed for a conciliatory tone, but hurt by his ill will, I may well have fallen short.

To me, I wrote him, the most egregious *political* misstatement in his book was his insistence that I viewed bisexuality as a cop-out and a sham. That may have been true of *his* experience, I pointed out, but it was a gross misreading of mine: I'd clearly stated *in print* my view that "a bisexual capacity was probably intrinsic to human nature" and had even suggested that those "who claimed that bisexuality was a function of 'lower consciousness,' the preserve of cowards and poseurs, might themselves be trying to avoid coming to grips with their own erotic impulses toward members of the opposite gender."

In his brief and airy response to my letter, Paul largely ignored my complaints, insisted that his account had been "basically admiring," and—giving arrogance a whole new dimension—chastised me for not appreciating that "out of dozens, more likely hundreds, of gay auto-biographies, I picked yours as one of a handful worthy of serious and considered analysis." *Gee, thanks*, I wanted to reply, *but henceforth spare me such honors*. In my actual reply I aimed for a conciliatory tone—in retrospect perhaps too much so. Not that it mattered, since Paul never bothered to respond. Still, his weirdly malevolent attack threw me off balance, and I took my distress to Sue, my therapist, with whom I'd now been working for about a year and had learned to trust.

"Paul's nastiness has depressed me," I told her. "Made me feel like a fraud."

"Of course you do. He's played right into your long-standing anxiety that you're not right, that you're faking it. This may surprise you," Sue calmly added, "but I don't think of you as very neurotic, though I know you've been taught to see yourself that way."

That came as a surprise.

"Look, it's like this," Sue went on. "Your reality-testing is decidedly intact. Your sense of humor is keen. Your ability to explore your tics and foibles unusually full. Your willingness to let people see you in a less than idealized light is profound, and suggestive of neither masochism nor narcissism. None of that adds up to being 'very neurotic.'"

During my long march through psychiatrists' offices, I'd never heard a diagnosis so emphatically affirmative. I loved every word of it, but what I said was, "I've always felt more comfortable itemizing my shortcomings."

"You mean exaggerating them. And I'll add one more thing: you minimize your own attributes because you genuinely don't want people to feel badly about themselves. You'd rather carry the additional pain of self-deprecation than produce pain in others."

"That's about the nicest thing anybody's ever said to me. Can I write it down? Otherwise I'll forget it as soon as I walk out."

"By all means."

"You're sure it's not just a *tactic* for lifting me out of depression and getting me to write again?"

"I don't deal in false flattery."

True or not, the tactic worked. *Really* worked. With each passing day I felt lighter and more cheerful. I even signed up at the Actors' Loft for several acting classes (theater was still in my bones). I wasn't dreaming of becoming an actor again—it was a wee bit late for that—but I did hope to give my emotions a good shake: if I was ever to carry off my next project—a novel about the Haymarket Affair—I'd need to unearth a whole palette of them. At the Actors' Loft I signed up for two classes, one on technique and scene study, the other on movement—the equivalent of barre exercises for beginners. I especially loved the movement class, with its bits of everything from Tai Chi to yoga to Laban. I tended, naturally, to overdo it and at one point nearly sprained an ankle.

The good feelings carried over into a fundraising benefit for CLAGS in our new apartment. It coincided with the first pleasant spring day in late March. An overflow crowd of 150–180 people showed up and the CLAGS staff outdid itself in erecting a festive blue-and-white striped tent over the garden, along with providing a mellow jazz trio and platters full of fancy hors d'oeuvres. The event *netted* $17,000 for scholarships in gay studies—a fortune for a new field still lacking funding resources.

Only the sight of a forlorn Kate Millett, standing alone in one corner of the apartment, brought me down a bit. I hadn't seen her in half a dozen years and it was nearly ten years since she'd had me over for dinner, during which she'd drunk a lot, veered back and forth from grandiosity to vulnerability, expressed anger that "more young scholars" weren't interviewing *her* instead of "writing yet one more paper on Jane Austen," loudly denounced the view that "there's any such thing as mental illness"—and eloquently deplored the "disastrous" role of the United States in the Middle East. I'd always admired and liked Kate but didn't like being around her: too often her massive equanimity seemed about to explode into belligerence.

At the CLAGS party, though, she looked as if she'd lost some thirty pounds since I'd last seen her and was temperately clear-eyed—nothing like the grim speechifier I'd last had dinner with, nor a trace of the belligerence that had turned me off. But she did look desolate, almost near tears. I tried to round up some of the exuberant younger guests to go over and greet her, but they (predictably, alas) responded with "Kate *who*?"—making me want to throttle them. Possibly worse was my attempt to join her up in conversation with the composer David Del Tredici, which proved a case of oil and water. Orange-haired, natty, and smiley, David clearly did not appeal to Kate, though he seemed not to notice. By this point I'd gone over my two-drink limit and in a true throwback to yesteryear found myself hitting on a hot young Black reporter from WBAI, who smoothly extricated himself. I chose to look on the bright side, viewing the attempted seduction as a "welcome rebound" from the blues.

Spring passed into fall, with only minor disruptions in a placid routine. My collection of essays, *Left Out*, was published, I started work on my Haymarket novel, and I shifted from the Actors' Loft to the Herbert Berghof Studio to take a class in advanced theater games—that is, "improv." Surrounded by an intimidating group of professional actors in their forties, I felt a five-year-old's terror at being called on, and when inevitably I was, did badly. The teacher—who pulled no punches— reminded me, out loud, that "rationality and logic are valuable, Martin, but you overuse them. And you're too negative. Instead of challenging your partner's inventions, try committing to them, find something in them of positive interest and value." Talk about a life lesson! I'd found myself a second therapist. . . .

Therapist number one, meantime, summed up the relatively peaceful interlude of the past few months: "In the past," Sue said, "you veered between being (overly) compliant and (impulsively) incendiary. These days, you inhabit a middle ground that's less vivid but less arduous." That seemed to me just about right. On my sixty-ninth birthday, I wrote up my own summary: "And so I enter my 70th year. An astonishing number given how un-old I feel—at least these days, with depression and anxiety battened down. I'm very conscious of my wealth of blessings— health, work, Eli, financial security. I'm tempted to say that everything is 'good enough'—but that conjures up the mirage of life ever having been or possibly ever becoming 'better'; it reveals the ingrate's hidden belief, contra history and temperament, that some transformative energy awaits, and is deserved. My declared, insincere wish is that nothing at all changes, and for as long as possible."

When the collection of my essays, *Left Out*, was published in 1999, I felt (like most writers) disgruntled with the publisher's efforts on behalf of the book. This time around the fuckups were so encompassing that my annoyance, even in retrospect, seems more or less justified; it was, as I later put it, "The worst experience I've ever had in publishing." Ad copy was delayed so long that several crucial deadlines were missed, and the publicity department's efforts to schedule readings and the like were so ineptly half-hearted that by the time they roused themselves, almost every major media outlet was already booked.

Among the few events they managed to arrange was a speaking engagement at the gay synagogue Beit Simchat Torah. I didn't think it was exactly *my* audience, but I was eager to play author again. My instincts were right: the attendees, all members of the congregation, were so conservative and cantankerous that I felt as if I was back in the 1950s. Everyone, it seemed, wanted not to ask a question but to give a speech in response to my speech. I was serially chastised for "caricaturing" the American right, for not understanding that socialism equates to Stalinism, and for daring to have made a parenthetically positive remark about the Palestinians.

The limited round of radio and TV appearances was mostly on the third-tier circuit, with two notable exceptions: Doug Henwood's program on WBAI and Sam Roberts's show, *The New York Times Close Up*; both were serious minded and sympathetic, and both hosts had clearly read at least some of the book. The other interviewers had obviously relied on the press kit for information or, worse still, fallen back on some prototypically vapid, unanswerable cliché. Sample: "What will be the most important issue facing us in the future?"

The book got only a few reviews, and none in prominent left-wing publications; the coverage, such as it was, appeared online (to my pre-digital brain, worthless) or in scholarly journals. Though I was grumpy at the limited response, it was largely favorable: "a complex and nuanced understanding," "a remarkable job of blending personal goals and public ones," and so on—though the Marxist publication *Science & Society* took me to task for lacking "a dialectical framework," which I considered a commendation. As for the promised "tour" for *Left Out*, it consisted of appearances at two Borders bookstores: one in Boston, the other in Arlington, Virginia. Though the 9:30 AM Amtrak would have gotten me to Boston with plenty of time for a leisurely meal, the publisher put me instead on the 10:30 train, well known (I later learned) for taking a back route that, due to construction, was notorious for *always* being late. Arriving at South Station at 5:30 PM, I called the car service number the publisher had given me. On came the canned message: "The number you have dialed is not a working number." I managed to locate the service's home office, and my driver and I did finally connect—just in time for me to drop my bag at the hotel (at which point I realized it was *one block* from Boston's Back Bay Station, which is obviously where I *should* have gotten off the train). At this point, with no time to unpack, eat, or even go to the bathroom, I dashed off for a scheduled 6:30 PM reading at Borders—or so said the publisher's instruction sheet.

When I arrived at the entrance to Borders, I was greeted by a frantic employee who blurted out, "Where *were* you?!" It turned out the reading had in fact been scheduled for *6:00*, and by 6:30 only seven people remained in their chairs. Later I asked the employee how many people had originally shown up. "No less than nine," he said. Crestfallen, I asked him if the promised ad in the *Boston Phoenix* had been placed. "Oh, yes," he reassured me. Yet when I later saw the ad, it contained no mention of an upcoming reading at Borders. Back at the hotel, feeling exhausted, misused, irrelevant, I called Eli at home and he calmed me down.

I still had the Arlington reading to do. It proved more humiliating still. Borders had taken out no ad, nor put up any sign or book display in the store's window. Net attendance: a perfect zero. I thought briefly of forcing the store's manager to sit alone in the front row while I read the entire book aloud, but decided I preferred to go to sleep. The next day I woke up with bronchitis. Never again, I swore, never again would I subject myself to a publicity machine designed (unless you were Toni Morrison) for minimal exposure and maximal mortification. But of course I subsequently did, as ignominy faded and adolescent dreams of glory resurfaced.

Still, I felt in better balance than usual; equilibrium, I decided, is the true definition of happiness. I trusted myself more—trusted (thanks, Sue!) my essential decency, character defects and all, and the essential health of my body, despite bouts in the past of serious illness. I liked myself better—that was the bottom line. And because of that I no longer had to rely on a driven, packed schedule to keep anxiety at bay—nor berate myself to atone for unspecified but cosmic crimes. Still, the lack of reviews for *Left Out* and my ignoble "book tour" did make me feel for a while that I'd slid off the face of the earth.

Sue gave me another way to regard my steady disappearance from public view over the past few years: it had been my own—unconscious—choice. When I'd first come to her, she said, I had a powerfully clear, if not articulated, goal: to work on my intimacy issues. I didn't want to go into old age, I'd told her, feeling "not good enough" in my closest relationships. Since then Eli and I had, despite run-of-the-mill interludes of misunderstanding, made significant strides. Sue doubted if I could have simultaneously continued my frenetic public life *and* gone deeper within. Besides, she added, "there's every reason to think you *will* reemerge, and with renewed readiness for a public role. I think the time is rapidly approaching," she added, "when we can consider ending individual, though not couples, therapy." And soon after, approaching the three-year mark, we did.

———————

As if on cue, I had what felt like a breakthrough on the Haymarket novel—a feeling writing teachers tell us *never* to trust. Yet I did; for the first time in ages the flow of words felt organic: instead of forcing myself to the computer (yes, I'd at least managed *that* transition), I couldn't wait to get there. And almost simultaneously, the prestigious New York Theatre Workshop called to say that they wanted to give *Mother Earth*, my play on the life of Emma Goldman, a reading. They'd had the script for some time, and I'd given up any hope of hearing from them. Almost simultaneously, the Rattlestick Theater expressed interest in mounting another of my plays, *Visions of Kerouac*. Was the year 2000 about to validate—just in time for my seventieth birthday—my ancient longing for "a life in the theater"?

The answer would ultimately be a resounding "no," though it would take a while for the verdict to arrive and prove all the more painful for the promising start. The New York Theatre Workshop chose Michael Greif to direct the *Mother Earth* reading. Greif had already accumulated an impressive list of credits (including Tony Kushner's *Slavs!*, the original production of *Rent*, for which he'd received an Obie, and the rock musical based on Jay McInerney's novel *Bright Lights, Big City*). Greif confided to me that the Workshop "is eager to form an ongoing relationship with you and the play—their interest is considerable." For the first few weeks Michael and I worked well together on script revisions, even though "urgent phone calls"—well he *is* a hot property, I told myself—kept constantly interrupting our process.

Then came the day when, so I assumed, one of those multiple phone calls conveyed an offer he couldn't refuse, and Michael abruptly disappeared. Rehearsals were canceled, and casting wasn't completed until *three hours* before the reading (NYTW's last-minute, largely arbitrary role assignments included hiring a decidedly glamorous actress to play the stolidly earthy Emma Goldman). The date of the reading was changed—without notifying the Workshop's subscriber list—and a tiny audience of my friends filled in for potential backers and luminaries. Yet against all odds the script somehow managed to sound pretty good. More remarkably, Jim Nicola, head of the Workshop, invited me to meet with him the following week.

We talked for an hour and a half, and constructively. Nicola felt I hadn't fully decided between a documentary format and a "subjective" one, and seemed to think, as I did not, that a decisive choice between the two was needed. He looked blank when I said, "A 'documentary' is *also* subjective." In the upshot, we agreed on a "studio production," which he defined as a "middle ground" between another one-shot reading and a full production. There would be a three-to-four-week intensive workshop with the actors paid for their time, followed by several invited performances, but no critics. "Give me a little time," Jim said, "to think through budget, schedule, and space, and then we'll get back to you."

In the interim I moved directly into putting together the one-shot reading of *Visions of Kerouac* at the Rattlestick Theater. The excellent cast allowed me to hear what did or didn't work in the script, and for the first time I saw Cody (based on Neal Cassady) less as an energizing force of nature and more as a self-absorbed emotional thug. The reading came off well (which is rare in my experience, since unpaid actors can't devote any substantial amount of time to preparation), and David van Arselt, the head of Rattlestick, felt the play was "strong." He told me that he wanted his theater "to have a role in its future." The next step, he thought, should be a rewrite. I initially drew back: my plate was full (along with polishing the plays, I was trying to complete my novel, *Haymarket*). Besides, I'd already been around the block several times with rewrites and workshops of *Kerouac*. Concealing my reluctance, I agreed to a rewrite. David's enthusiasm, after all, seemed very nearly miraculous, given my history of mishaps in the theater. (Only my first play, *In White America*, had had a smooth path from completion to opening night.)

I did the *Mother Earth* rewrite first and then spent the rest of the spring and summer finishing *Haymarket*. Eli (a tough critic) thought it "*very* good" and Frances, my agent, loved it. I did, too, though I tried to remember that the odds of success for a first novel at age seventy were out of the ballpark. Yet Frances was confident. She sent the novel out on a two-week exclusive basis to Gerry Howard, her first choice as editor, and "just to play it safe" drew up a backstop list of five others on the off chance it didn't sell immediately. Meanwhile NYTW came up with November 26 as the starting date for the three-week workshop of *Mother Earth*. I was flying *very* high. While awaiting my double Pulitzer, I kept busy with rewrites of *Visions of Kerouac*.

Two weeks passed. No word from Gerry Howard. Angered, Frances rescinded his exclusive and moved on to her "backup" list of five. I completed my revision of *Kerouac* and sent it off to a typist. Still no word. By this point NYTW had picked Michael Sexton to direct *Mother*

Earth and—a signal of danger ahead—I had to chase him for ten days even to get a return call. When we finally met, I had instant misgivings. He seemed a classically arrogant young hotshot who *pronounced* at length and *listened* reluctantly. Uptight and tight-lipped, he wasn't at all a natural for understanding or even liking the ebullient, passionate Emma. Nor could I imagine him being any good with actors—with helping them as they struggled to explore and inhabit a given role.

Waiting for the other shoe to drop, I agreed to moderate a panel at Joe's Pub at the Public Theater on that chestnut topic, "The Artist as Sexual Outlaw." So who's an "artist"? So what's a "sexual outlaw"? In my opening remarks I suggested that these days, at least in much of Manhattan, anyone still committed to the model of lifetime monogamous pair-bonding should be regarded as representing a truly deviant minority view—and was therefore today's version of an "outlaw." Yes, it was all as dreary as that. Only the sparklingly articulate director Moisés Kaufman managed to catch the fancy of what was a surprisingly large audience. Didn't they have anything better to do?

Afterward, George Wolfe (then head of the Public Theater) came rushing up to me. The few times I'd ever talked to him I'd felt the mad urge to describe *all* my plays, announce my genius, and demand a production contract. None of that, strangely, ever seemed to be on George's agenda. That night he wanted to tell me that he'd just finished reading my Robeson biography and had found it "brilliant and enthralling." Bah! Phooey! I felt insanely hurt that he didn't know that *Mother Earth* was about to be workshopped at NYTW, and hadn't begged me to save him a ticket. So hurt that I inanely—that is, out of the blue—brought up the workshop myself and asked him to attend. He looked instantly stricken at what was doubtless the hundredth request that day from a playwright to read/see/applaud a script. Flustered, he beat a quick retreat.

Soon after that, the chosen "top five" editors began to phone in to Frances their reactions to my Haymarket novel. "Spirited and accomplished" was the closest any of the five came to a compliment, and "spirited" did not want the book either. I hadn't expected massive enthusiasm (awright, I had the *occasional* fantasy of bidding wars and auctions), but had felt confident of getting one or two enthusiastic bids.

"Politics!" an angry Frances fumed. "The book's too damned radical for their comfort!" I wanted to believe her but found my own take more persuasive: "A first novel at age seventy? Talk about a long shot." Frances, ever proactive, immediately set to work drawing up a new list of potential editors and publishing houses. I was disappointed but not devastated—*that* emotion found focus instead on the results of the presidential election. I thought Bush a nincompoop, a fraternity boy down to his loafers. But I *loathed* Ralph Nader, a smug priestly type, for having run on a third-party ticket—thereby helping to defeat Gore. Nader's grandiose post-election announcement that he had "no regrets" was exactly what I'd expected from him. His supporters liked to describe themselves as *radicals*, but in my view were more accurately seen as *cultural* conservatives: *Nach Hitler, uns*, they smilingly announced—the jackasses! As for Gore, I found his "statesman-like" concession speech far too bland; he should have fought the theft of the election, rather than readily acquiescing to it. And now, I thought, we're really in for it. . . .

Disgruntled, I turned in late November to the start of the *Mother Earth* project at the New York Theatre Workshop. It began badly and got worse. From day one Michael Sexton, the director, pontificated at length about the need for "visual framing devices" to counterbalance a play he characterized as "insistently political." He showed no sign of interest in either the historical Emma Goldman or the play that tried to tell her story. But I didn't rock the boat. I'd waited too long to get *Emma* a hearing. Like twenty-five years.

Still, during the first few days of rehearsal I was surprised at how remote I felt from the proceedings. Having longed for "just one more chance" to enjoy the collaborative rehearsal process, I wasn't enjoying it much at all. Sitting hour after hour in the empty theater, I felt mostly bored, and wanted out—like I was being kept away from something genuinely important that I should be doing. I chalked up my disengagement to exhaustion. I'd gone directly from completing *Haymarket* to doing script revisions for both *Mother Earth* and *Visions of Kerouac*—and to a generally apathetic reception on all counts: the novel threatened to go unpublished and the multiple play revisions had fallen into uncomprehending hands.

Jenny Bacon and Mike Stuhlbarg, who played the leads in *Mother Earth*, complained to me directly over dinner one night about how badly Sexton was treating them, and how indifferent he was to their explorations and suggestions. The more his staging took shape, the more my own concern grew. Yes, he had a gift for creating group tableaux, but he overused it. His distracting "stage scenes" and "backdrops" competed with, rather than complemented, the script, calling attention *away from* critical moments in the dialogue. I again tried talking to him, but with seignorial disdain, he "granted" me no more than a minute or two on the fly. When he finally did alight, briefly, he was defensive and argumentative; his aim was to *win* every discussion, not profit from it.

Jenny and Mike, near tears, complained to me that so much time and energy were being invested in everything *but* the exploration of character that they were "floundering, unassisted," their anxiety mounting. *Finally*, a mere week before the scheduled performances, I actually got Sexton to sit still long enough for a session on the script itself, but there was no time left to try out revisions. I spent nine straight hours at the computer reworking Act 2, but by hour five I had no idea whether I was damaging or improving the play. Besides, Sexton never *got* to Act 2. He'd obsessively fiddled for so long with the externals of his bloody "stage pictures" in Act 1 ("Should five people or four be clapping in this scene?" "Should the chair be placed less on a diagonal or more?") that he simply ran out of time. Act 2—which in fact had needed the most work—was left untouched, the actors reduced to a seated reading, scripts in hand.

The actual workshop performances were flat to the point of tedium. Jim Nicola left the theater without a word, which struck me as needlessly rude. *I* had to ask *him* for a meeting, and it proved unhelpful. He said the "architecture" of the play was now visible, "a production vocabulary" established—whatever *that* meant. Act 2, he added, needed "a major adjustment," and after I'd completed it, Nicola said, NYTW would be glad to have "another look;" but he warned me that in regard to an actual production, they were booked for the next eighteen months.

I had a different reaction: that my preferred medium really *was* print. I decided to give up the battleground of theater and instead put together a volume of my political plays (the New Press would publish it in 2008 as *Radical Acts*)—and to leave the rest to heaven.

A period of hyperactivity had ended abruptly in a roadblocked state of limbo. I was stalled, back in the doldrums. As usual, a plethora of physical symptoms promptly appeared to serve their usual purpose: to both represent the gloom and distract me from it. Abdominal pain led to GI/esophageal tests ending with the diagnosis of a large hiatal hernia and "a mess of currently inactive gallstones," which led to additional tests that put any decision about surgery on hold. My abdominal discomfort dutifully converted into attacks of chest pain. My trusted cardiologist ordered a thallium stress test, and when the results were "not entirely normal" decided "it would be a good idea finally to have an angiogram," though he felt "95 percent sure" that my chest pains were *not* heart related.

The test results were spectacular. One of my three heart arteries was indeed "entirely occluded" due to the heart attack I'd had in 1979, but to compensate I'd succeeded through exercise in developing a *replacement* artery. Just as "miraculous," the other two heart arteries were only 20 percent blocked, "which for someone your age," the attending doctor beamed, "was tantamount to none." It was time to get off the medical merry-go-round that had hijacked months of my life, and to look elsewhere for distraction from my sinking spirits. I booked an appointment with Sue for a "checkup."

Yes, she confirmed, our exasperating president and his Cold War cabinet had been making a number of her patients uneasy, but no, the political scene alone was not a sufficient explanation for my malaise.

Nor was the continuing rejection by the latest group of publishers of my novel, *Haymarket*. Sue suggested that we focus for a limited number of sessions on two conundrums: First, why did I—"capable of and needing intimacy" (Sue's words)—have so few deep friendships? Yes, she acknowledged, our adolescent-oriented culture puts scant emphasis on intimacy of any depth, but was I myself throwing up some barriers to what I longed for?

Second, how does a "golden boy," used to attention, deal with its sharp decline at age seventy? With flagging interest in anything I might have to say or contribute, how could I continue to get pleasure from work and life, however diminished in scope? Sue suggested that the reality of aging, of not being much in demand compared to earlier periods in my life, may be inevitable, but depression and self-pity weren't the only possible responses, even though my temperament naturally leans toward lamentation—toward feeling forgotten and futureless. We needed to try and figure out why I persisted in experiencing inevitable lulls and downturns, bound at my age to multiply, as the emotional equivalents of permanent obscurity and creative death. The answer, Sue felt, surely lay with having been treated from an early age and for a long period of time as a golden boy immune to life's ordinary travails, even though, paradoxically, I've experienced a fair share of them, from a heart attack and bouts of depression to a variety of professional disappointments, especially in regard to my plays.

Sue's double-pronged challenge to "go deeper" into the issues she'd posed was abruptly halted when an MRI revealed that the severe back pain I'd been dealing with was due to a—or rather three—slipped discs. The pain was agonizing and stopped me on a dime. I could barely stand or sleep, unable to take a step without pain coursing down my left buttock, thigh, and leg. The back specialist I went to see thought that a combination of physical therapy and a set of three epidural shots into my spine *might* make it possible for me to avoid surgery. While awaiting results, he put me on codeine to ease the pain (which it did—along with wrecking my stomach).

Within two weeks I was able to have the first epidural, and it dramatically reduced the level of pain. That night I slept a blessed six hours. Plus the doctor replaced codeine with Darvocet. Movement was still restricted—I was mostly on the couch reading magazines (with Eli uncomplainingly taking over *all* the household chores)—but my head was clearer and my mood more optimistic. With the second epidural I was able to return to teaching, though between classes had to lie flat on the floor of my office—and was happy to be there! After the third epidural, I definitely turned the corner.

By mid-May, three months after the initial attack, I seemed to have reached a plateau, getting neither worse nor notably better, though I'd remained super dutiful about physical therapy. I'd never had much trust in the integrity of my body, and the trauma of prolonged pain exhausted me emotionally as well. With my spirits still pretty low, Sue thought it might be a good idea to consult a psychopharmacologist. I did, and a low dose of Wellbutrin was added to the bulging cabinet of medicines. It didn't seem to help at all, and I soon gave it up.

With the level of pain refusing further to budge and my spirits sagging, where would a naysayer intellectual turn for solace? To "figuring it all out," of course, and, in my case, to coming up with a satisfyingly negative explanation. Depression, I decided, is a by-product of the realization at a certain age that nothing is going to get better; no magic wand is going to wave away the disappointing shape of one's life when compared with the optimal version we once cherished. For many, the realization is too barren, too painful to sustain. We need to push it away, to project it outward or to bury it—so we smack the kids or drain the six-pack. Some of us, alas, aren't good at denial; we have trouble erasing reality. Our incessant complaining increasingly annoys friends and family; they're angry at being put in touch with their own discontent. "Grow up!" they growl. "Count your blessings!" "Stop complaining!" "But we *can't*," we whimper. "That's IT!"—their patience at an end, they retract their sympathy, disappear. Abandoned, we sink further down.

In a session with Sue, I began by accusing her of fatuous optimism—which then, to my astonishment, turned into a torrent of drenching sorrow. "You told me I was 'well,'" I shouted, "and I'm a basket case, more desperate than ever! . . . I'm seventy, for God's sake, and I haven't learned a fucking thing!—still the golden boy immune to ordinary problems!—or so everybody thinks, including you!"

Once my tears and accusations had run their course, Sue quietly said, "We *did* win the big one: you finally believe you're a good person. No small accomplishment!" I hadn't seen it that way, and it helped. It broke the logjam. After the session I felt lighter than in months. I saw clearly that although my options in life had considerably narrowed, my blessings were still multiple. I should be bathed in gratitude, not tears.

The universe, in its magnanimity, instantly arranged for a sudden change of fortune: enthusiastic word abruptly arrived from the small, left-wing South End Press that they wanted to do a paperback edition of *Left Out*. Next up, following months of silence and having resigned myself to *Mother Earth* being dead in the water, Jim Nicola of the New York Theatre Workshop got back in touch to suggest yet another reading of *Mother Earth* in the fall. His plan was to invite the heads of two highly respected regional theaters, the Arena Stage and Trinity Rep, to the reading; if either proved enthusiastic, NYTW would then join in cosponsoring a production the following year. As I'd learned, the number of possible slips between the cup and the lips was vast.

Never mind. I was reenergized. I picked up the much-maligned manuscript of *Haymarket* and gave it another whirl. This time around, I had what felt like a breakthrough. At the point where I'd earlier gotten stuck, I now had the idea to switch from the narrator's voice to selections from a diary I invented for Albert Parsons (the leading character). I thought the shift worked; the next day I *still* liked it.

The optimism carried over into other areas. I felt on a more even keel in general, even renewed trust in the essential health of my body. Best of all, Eli and I reoccupied a good place where mutual caring strongly resurfaced and mutual defensiveness receded. Sue and I agreed that we should continue couples therapy a while longer, but that it was time to end individual therapy. To help me avoid slipping back into depression, she cautioned me against excessive isolation—against continuing to fall back on my outworn boyhood survival strategy of retreating to my room in order to avoid family turmoil. The strategy had once served a purpose, but it had long since curdled into a recipe for starvation.

Quite suddenly I also had some ideas about how to reconnect politically. I'd recently reviewed the anthology *Out at Work* for the *Progressive* and had been struck by the editors' (Patrick McCreery and Kitty Krupat) indictment of the national gay movement for its lack of awareness that most gay people were *working class*; they held low-paying jobs with minimal benefits in workplace environments that remained strongly defined by heterosexual norms. If they dared "to come out" or if their gender nonconformity couldn't be hidden, they were subject to serious harassment by coworkers and could be *legally* fired. *Out At Work* argued that progressives active in class, gender, and sexual politics needed to recognize more than they currently did the *linkages* between their struggles and to form organizations that would fight for a common agenda. I'd long felt much the same—and in the late '70s had more or less cut ties with a national gay movement that seemed increasingly focused on winning mainstream acceptance.

I found a phone number for Pat McCreery and asked him how I might contribute to addressing the issues he and Kitty had laid out. He couldn't have been more receptive, and the three of us got together several times to discuss the possibility of forming a "think tank" to plan a gay-labor alliance. It turned out that they had hoped all along that their book might lead to some kind of organization-building and had been delighted at my getting in touch. They were keenly interested in how I'd managed to put CLAGS together and to sustain it against the odds, and were intrigued to hear that we'd begun with a handful of people meeting in my living room; they thought a comparable starting point might be the way to go in launching a gay-labor alliance.

In the weeks that followed, alas, it became clear that despite their undiminished enthusiasm, Kitty and Pat—already juggling graduate work and full-time jobs—simply didn't have the breathing room for another time-consuming project. We'd only gotten as far as agreeing on a list of some twenty invitees to attend an inaugural discussion when the World Trade Center was attacked on September 11 and reduced to rubble. Soon after that, all three of us got caught up in antiwar protest and reluctantly decided to "put our plans on hold." Alas, they were never resuscitated.

As was true for most people, the World Trade Center attack sent me reeling. Eli and I knew no one who'd been killed or injured, but we were staggered nonetheless. The heartbreaking stories that began to emerge about the individuals who'd died on 9/11 were soon matched by the murderous retaliatory policies that the Bush administration quickly put into play. Our descent on Afghanistan in 2001 to "punish" the Taliban, followed two years later by the invasion of Iraq to "disarm" nonexistent "weapons of mass destruction," was marked by a callous, almost gleeful indifference for human life. And the butchery was accompanied by the sickening triumphalist rhetoric of Donald Rumsfeld, Dick Cheney, and George W. Bush—"our fight is 'civilization's' fight . . . God is not neutral," and so on—with not a word said about the catastrophic loss of *civilian* life. Empty slogans and indiscriminate slaughter had become coin of the realm. Yes, Saddam Hussein's regime was barbaric, yet not a word—not even a pious "regrettable"—was issued from the White House in regard to the enormous casualties our daily bombings were inflicting, nor about our alliance with the differently vicious Saudi Arabian patriarchy. Only one member of Congress, Barbara Lee, dared to vote against the invasion of Afghanistan, while the mainstream news media, for its part, agreed to *self*-censor "disturbing" images emerging from the bombing.

And so the familiar cycle began again. Nightly TV interviews with gung ho American twenty-year-olds sounding their simplistic slogans— "We need to bring things to a head!" "Let's get this job done!"—that were all too reminiscent of the Vietnam War, to the endless body bags and to the mangled bodies that still fill VA hospitals. President Bush assured the country that our marvelous new weapons guaranteed "technological precision"—ours was purportedly "a lean war against military targets only"—as if there ever was or could be such a thing. As reporting in the *Nation* and a few other left-wing publications made clear, our

carpet bombings were killing thousands of Afghan and Iraqi civilians—
yet Bush maintained an approval rate of 80 percent. Vietnam had taught
us little or nothing; the profoundly American talent for forgetting its
own periodic cruelty settled over the land, and scholars, gay and straight,
were hardly immune—even if some of us thought we were.

In the midst of this madness—the moment could hardly have been
less opportune—the New York Theatre Workshop called to schedule
yet another reading of *Mother Earth* for January 2002, with (NYTW's
choice) Michael Sexton again directing. Stranger still, and almost to
the day, the well-known California producer-director Lee Sankowich
decided out of the blue that he wanted to do a full-scale production of
Visions of Kerouac in L.A. On the assumption that one or both sponsors would back out I gave both the go-ahead, though by this point
I'd lost all confidence in my ability to predict or even to influence the
maddeningly unpredictable fortunes of my poor, precious plays.

I did manage to do a thorough revision of Act 2 of *Mother Earth*
for the reading at the New York Theatre Workshop, and I sent it off
to Sexton, who, running true to form, remained silent. After hearing
nothing for two weeks, I called him. He was his usual unapologetic,
arrogant self: "Oh yeah, Marty, I did get the new Act 2, been up to
my ass in projects and anyway prefer the previous version." By this
point, only a few days remained before the planned reading—too few
to make any additional script changes. Molly Smith of the Arena Stage
did attend, and the net result was, as before, irresolution. Molly settled
for a few guarded, generic compliments ("an *interesting* play"), though
I thought I sensed a level of enthusiasm higher than she was willing for
the moment to verbalize.

I was wrong. In the upshot, she decided *not* to go forward. I came
up with the comforting theory that I'd been nuts from the start to think
that a Washington, DC, theater, reliant for ticket sales and funding on
the local powers that be, would ever dream that it could get away with

staging a play whose passionate heroine saw church and state as the archenemies of the working class.

By this point I'd become fed up with the whole theater scene, with the humiliation of constantly cooling my heels awaiting word from apolitical people unsure of their own opinions and even less attuned to ordinary manners. Lee Sankowich *would* eventually come through with a production of *Visions of Kerouac*, but that lay a few years down the road. For now, prospects were yet again minimal. I bought myself a copy of the *Dramatists Sourcebook*, chose a dozen vaguely plausible venues—knowing full well that for a script to have any chance of being read, it had to be submitted through a theater agent—and (not that anyone cared) tried to pretend that "I'd had it."

Print, it had been yet again made clear, was home base. Not that any new writing project had emerged. Nor had my completed novel *Haymarket* been able to find a publisher. If print was my medium, somebody forgot to tell the publishing world. The latest rejection had come from Nation Books, along with a three-page breast-beating letter whose bottom line was some semicoherent comparison between me and (God forbid!) Upton Sinclair. It began to look as if I'd be spending my post-seventy years *reading* novels and *seeing* theater. They were at least put "out there" when New Press published *Radical Acts*, a collection of my plays, in 2008; maybe at some future point they'd strike a chord with someone. What I needed now was to let go and reorient—above all, to again find meaningful political work.

———————

Fortunately for me, when I told my friend Terry Boggis about my disappointment that the connection with Kitty and Pat hadn't worked out, she told me about another group of progressive queers, the Economic Justice Network, and invited me to one of its meetings. It was there that I met Joseph DeFilippis. We immediately hit it off, and that same evening started to mull over the possibility of setting up a nonprofit that would center on the needs of the gay poor—those in shelters and prisons, unemployed or on welfare—but would also do bridge work to help mobilize what we hoped would become a movement demanding a guaranteed annual income.

Politically Joseph and I seemed very much on the same wavelength, and we both wanted to move rapidly ahead. At the start, in January 2002, we invited Kitty and Patrick to join us, but both, alas, had to drop out early on, and for the same reason as before: their overcrowded schedules. For a few months, though, Pat was centrally important in helping Joseph and me compose a mission statement that we could send out to some thirty like-minded people, hoping they would join us for an initial roundtable discussion.

Rereading our five-paragraph statement today, I still find its analysis compelling, and the new organization it hoped to mobilize badly needed. Central to the stated mission was the urgent matter, as we saw it, of making the LGBTQ+ movement more responsive to class and racial issues, and the labor movement, in turn, more willing to negotiate with employers for expanded protections and benefits in the workplace for queer people. Put more generally, the statement called for greater awareness of how people "understand, acknowledge, and express their sexuality in relationship to their working lives."

Currently, the statement went on, the misconception was widespread that LGBTQ+ people were largely White and middle class, and their employment mostly clustered in "niche industries." In fact, the large majority of LGBTQ+ people are working class—and this is true whether "class" is defined on the basis of income, education level, or job status. LGBTQ+ people were found throughout the spectrum of industries and workplaces and if welcomed, the statement argued, could potentially increase membership for a labor movement "that must organize in new sectors if it is to grow in influence and vitality." As a first step, the mission statement called for a meeting in May to explore "the insights of feminist and queer scholars to change the workplace into an environment no longer dominated by the values of a heteronormative culture." We emphasized that we were interested in having an initial discussion together and had no set idea of where the meeting might lead us.

In reply, thirty-two people checked the box for "strong interest" in attending such a meeting—which delighted us. Yet when May 23 rolled around, only half of them actually showed up. Most of the no-shows were people of color. To a degree, I wasn't surprised; the mission statement had put the stress on gay and labor constituencies, whereas the "primary emergency" for most activists of color was race. Joseph was particularly downhearted since he thought he'd gotten firm commitments from a number of Black and Latino activists. At the May meeting everyone agreed that we couldn't proceed further without first asking the non-White invitees to tell us whether this new venture felt congenial to them and, if not, how we could make it so. That meant putting off any discussion of applying for nonprofit legal status or planning a retreat. Having been down this road before with CLAGS I tried to caution myself against impatience. But it was hard; I *was* eager to plunge back into political activity.

Joseph did most of the ground-level work in reaching out to those who hadn't shown up and reassuring them that racism was indeed central to our agenda, even if the original mission statement had failed to fully convey that commitment. When we met again in late July, we took heart from the fact that eight of the fourteen attendees *were* people of color; by September we'd managed to create a board that was 50 percent female and 50 percent people of color. Only three of us were out of our thirties—with me, at seventy-two, *way* out. Our weak spot, as everyone acknowledged, was the lack of transgender representation. It wasn't for lack of trying: Joseph had gotten four transgender people to the point of saying they were interested and would try to attend, but none (due to overarching issues of survival) had been able to. It was otherwise an exhilarating day, especially in the respectful way people listened to each other. We reached consensus on nearly every issue, and good personal relationships—the real building blocks—got solidly established. The goodwill and political sophistication filled me with optimism, and I left the retreat feeling enthusiastic about the work ahead. "Queers for Economic Justice" (QEJ) had been born.

Not all who attended the July meeting would stick; others would weave in and out, often the result of do-or-die exigencies in their own lives. Nearly all were already involved in social justice movements, including Felix Gardon (UMDN), Lidell Jackson (OutPOCPAC), Ariel Herrera (Amnesty International), Michelle Matos (GMHC), Earl Plante (Gay Men of African Descent), Joo-Hyun Kang (Audre Lorde Project), Gabriel Martinez (FIERCE), Leona Williams (Health Force), and Andres Duque and Ingrid Rivera (both from the Latino Commission on AIDS).

As I excitedly wrote Joseph, "I don't know any LGBTQ organization that has managed (or even tried to manage) to create a board that was 50 percent female and 50 percent people of color—especially at the *start* of its history." Before the end of the year QEJ had, on a first try, gotten a $40,000 grant, spread out over two years, from the Open Society Institute. It wasn't enough money to hire a full-time staff person, but it was enough to get started in earnest on our work. We soon broke into committees that would operate during the interims between general board meetings. I myself was asked to join the Steering Committee, which served as a general clearinghouse and a conduit for carrying out the wishes of the group as a whole.

Thanks mostly to Joseph's unstinting efforts, we "rewarded" him (poor man!) with the title of executive director; by 2003 we were well embarked, incorporated as a nonprofit organization, and hopeful about our future. When Eli and I threw a fundraiser for QEJ, I was struck, and not for the first time, at how few straight White lefties showed up, or even bothered to RSVP. (Still, the fundraiser managed to clear $7,000.) Most heterosexuals on the left regard most queers as contemptibly frivolous, incapable of joining any alliance with a serious-minded purpose. Yet politically *radical* gays *do* exist, and in mounting numbers among the young. In direct contradiction to the straight left's widespread assumption that gay people are inherently featherbrained, radically minded gay people pride themselves on their *disaffection* from mainstream mores, on *not* being "just folks." Many of them go still further and suggest that radical queers, *in their differentness*, have much to tell *everyone*—though on this point the straight left's hearing aids have a way of going instantly dead.

As do those of the national gay organizations, whose mainstream agendas for the previous two decades have focused largely on assimilationist goals—and in the process have not only downplayed the ways in which we're demonstrably and richly different but have also ignored the large and needy numbers of poor people within our own communities. All of which is precisely why QEJ, in its radical opposition to mainstream values and tactics, appealed to me as a port in the storm.

I was a little surprised, given a decade of hard knocks at CLAGS, at my lack of cynicism; I chalk it up not merely to temperament but also to the fact that I was hugely touched and inspired by QEJ's other members. They were mostly young, urgent, scornful of moneymaking careers, devoted to helping those less fortunate than themselves. Almost all of them were already working full-time with progressive groups; they were "lifers"—committed to social justice work and obstinate in the face of roadblocks.

For starters, given our limited funds, we decided to focus initially on the poor in our own LGBTQ+ community, and to spread out from there to a more encompassing agenda. Our broad aim was to change the mainstream gay conversation, to expand its woefully narrow agenda (gay marriage and gays in the military) that lately had dominated the national movement, and to refocus on issues like prison and welfare reform, housing, and homelessness. We hoped to establish a legal clinic for low-income queers, provide greater access to health care for those of limited means, and hire a full-time community organizer to coordinate grassroots activity.

Our initial goal of establishing a queer antipoverty organization that would be multiracial stood in contrast to the powerhouse LGBTQ+ organizations that currently dominated the gay movement and (at most) paid lip service to the needs of the poor. We wanted to establish *as fact* that race and class were queer issues, that an appalling number of queer people were living below the poverty line and suffering from all the disabilities that characterize low-income life in our society (though neither the mainstream gay rights groups nor the "democratic socialist" movement seems to give much of a damn).

QEJ's stated goal was from the start focused on the needs of the least fortunate: "We seek to amend the conditions and policies of our economic system to prioritize the needs of the poor." We knew that it would be all but impossible to gain entry into the funding stream of the foundation world on which most nonprofits rely, and in the beginning our income derived almost wholly from individual donations, usually of small sums. Yet by 2004 a few left-wing foundations had come through with enough small grants for our annual budget, miraculously, to have reached $90,000. By 2004 we also had a hole-in-the-wall office, a number of volunteers, and one (badly) paid staff member, Jay Toole. Though this was a considerable accomplishment, rent on our office and salaries for Joseph and Jay consumed most of our budget, and the broad agenda we initially envisioned had to be confined for now to a few of the more pressing items.

Jay, fortunately, was a gem. Her primary mission was to empower homeless queers living in shelters to become more aware of their rights— for example, the right of same-sex partners to be housed together—and in general to make life in the shelters somewhat more bearable. Few of the gay homeless were "out," and for good reason: homophobia in the shelters was pronounced, as Jay herself knew firsthand. She'd lived in a shelter as an "out" lesbian, and for her courage had been beaten up and thrown down a flight of stairs.

Jay exemplified the attitude that characterized everyone connected to QEJ: we weren't going to be another top-down organization in which we, the privileged, spoke for the needs of the less privileged. We defined our job as teaching the skills needed to empower the powerless to find the voice they hadn't had—to enable *them* to run the show. The poor people's movement had to be led by poor people themselves. We believed the theory, but putting theory into practice became, as it usually does, more difficult than most of us had expected.

I can say in good conscience that the discussions we had during our Steering Committee meetings were less redolent of noblesse oblige than those I'd sat through in the past on the boards of other gay organizations. Yes, we too at QEJ had our pontificators—we were, after all, products of the same culture that we were trying to change. A couple of the older members had picked up some bad habits from earlier movement work, and tended to assume that their views needed to be heard on *every* issue that arose—and at length. Yet they, too, were often eloquent in reiterating the need we all felt "to help others find their voice so that they can represent themselves."

———————

Absorbed as I was in QEJ, I was simultaneously juggling some unexpected, unrelated developments. Lee Sankowich in L.A., after much back-and-forth pondering, did finally offer me a full production of *Visions of Kerouac* at the Odyssey Theatre—and actually gave me a formal contract and an advance! At nearly the same time, Dan Simon, head of the small left-wing press Seven Stories, reported to my agent Frances that an outside reader he'd sent the *Haymarket* manuscript to had weighed in with a "highly admiring" report; "others" were now reading it. A few weeks later Dan called in the verdict: *Haymarket does* deserve publication—that is, *after* some needed revisions. Still *more* revisions?! I was longing to work, not rework, and silently groaned. Did I have another revision left in me?

Though feeling stale, I of course *did* go back to work on the manuscript. But what made it unusually difficult this time around was that just weeks before I'd finally come up with a major new project that deeply engaged me: a biography of Lincoln Kirstein, the gay cultural impresario who'd brought Balanchine to America. When I first got the idea, seemingly out of the blue, I was afraid both that someone was already at work on a Kirstein book or that no large, unexplored archive existed that would allow for an in-depth biography. I put in a raft of phone calls and quickly learned that someone had indeed been working on a biography but *just three weeks earlier* had decided to call it quits. (She was quoted as saying, "I just don't like him well enough.")

And an archive? I found out that not only did one exist but it was vast, essentially untouched, housed at the New York Public Library for the Performing Arts at Lincoln Center, and guarded over by Kirstein's executor, a professor of English at Stanford named Nicholas Jenkins. Would he give me access? Had he decided to take on the project himself? Was he "difficult" (as one informant claimed) or "charming, gifted—and *not* gay" (as others reported)? Frances (my agent) straightaway called Bob Gottlieb, who was soon to leave his post as head of Knopf to become editor in chief of the *New Yorker*, had known Kirstein well, and had close ties with the New York City Ballet. Gottlieb told Frances that he thought "Kirstein-Duberman" was a good combination. Nicolas Jenkins—charming, *not* difficult—thought the combination "ideal" and promptly agreed to give me exclusive access to the archives. Knopf immediately offered a contract.

Having recently been traveling over a pretty bumpy road of rejections and blind alleys the last few years, I was thrilled with the new project: it felt absolutely right for me, and I plunged into reading background literature that would help to prepare me for an assault on the archives. I also had to clear the decks in regard to *Haymarket*. With the indispensable help of Jill Schoolman, a Seven Stories editor (and later the founder of Archipelago Books), I made a number of needed adjustments to the manuscript. Dan Simon, the head of Seven Stories, became an enthusiast, and the book was fast-tracked to publication in 2003. It got a good critical reception—though the *Chicago Tribune* felt that I "over-sanctified" the workers shot down by the police, and several historians expressed concern that I'd gone beyond the "known historical record."

As indeed I had—though my additives strictly derived from that record. Besides, as I'd been arguing for many a decade, archival material is usually either scanty or nonexistent when trying to re-create a subject's *inner* life—about which most historians seem, in any case, uninterested; those who *are*, need to risk a certain amount of learned guesswork (which academic historians indulge in all the time, but rarely acknowledge, even to themselves). But I wasn't going to fight *that* old battle again, not with Lincoln Kirstein awaiting me in the batter's box.

I stayed active with QEJ for another three years, until the Kirstein biography reached the stage where it needed my full attention. I also cut socializing to the bone, but that was no hardship: I rarely enjoyed parties, and my circle of close friends had long since narrowed to a few intimates—plus Eli, of course; they understood that although my hermit side periodically needed airing, solitude had a strong pull. Besides, as I saw it, "friendship" as currently practiced in New York had mostly become a shallow thing; when friends did meet, discussion of our aches and pains, or, alternately, the latest movie or TV show, commanded far more attention than any deeper political or personal exchange—though as a loner by temperament I may exaggerate.

Six months after gay couples won the right to marry in Massachusetts, opponents of same-sex marriage in eleven other states passed constitutional amendments that codified matrimony as an exclusively heterosexual institution. Although I opposed making marriage a primary issue, the antigay vote was to me primarily important for signaling the depth of opposition to extending even mainstream civil rights to gay people. The degradation of political life was further exemplified by the fact that Bush managed to become the only incumbent president to win reelection after losing the popular vote in the previous election: in other words, the war in Iraq had made Bush *more* popular than when he'd been a peacetime president. The sole comfort was that he'd failed to win a single electoral vote in the Northeast (i.e., God's country). All of which meant that the "war against terrorism" would continue, or perhaps further escalate.

My disaffection from mainstream politics—gay *and* straight—went up another notch when Eli and I hosted a benefit party for the Sylvia

Rivera Law Project, the pioneering trans organization. Of the two dozen or so invitations I myself sent out, mostly targeting prosperous gay White males, not a single person showed up or sent a check. As I saw it, "queers"—gender noncomformists—frightened them, whereas I myself tended to regard them as the cutting edge of evolutionary change. The trans people at the party seemed to me a warmer, more caring, sensitive bunch than any collectivity I'd known—certainly more than the gay White men who didn't show up.

The return of back problems and an unexpected diagnosis of spinal stenosis put me more or less out of commission for a few months and temporarily dampened my spirits. But fortified by my renewed political engagement and my ongoing work on the Kirstein biography, I kept a full-scale depression at bay. It further cheered me up when Eli and my close friend Marcy Gallo put together a fundraising celebration in a downtown loft for my seventy-fifth birthday and my retiring from teaching. The event raised several thousand dollars to add to the Duberman Fellowship, already established at CLAGS. I scolded myself for my recent downturn in mood, for not appreciating that it had been a full twenty years since I'd had a *disabling* bout of depression, which in comparison made my current decline in energy and optimism appear modest.

Still, I decided it would be wise to have a "refresher" session with Sue. After hearing me out, she startled me by saying that she thought I was "at the lowest ebb" she'd ever seen me, and she didn't think aging was primarily, or even marginally, responsible. What was? Maybe I couldn't stand (didn't "deserve") all the good things that had recently happened to me, as topped off by setting to work on the Kirstein project? That seemed too pat, outworn—little more than well-rehearsed platitudes. Maybe my imprinting, I suggested to Sue, had been too deep to alter in any characterologically significant way. The insights of psychotherapy, I said accusingly, were as overrated as the comforts of friendship. Neither, I added, was capable of rearranging reality. Yet here I was, lamentably, still offering myself for still more rites of self-improvement. Finally, I glumly concluded,

I was left with having to white-knuckle it and simply wait out the downward turns in the cycle. No, Sue said, with some force, we can do much more than that. Reluctantly, I agreed to start seeing her again on a regular basis.

Only a few weeks later my low spirits, rather than rebounding, as so often in the past, instead suddenly plunged into the worst, most engulfing, and longest-lasting depression of my life. Over a period of roughly six months, I was in truly terrible shape, frequently in sobbing despair, often in bed, shuffling from medicine to medicine and (always accompanied) from doctor to doctor. For toppers, I developed fibromyalgia (severe body pain and fatigue), with no known cause or treatment, and temporarily relieved only by that latest medical miracle: warm baths. Now and then I did briefly improve, and when I did—my writing compulsion intact—recorded my ongoing misery in my diary. It captures something of the deep wretchedness—encompassing, inexplicable—that had me in its grip:

Sept. 15, 2005

A terrible time . . . can barely write . . . aches and pains everywhere, exhaustion total, severe nighttime pain . . . treatment a grab-bag: Elavil plus pain management. . . . Eli has been an angel, deeply empathic and devoted . . .

Sept. 28

First day feeling any optimism, after more than 2 months of sleeplessness, aches & pain everywhere, endless, fruitless doctoring, total inability to work or even read, periods of scary despair, wanting to check out. . . . I've finally landed in the hands of Norman Sussman, big-shot psychopharmacologist, and finally feel some hope from the medical quarter. . . . Ron & Beth [my cousins] came through in a big way, but I wouldn't have made it without Eli. . . . Several others came by or phoned once or twice; the indifference, to someone sobbingly desperate, did surprise me. . . . I just don't have a network & a lot of that has to be my fault. Self-isolated, always working, reluctant to go out, how can I expect the magical appearance of droves of devoted friends? . . . The depression—by far the worst of my life—a truly engulfing black cloud . . .

Oct. 4

Radical ups and down. As recently as yesterday morning, back in bed crying & immobilized. Yet today able to do some reading . . . some reduction in pain but my back is agonizingly worse. . . . An endless cycle, hard to punch through . . .

Oct 12

Coming back, though I've now learned to expect further setbacks. . . . Yesterday, one of the worst days ever, I broke down sobbing at Sue's, my speech slurred, unable to find words . . . she called Dr. Sussman. He had her put me on the phone & ordered me to go directly to an emergency room. "No way!" I all but shouted—me, the purportedly fragile, emotionally spent, exhausted one (below all of which, apparently, a layer of steel remains)—"I'm going home!" And did . . . slept ten hours. Today I feel more energy than in months . . . determined, even if only for an hour, to at last write a few sentences on Kirstein . . .

Oct. 15

First day of doing any significant amount of work (2–3 hours, off & on, of actually writing—well, revising). Hoping from here on in for steady improvement, and decreasing focus on my private plight. . . . One clear sign of improvement was being again able to summon up enough energy to denounce Bush: ". . . his 'emotions' are an ersatz compound of fake (and deadly) 'compassion' and a stubborn self-righteousness encompassing enough to swallow all else. I loathe the man . . ."

Nov. 29

Can't seem—still—to get a steady run of days. . . . I seem stuck on a plateau of recovery, no terrible days but no energized ones either. I'm able to do some work on Kirstein most days, but it's uninspired. . . . The cold weather & early darkness don't help . . .

Dec. 25

Well into my 76th year, I feel the dawn of maturity (dawn only). By which I mostly mean that the junk judgments that fill my diary pages show scant empathy for the early traumas my antagonists experienced when younger that (I'm guessing) account for the bizarre behavior of so many of the people I've crossed swords with over the years—their projected anger at me is in truth discharged recompense for the lack of love they experienced when young, the lack of comfort and support, the emotional (and sometimes physical) mistreatment.

By the start of the new year, I'd finally emerged from the depression, though now and then still felt shaky. I managed somehow to finish the first draft of *The Worlds of Lincoln Kirstein*, and sent it off to both Bob Gottlieb and Nick Jenkins (the Kirstein executor) for comment. While they were reading the manuscript, I decided that for *my* good it was time to get reinvolved again in some sort of political work. Interacting more with people instead of remaining isolated in front of my computer would, I felt, further solidify my recovery. I signed on for a berth on Queers for Economic Justice's new Public Policy Committee, but the organization hadn't flourished, and such resources as it had were still too meager to work on anything more than improving conditions in the homeless shelters. The enforced limitations directly reflected the sickening truth that there was scant interest among the more prosperous national gay organizations—let alone the straight foundation world—for improving the lot of the queer poor.

Hoping to give QEJ a shot in the arm, Eli and I did a benefit fund-raiser in our apartment. In her pitch, Amber Hollibaugh made it clear that the organization was at a crisis point and blamed several foundations for having reneged on their promises. Some good-sized ($500) pledges were made at the fundraiser, but in the follow-up few actual checks arrived. Six months later, in December 2013, QEJ closed its doors. It simply ran out of money. One offshoot did, for a time, survive: Jay's House, named for Jay Toole, the first LGBTQ+ homeless shelter for adults in New York City.

Writ small this mirrored the country's current attitude toward poverty: cut both food stamps and unemployment payments, but continue to give billions to monopoly agriculture and the defense industry. The mainstream gay movement was simply replicating national values instead of—as it once had—challenging them, which was precisely why our "acceptance" has continued to grow by leaps and bounds. The more we act like dutiful citizens, the more we cease being Other, the more we're welcomed into the clan, the more likely we become like them— the clan that lets its children go to bed hungry at night, the clan that trains eighteen-year-olds to become killers and then, after their bodies are smashed, locks them away in VA hospitals.

Where else to align politically? As my health improved, I tried volunteering to teach at the women's prison on Twentieth Street in Manhattan, but my application somehow got "lost" in the bureaucracy. Nor could they find anything for me to do at CLAGS. They seemed reluctant to assign me "drudge work" (though I'd done plenty of it in the past), not recognizing, apparently, that they'd be doing *me* a favor. When I had lunch with people at the Gay Center on Thirteenth Street to figure out how I might be useful to *them*, they promptly converted my offer of anonymous volunteer work into a grandiose set of Conversations with Martin Duberman (example: me and Victor Navasky discussing "The Gay Movement and the Left"). I assured them that (a) no one would attend, and (b) I'd get instant dry mouth and succumb on the spot. I vetoed the Conversations idea.

Several other possible projects came along, but none that had a political dimension. James Atlas, publisher of a series called Eminent Lives—short biographies of certified world-beaters—sounded me out about doing one of the volumes and declared himself "thrilled" when I expressed interest; but he then proceeded, increasingly brusque, to veto every suggestion I made—until I finally stopped making them. I also dithered, and then cut bait, when Anne Prescott offered to let me have the accumulated files she'd inherited on the death of her husband, Peter, who'd been at work on a dual biography of Alfred and Blanche Knopf. I got as far as looking over the files but soon decided that in the absence of any queer or left-wing dimension to the project, I'd prefer to read novels a while longer.

I went somewhat further with a few other projects that were politically more substantive. For a time I thought of doing a book—I tentatively called it *Sunset Dreams*—on the burgeoning movement to build gay retirement communities. I made lots of inquiries, browsed through the secondary literature, and got connected enough with one group in Boston to sit in on a planning session. It soon became clear to me that with a very few exceptions, the retirement communities that were up and running were essentially privileged compounds closed off to those with limited incomes. The realization drained off my interest in the subject, and I moved it to the "reject" file.

I also tried hopscotching for a number of months between the various "talk" groups, mostly divided by age and gender, sponsored by SAGE, the organization focused on serving the needs of the senior gay community. I had some pleasant encounters, especially in the seventy-five-plus mixed-gender group, but the traditionalist values that held sway—for example, the absolute conviction that biology alone ("We were *born* this way") explained sexual orientation—led me to drop out.

Yet the subject of gay aging continued to interest me, and as an alternative way of exploring it, I told CLAGS that I'd be willing to organize a conference for fall 2007 on the subject. They immediately OK'd the proposal and put me in touch for further exploration with David Serlin, a board member and young professor of communication at UC San Diego, who I already knew and liked. Over several months David and I sketched out a promising daylong conference consisting of three panels: (1) "What are the class dimensions of the gay retirement movement?" (From gated communities for the rich to squalid rest homes—and a return to the closet—for the less well off?) (2) "Is segregation by sexual orientation *and* gender actually desirable?" (3) "Do gay people age differently from straight people?" (Are there real or merely perceived differences in regard to loneliness, celibacy, and depression?)

After some months of work, David and I both got entangled in too many side projects—for me it was revising the Kirstein manuscript—and we decided to put the aging conference on hold for a semester or so. But we never did get back to it, which was regrettable; we'd done some good spadework on a topic that needed—and still needs—more serious scrutiny than it's gotten.

Another casualty during this period was my partnership with my long-time agent, Frances Goldin, leading to my decision to represent myself in the future. It was a tough choice; Frances and I had worked together successfully for some twenty-five years and had been staunch allies—and friends. But of late, at least as I saw it, with her agency prospering and representing a number of prominent writers, I seemed to have fallen off her radar. As early as 2002, when *Haymarket* was still unsuccessfully making the rounds, many weeks would go by without my hearing any progress report from her; when I would finally call and ask her for an update, she usually had no idea which house was currently considering the manuscript. Essentially, she'd given up on it, and I was the one who had to suggest sending it to Seven Stories—where, finally, it met with enthusiasm and eventual publication.

Since then, as I neared the end of my five-year project on the Kirstein biography, I'd begun to think about ideas for my next book and had been sending Frances an assortment of proposals, several of them worked through in considerable detail. Week after week passed and I heard nothing. Well aware that I can be impatient, I let a full three months go by before deciding that yes, any fair-minded person would conclude that I was being ignored. Given our long history and friendship, I felt hurt and unhappy; finally in late August I wrote to her: "I gave you three proposals back in May and not having heard a word from you, I've decided to go ahead and contact publishers on my own."

That got Frances's attention: she immediately called and insisted that she *had* told me that two of the three proposals would be "too tough a sell," though it was apparent that she hadn't tried.

The third proposal, the one closest to my heart, I tentatively called *Unofficial Heroes*. It centered on a dozen "second-tier" historical figures who'd identified with social justice movements, had faced calumny in their own day, and had been forgotten in ours (though in most cases their views had long since become mainstream). Fran said that a young agent in her office was currently working on a proposal "competitive" with mine. She didn't say to what extent the two actually duplicated each other, yet made it clear that she wouldn't be attempting to interest a publisher in mine—though she didn't bother to explain why I should be the one to take a back seat.

That did it for me. I didn't doubt that Frances cared about me personally and valued me as a client, but it had also become clear that her attention had shifted. When I told her I was leaving the agency, she repeated what she'd often said before: that she credited the sale of my Paul Robeson biography to Knopf with putting her agency on the map and would feel "heartsick" if I left. "I, too, feel heartsick," I wrote her, "I love you dearly and didn't want to bring any needless pain into your life. But you really haven't left me any choice. . . . I have to stand up for my own work." Frances and I both tried hard to keep our personal relationship intact, and did manage it for a few years, though we gradually drifted apart.

My first call after deciding to do without an agent was to Ellen Adler, recently named to head up the New Press, which I'd long admired for its championship of left-wing writers. I didn't know her personally but had heard good things about her. She suggested that we meet without delay. Within less than a month, we signed a contract for what became the first three of six books that I'd do with the New Press over the next seven years: *Radical Acts,* a collection of my plays (2008), *Waiting to Land: A Political Memoir* (2009), and *A Saving Remnant: The Radical Lives of Barbara Deming and David McReynolds* (2011). It was a welcome change from brooding alone in an echo chamber.

While Bob Gottlieb and Nick Jenkins were reading my Kirstein manuscript, Eli and I decided to attend the New York City Ballet's tribute to Kirstein. It proved the nonevent of the century, consisting of nothing at all. No pre-curtain speeches or reminiscences. No film or slides depicting his life. No appearance by His Eminence Peter Martins (then head of the company) to suggest this *might* be something of an occasion. A meager program note substituted for all of that—plus a mediocre new ballet (*Tribute*) by Christopher d'Amboise that was bafflingly empty of any dance reference to Kirstein. It could have been a tribute to the Dalai Lama—or Hedy Lamarr.

Soon after that, Bob Gottlieb finished reading the manuscript and pronounced it "a fabulous job." Still, he had "lots" of suggestions for improving it further, and he and I began an editorial process that lasted six months. It was mostly pleasant: Bob can be engaging and funny, though he also has a peremptory side and I sometimes had trouble holding my ground, particularly when it came time to choose photographs.

In the middle of the process, I got briefly distracted by a more or less friendly imbroglio with Katrina vanden Heuvel, editor and publisher of the *Nation*. I'd written fairly often for the magazine over the years, and read it regularly. One day, leafing through the current issue, my eye caught an ad for one of the income-generating cruises that the *Nation* periodically sponsored, complete with assorted experts as on-site guides. It suddenly struck me—as I wrote Katrina—that *Nation* cruises never seemed to include *gay* speakers or topics. My query, I emphasized, was "meant to be constructive, not churlish."

It seemed to me, I then (churlishly) added, that "large issues are at stake," in particular the fact that "although the straight left *of course* 'accepts' us, they also ignore us; they refuse to take the next step and make any real effort to *understand* us, to appreciate the ways in which our history, cultures and lifestyles not only differ from the mainstream but have a good deal to teach it"—and in particular about domestic relationships, sexuality, and gender. The long absence of any gay voice on a *Nation* cruise, I added, seemed symptomatic of "the magazine's failure *regularly* to cover the 'gay beat.'" I further remarked that "a substantial leftwing coalition will never come into being if potential constituencies feel they're being smiled at—and looked through. These matters are mostly dealt with at present through silence. They need discussion—lots of it. I can't think of a better place than on a *Nation* cruise."

Given the tart tone I'd taken, I thought Katrina's response was gracious. She acknowledged that I had a point about the lack of gay representation on the *Nation* cruises, and then promptly—to my hor-ror—invited me to participate in the next one. She couldn't have known that I'd never been keen on travel and that now, in my late seventies, was positively allergic to it—let alone hopping on board an ocean-bound ship! I hastened to assure her that extracting an invitation had *not* been my motive in contacting her, and offered to provide a list of possible replacements "who could cover the 'beat' in an expert, scintillating way."

In yet another regard, our (cruise) ships passed in the night. Hav-ing acknowledged my point about the lack of gay speakers on previous *Nation* trips, Katrina muddied the admission by pointing out that Laura Flanders, the radio and TV host who was openly lesbian, had "been on at least three, perhaps four, cruises." I knew and liked Laura; I'd been a guest on her TV show, and she'd served as the MC at one of my book-signing parties. But none of that, as I wrote Katrina, made her remotely a spokesperson for the gay community; LGBTQ+ issues had never been at or near the center of Laura's political agenda.

Katrina didn't respond. Never mind; I felt the entire exchange was already something of a tempest in a teapot—a rather amusing one. I did subsequently notice, though, that no request from Katrina arrived asking for that list of possible gay candidates to serve as a replacement for me.

———

The Worlds of Lincoln Kirstein appeared in April 2007. First out of the gate was a long, featured review, replete with multiple photos, in the *New Yorker*. The reviewer was none other than Claudia Roth Pierpont, the very person who'd herself started to research Kirstein's life and then given up on the project. Few people knew him as well as she did—and also the various pitfalls that awaited anyone undertaking his biography. "The happy news," Pierpont reported in her review, "is that Duberman has proved equal to the difficulties both of the job and of the highly outspoken, often irascible man. . . . Like all good biographers, Duberman is part detective and part judge." She added, hauntingly, that "the most appealing aspect" of my book was that I seemed to love my subject "more than Kirstein ever loved himself."

She did have some criticisms of the book: she thought I sometimes went into "excessive detail" on minor matters, at the expense of skimping on some major ones. Among the latter she specified—justly, I thought— my lack of in-depth analysis of Balanchine's individual ballets; the failure to point out that Balanchine's will left the body of his work not to the New York City Ballet but to his former wife, the brilliant Tanaquil Le Clercq, and his longtime assistant Barbara Horgan—which had deeply wounded Kirstein; and, finally, my skimpy description of the landmark Stravinsky Festival of 1972—which she viewed as "one of the major cultural events in New York during the second half of the century."

During the first few weeks after the biography appeared, the reviews were nearly all positive ("a great accomplishment," "a superb biography," "a splendid achievement"). But then the art historian Jed Perl weighed in for the *New Republic*. He began a long review with generous praise: "A book that is fluid, lucid, and intelligent . . . [Duberman] evaluates the tangled strands of Kirstein's private life with sensitivity and generosity." Blushing with pride, I read on, only to watch the compliments abruptly melt away before my eyes. Perl decided mid-review that I hadn't been able "to grasp the almost anarchic nature of Kirstein's free-spiritedness." I found it difficult to grasp what Perl meant. Was he calling me a fuddy-duddy? That would be news to some, but my mother might have been proud.

As for Kirstein's "free-spiritedness," what definition was Perl employing? Kirstein's taste both in art and politics was sharply circumscribed. In the '30s, like so many intellectuals of the day, he leaned toward socialism, but never to the antiauthoritarian anarchism of, say, an Emma

Goldman (now *there* was a "free spirit"). As for the emergent school of abstract art, Kirstein accused the Jackson Pollock crowd of lacking "general culture, historical and scientific," and he deplored the elevation of "chance into a canon." Spontaneity and immediacy were not, in Kirstein's view, prime virtues—not, that is, when compared to "mindfulness" and technical mastery. His own pantheon was largely reserved for naturalistic painters and sculptors. He did champion the modernists Gaston Lachaise and Elie Nadelman, but dismissed Derain, Matisse, Soutine, Beckmann, Ernst, and Dalí. And many of those he strenuously admired—academicians like William Rimmer, Dan Newman, William Brice, and Henry Koerner—have not gained enduring reputations, nor could any of them be remotely viewed as "free spirits."

Perl employed the term "liberalism" with the same vagueness he did "anarchism," suggesting unfamiliarity with political language or involvement. I had failed to grasp, he wrote, "liberalism's darkest truth"—no, not *that* truth, not its basic and misguided assumption that only *limited* social change is ever practical or desirable, but rather "that no matter how we may search for the patterns in art and life, there are finally no dependable patterns" (a nominalist attitude with which I felt entirely sympathetic—as did many *radicals*—though *not* many liberals).

According to Perl, I also failed "to underscore Kirstein's preoccupation with sculpture" (perhaps because he didn't *have* one—certainly not at the expense of his primary interest in painting). Perl also asserted that Kirstein had been determined "to define the timeless forces [unspecified] that fueled the rapid-fire artistic discoveries of the modern century [unspecified]"—but made no effort to define such vacuous abstractions.

And so it went, with the homosexuality of both subject and author obviously a disconcerting factor for several (heterosexual) critics. Dwight Garner in the *New York Times* described me as a "talented" biographer who "faithfully captures the busy doings of a 20th-century cultural angel," but he also complained that *Worlds* "reads, at times, like a long string of late-night cruising scenes, visits to Turkish baths and assignations with young blonds" (Garner even managed to work in the fact that I had myself "publicly announced . . . [my] homosexuality in 1972").

Terry Teachout picked up the gay theme in *Commentary* magazine, announcing that Kirstein's "private life, complicated though it was, does not bear recounting at such enervating [unnerving? exhausting? embarrassing?] length." Yet another well-established critic (straight, of course) complained about my featuring "Kirstein's life as a gay man" as a "major theme . . . tell[ing] us more than we really need to know about Kirstein's romances." To point out that Kirstein's love affairs and sexual escapades *were* a major theme of his life was simply to tell the truth—which, to be sure, can guarantee a mixed reception.

But enough. A number of individuals who'd been close to Kirstein at various periods in his life—including Donald Richie, Jerry Thompson, and Jensen Yow (who knew him the longest and most intimately) wrote me to express their admiration for the book and to tell me that, as Jensen put it, I'd succeeded in "bringing him back to life." The critical appraisal, taken as a whole, was less subject than usual to the reviewer's penchant (which every writer faces) for promoting the critic's personal agenda at the expense of the subject at hand. Yet one episode did bother me more than any single review. In honor of Kirstein's centenary, the New York City Ballet, having earlier done a content-free "tribute to Kirstein," announced an evening panel devoted to the topic "Lincoln Kirstein: Art and the Man." It so happened that the person chosen to chair the panel was someone I knew. He confided to me that Peter Martins (who would soon be disgraced as a sexist predator) had issued a ukase officially barring me from participation in any and all of the planned centennial events. (Or in the official words spoken to my friend: "Due to his hostility to the current regime at NYCB, we will not be inviting Mr. Duberman to participate in any of our events.")

Martins's animus was in part the result of my including in the biography the well-known fact that during a domestic altercation he'd roughed up his wife, the ballerina Darci Kistler, and she'd called the police. On top of that I'd also revealed in the biography the previously unknown fact that Kirstein had regarded Martins as a bad choreographer *and* a bad manager, and had pressed Ted Rogers, the NYCB's chairman of the board (who passed on the information to me) to replace him.

Martins could prevent me from participating in centennial events, but no one could prevent me from sitting in the audience during the Kirstein panel. It proved a throwaway event, a "testimonial" in the most traditional sense—which is to say, boring and banal. In advance I'd been naive enough to think that in sophisticated Manhattan in 2007 *some* discussion of Kirstein's tumultuous personal life might be mentioned; I even thought it conceivable (no more than that) that his sexuality might be part of that discussion, however skittishly sidelined. But no, not a word.

Similarly, when the Whitney Museum invited me to do a talk on Kirstein and accompanied it with a slide show illustrating his influence in the arts, the narrator of the show blandly described a slide of Paul Cadmus's homoerotic painting *The Bath*—replete with gorgeously muscled male buttocks—as demonstrating "his interest in the human figure"! What struck me as particularly irresponsible was the entire omission at both the NYCB and Whitney events of any reference to Kirstein's erotic preference—as if to imply that it had no bearing on his aesthetic or, for that matter, his life.

In regard to *Worlds* itself, the icing on the cake came several months later, when a man I didn't know came up to me at a public event to say that he'd been a judge on the biography panel for the Pulitzer and had himself voted for *Worlds*, though it lost by a 2–1 vote. Other awards did follow, including Lambda Literary's Pioneer Award and the American Historical Association's lifetime achievement award—the two rarely if ever, I immodestly note, landing side by side on the same brow.

That was the ideal moment to move on. And I knew exactly where I wanted to land. I was eager to start in on a project that had been brewing for some time: a political memoir that roughly covered the years 1985–2008. (It would be published in 2009 as *Waiting to Land*.) I decided, too, to give up for at least a while keeping any sort of diary; in recent years I'd in any case only been making occasional entries. As I wrote in September 2007—the last entry for a full five years—"These days my activities and reactions don't interest me enough (don't seem special enough) to warrant recording. Besides, in outline, saved e-mails these days cover the territory pretty well."

Life quieted down to a contented standstill. Most days I worked away steadily on *Waiting to Land*, most nights Eli and I ate dinner at home and watched TV, occasionally interspersed with traipsing off to see the latest raved-about (and usually grossly disappointing) movie, play, or gallery exhibit, or having an occasional meal with longtime friends. We didn't own a car, didn't have a summer getaway, didn't have hobbies, hated shopping and attending parties, didn't travel—other than me to an out-of-town archive or Eli to visit Gary Gardenhire, his closest friend, who lived in Italy. In my case finding a soul mate had, happily, meant finding a fellow hermit.

PART IV

2008–2012

Then, out of nowhere, our contented seclusion was interrupted. After recovering from depression-induced fibromyalgia (or was it fibromyalgia-induced depression?), I had a good number of healthy years, with nothing more serious than a once-a-winter cold. I continued, though, to have yearly physicals, and as one way of celebrating my seventy-eighth birthday in August 2008, I dutifully took myself off for a checkup. Everything seemed fine, but two days later I got a surprise call from my doctor: "Your PSA [prostate-specific antigen] is elevated. Nothing particularly alarming, but we should keep an eye on it. At your age a 4.5 reading is essentially normal, though a bit on the high side. You know, come to think of it, to be sure we should have a urologist check you out."

And so off I went to the designated specialist, a Dr. Paul Isenberg. A dignified, pleasant man, he too seemed unconcerned, though "just to be sure" he had his technician redo the blood tests. When the results came back, Isenberg, his tone a bit less lighthearted, told me that to his surprise I had a "Gleason 7" score. In layman's terms, he explained, that means *some* possibility of a malignancy. "Frankly," he added, "I very much doubt it, but it does signify something abnormal that requires further evaluation." That meant a biopsy. "You won't feel a thing," Isenberg reassuringly added.

And I didn't. It helped that just as the anesthesia kicked in, Isenberg bent over and whispered in my ear, "I shouldn't say this, but I'm all but certain you have nothing to worry about." He was wrong: the biopsy confirmed a malignancy. The next step—after a six-week delay to allow the prostate to heal from the biopsy—was an MRI, and it, too, verified the presence of cancer. I then had to sit around for nearly a month before one of the prostate specialists at Sloan Kettering hospital decided on a treatment option. In all likelihood, I was told, I was headed for a combination of seed implantation and external beam radiation.

But no, for reasons I didn't care to probe and which were never offered, it was finally determined that I would be given forty-eight external beam radiations, one every weekday for approximately ten weeks. In early June 2009 I began treatment. Not auspiciously. I received a phone message prior to the first treatment informing me that "although your appointment is for 2:00 PM, you must arrive at 1:15 in order to drink liquid." Being prompt in my family had always meant arriving half an hour early, so I presented myself at the desk at 12:45—only to be curtly told to sit in the waiting room until they were ready for me to change into a hospital gown. Ah, the waiting room—how familiar that drab gray interior would become, and how quickly I would adopt a routine as close to catatonia as I could manage: eyes buried in a book, my back to the clock, and avoiding all eye contact with the other patients. That first day, before I knew better and learned to bring along a book (the hospital provided nothing as shallow as a magazine rack—You have cancer! Get serious!), and after twiddling my thumbs for an hour, I went back to the desk and politely asked, "Can you estimate how much longer it will be?"

"Your appointment is for 2:00. You're *very* early."

"I was told I had to be here at 1:15."

"For what?"

"'To drink.'"

"You don't drink today. Today is X-rays."

"So why was I left that message?"

"I have no idea, sir."

The X-rays took only half an hour, and I was ready to leave by 2:45. The nurse told me that the remainder of my appointments for the week would be between 7:30 and 8:00 PM.

"But, but . . . I was told that twelve to two would be my regular time."

"Sorry, sir."

The following week the powers that be were twice able to accommodate my preferred time, but a penalty was enacted: though the treatment itself lasted eight minutes, I sat in the waiting room for four hours, my afternoon appointment having been converted to an evening one. By treatment number six, the entire process had become more mechanical, though it would be a while longer before I was told that I now had enough "seniority" (in age? in the number of treatments? in the escalation of my Gleason scores?) to have earned a stable time slot. With Eli in London during the early days of treatment, I had to race around between trips to Sloan Kettering, picking up our dog Emma (yes, she was still with us) from the kennel, taking her for a run, dashing to the bank, the grocery store, and so forth. At this pace, I decided, a heart attack, not cancer, will nail me. The radiation technicians tried, in their way, to cheer me up: "In a few more weeks, you'll be too tired to do much more then couch sit."

The exhaustion *was*, as predicted, cumulative, and even after the treatments ended late in 2008, I needed another few months to regain my energy. Contrary to my own expectations, I remained even-keeled, even placid throughout; the *lack* of mood swings surprised everyone who'd seen me during my despairing bout with fibromyalgia. Who could explain it? I couldn't, though I suppose the obvious candidate was Freud's "unconscious death wish"—which I didn't believe for a second, though the theory held considerable appeal to my theatrical side.

The results easily compensated for the fatigue and idleness: my PSA level rapidly receded, and at the end of six months all the tests showed that I was cancer free. By the time *Waiting to Land* arrived in bookstores in spring 2009, my energy had fully returned, though as it would turn out, I needed very little of it. The book barely made a dent. It got some nice blurbs from Frances Fox Piven and Howard Zinn, but outside of a few reviews in the gay press, it was largely ignored. Ellen Adler, head of the New Press, cited a number of factors: the worst book market ever at a time when newspapers were in crisis and no longer reliably reviewing books; a credit crunch among booksellers, especially independent ones; the hesitation or downright unwillingness of much of the so-called progressive straight media to cover gay-themed books; the conservative, assimilationist turn of the gay movement itself, making my perspective less digestible; "the challenge" (as Ellen put it) "of doing a serious nonsalacious memoir with left/gay political concerns at the core." She was as disappointed in the reception (or lack of one) as I was.

Still, I was content to stay with the New Press; it felt like "home" in comparison to my experience with other houses. Solidly left wing, TNP was ideologically compatible, and its devoted editors actually *did* edit—a disappearing skill in the publishing industry, where copyediting (grammar) often usurps "old-fashioned" concern with style and argument. Between 2011 and 2014 I did four more books in a row with TNP, always in a cordial spirit.

Having retired from teaching when I turned seventy-five in 2005, I had more free time to write than ever before. There was nowhere I had to be at a certain time—no place I *wanted* to be other than in front of my computer. External obligations and demands were minimal. No adult children expected us for "the holidays"; no grandchildren demanded constant adoration. Eli's temperament matched my own. In earlier years we'd both (like most human beings) suffered our share of loneliness, and thought of it as the great disabler, the prime source of misery.

Yet constant "togetherness" wasn't our thing either. He maintained a larger circle of friends than I did, and our closest ones only partially overlapped—to a greater extent, I think, than is true of most couples. Eli had a burgeoning set of professional friends, while I was no longer in regular touch with colleagues—which was appropriate to our different stages in life (Eli was twenty-four years younger) and to my greater penchant for solitude. Neither of us, though, was a gadabout. Most evenings we were both at home (which we both infinitely preferred to social chitchat), and often in comparable states of exhaustion— Eli, after an emotionally draining day with therapy patients; me, after my daily combat at the computer. We were in sync; we both derived great comfort from knowing that the other person was in the next room, but didn't need to do extended rehashes of our day or maintain constant conversation in order to reassure ourselves that we belonged together. We did have *some* friends in common and would see them for dinner pretty regularly, though at well-paced intervals. Generally, though, we preferred a cozy evening at home watching TV, which was for me—who'd bought my first TV set at age fifty, when immobilized by a heart attack—a remarkable shift from the night crawling of my decadent youth.

During the day I was contentedly alone in my study absorbed in writing, the one pursuit I could count on for steady satisfaction—except when the blank screen remained aggravatingly blank, at which point I'd sweat it out at the gym or schedule lunch with one of the few friends (like Marcy Gallo or my cousin Ron) who'd survived the final cut. At one point I dutifully bought a cell phone—and within two weeks gave it away, exasperated. Who needed the inane distraction—multiple times a day, no less—of hearing a friend complain about the disappointing omelet he'd had for lunch, or listen to a detailed recounting of a glorious trip to the Yucatán? Living with Eli since 1988 had put an end to the coke-filled night crawling and crisis-ridden affairs characteristic of my middle years—usually accompanied by marathon lamentations with Leo or Dick, angst-filled and extended confessionals to bind up the emotional wounds. Leo had moved to California long since, and the close friendship with Dick had fallen victim to his abrupt disappearance when I'd had a heart attack in 1979.

I was among the lucky few—the very few—able to devote the bulk of my time to doing pretty much what I wanted. I found it deeply mystifying, as I headed into old age and after a number of close calls, medical and otherwise, that I'd come out on the other side, still able to function more or less fully. Declared cancer free, my energy restored, I had a secure income, a comfortable home, and absorbing work. I felt profoundly grateful (*not* a characteristic of my younger years) for what I knew was uncommon good fortune. I even enjoyed an aberrantly calm sense of contentment that now and then, ridiculously, felt something like serenity.

———————

Having taught the history of US social justice movements for many years, I'd become intrigued by the fact that during the mid-twentieth century the ranks, and sometimes the leadership, had included a number of (mostly closeted) gay people. In the years before Stonewall those gay people involved in political activism were mostly invested in struggles for nuclear disarmament, Black civil rights, and ending the war in Vietnam. *Post*-Stonewall, with the emergence of the modern gay movement, some of these activists added gay liberation to their agenda. But most gay people of my generation, having grown up when homophobia was rampant and having internalized its belittling message, had never been politically active and when the gay movement emerged had preferred to remain in the closet; some even dismissed "gay liberation" as misguided, as asking for trouble.

I thought for a time of doing a book about a half-dozen earlier radicals who *happened* to be gay and the role they'd played in a variety of earlier social protest movements. But I soon had too large a canvas on my hands and worried about sacrificing depth to breadth. Besides, two of the radicals I had in mind, Barbara Deming and David McReynolds, soon became particularly attractive to me. The two had known each other over the years and shared a commitment to nonviolent struggle—though they'd reacted to the emergence of the feminist and gay movements very differently. Both, moreover, had amassed large archival collections (Barbara had given hers to Harvard's Schlesinger Library, David to the Swarthmore Peace Collection) that to date had gone largely unexplored. I'd never met Barbara, who had died in 1984, but David and I had crossed paths several times in the past, and once I settled on a joint biography of him and Barbara, he gave me access as well to the residual material in his apartment and at the War Resisters League (which remained the central focus of his own activism).

Full immersion in research and writing has always been the key to contentment for me. And now, after a difficult time-out for health reasons and approaching eighty, I was free of any major distractions and able to lose myself again in research. Over the next four years I researched and wrote the dual study of Deming and McReynolds (*A Saving Remnant*) and then a biography of Howard Zinn. In between I chose the contents for the New Press volume *The Martin Duberman Reader*.

Of the three, my biography of Howard Zinn proved by far the most controversial. That much was predictable: Howard's own 1980 book, *A People's History of the United States*, had challenged the traditional narrative of America's unvarying goodness and virtue and had for several decades been producing both cheers and brickbats. As of 2020, *A People's History* had sold over two million copies—and had continued to receive a fair share of hostility. In that same year Mary Grabar published her polemical (and shoddy) study *Debunking Howard Zinn*, which to date has received some five hundred online reviews, a whopping 78 percent of them five-star favorable—that is, *anti*-Zinn.

I'd known Howard, though never more than casually, from as far back as 1964 when I'd persuaded him to write one of the essays in a book I was putting together (*The Antislavery Vanguard*) that presented a far more positive view of the abolitionists than had previously held sway. Then, in 1972, Howard and I had been part of a group that got arrested and sent to jail after carrying out a sit-in on the US Senate floor to protest the war in Vietnam. As recently as 2008 Howard had even blurbed one of my books, *Radical Acts*, a collection of my plays. (Howard, too, wrote plays.) Though our political views usually coincided, Howard was indifferent—though not overtly hostile—to feminism and gay rights, the two movements that in recent decades had most absorbed my own attention.

When Howard died suddenly in 2010, I knew immediately that I wanted to undertake his biography; to explore his life in depth would be tantamount to excavating much of my own political history, the values and activities he and I did—or did not—share. As in all my biographical works, I started out expecting to explore Howard's personal life as well, but obstacles soon arose. His daughter had led me to believe that he'd left behind a substantial archive rich in correspondence—seemingly confirmed by the competitive bidding between several manuscript libraries for his papers. The Tamiment Library at NYU won the competition, and Howard's family gave me full and exclusive access.

I soon learned, unhappily, that in the last years of his life Howard had destroyed nearly every scrap of paper relating to his private life—including his marriage, his parenting, his friendships, and his affairs. I was able to piece together from other manuscript collections and from interviews with his close friends (a few of whom shared private correspondence) enough material to do a *somewhat* rounded portrait. Yet in the upshot, the available evidence—and the biography—necessarily focused on his public life. Which is obviously what Howard, as he weeded and discarded, had wanted—though I would have preferred otherwise.

The limited content of his archives dictated a focus on narrating his political life—the public figure, not the private man. And that emphasis also determined the book's reception. The right-wing media, predictably, pretty much ignored the book; reviewing space had become notably scarce in the digital age, and none could be "wasted" on a "simple-minded" leftist like Howard Zinn. The real division among the critics was between "liberals" and "radicals" on the left. The liberal group around *Dissent* magazine—though the word "group" may be unduly homogenizing a diverse crowd—was epitomized in the work of the magazine's coeditor, the gifted and contentious historian Michael Kazin.

In his book *American Dreamers*, Kazin took off on Howard with the zeal of a kamikaze pilot. From a vast height he leveled the ground below, in the process doing significant damage to Howard's reputation. Kazin's scorched-earth polemic included some incisive criticism, and in particular his denunciation of Howard's Manichaean tendencies (which I too deplore in my biography, though within a more appreciative context). Yet I also argued that Kazin had gone too far in his combative insistence that *A People's History* was "hardly as pathbreaking as [Zinn's] . . . admirers supposed." Kazin based his disparagement on the fact that Zinn depended "on the research of hundreds of liberal and radical scholars." Well, yes—but whose scholarship does not? Had Howard *not* included them in his list of sources, he would have been accused of superficial research.

Kazin further contended that "Zinn's book was stronger on polemical passion than historical insight"—a judgment based on the dubious assumption that value-free, "objective" historians *exist*—though many in the profession would (misguidedly) claim that status for their own work. Strong feelings, moreover, do not necessarily signify distortion, special pleading, or lack of insight. The charge that Howard's account is one sided—that it lacks academic neutrality—is to some extent true. But what are we comparing it to? Where is that exemplary work of history that does *not* reflect the values of the individual historian writing it as well as the value-laden perspective of the time in which it is written? Howard's active participation in the struggles for social justice of his own day offended those academics who stick close to the campus and avoid confronting the country's inequities, claiming that they do so in the name of remaining above the fray, of fulfilling the scholar's purported duty to maintain an "objective" voice (as if there ever was such a creature).

Historians, like it or not, deal in *opinions*, not agreed-upon truths. Today the profession acknowledges more than it once did that "objectivity," though a worthy goal, is also an unattainable one. It can be *approached*, but never achieved: too many distorting factors are in play—like incomplete evidence or the historian's own inescapable subjectivity—guaranteeing that each generation will find the need to revisit and rewrite the previous generation's "partisan" version of past events. As for indicting Zinn for his "strong feelings," one can justifiably ask, "Why is it that most historians manage to describe cruelty and injustice in a tone so *devoid* of passion that the reader barely blinks in response—or, out of boredom, stops reading altogether?"

A People's History unquestionably has its shortcomings, and I took care to discuss them in my biography. Howard's version of events sometimes lacks nuance, overstates the solidarity of working-class protest, suffers from inexplicable omissions (like a sustained history of communes), and avoids dealing substantively with issues relating to gender and sex. Yet in the end, as I see it, we owe Howard a considerable debt for boldly challenging the standard textbook's triumphalist version of our past, one that minimizes our periodic savagery and repeats the false message that in our "open" society those who fail to get ahead have only themselves to blame. Howard includes what too many other texts leave out: the struggles of the working class, the brutality of slavery, the genocidal war against Native Americans, the oligarchic control of the economy, the sanctimonious insistence on the morality of our "benign" interventions abroad.

When my sympathetic biography of Howard appeared, the liberal/radical divide had deepened into a chasm. The division was exemplified by David Greenberg's lengthy, smart review in the *New Republic*. Greenberg, a liberal professor of history at Rutgers, credited me with narrating Zinn's life "fairly and dispassionately," for "navigat[ing] artfully between sympathy and criticism, recognizing complexity where Zinn prefers simplicity." Greenberg applauded, too, what he described as "the fierce questioning by radical historians that had emerged during the 1960s of conventional academic history . . . it had transformed historical inquiry."

Up to a point, that is. In Greenberg's opinion that radical questioning had degenerated into "a conspiracy-laden tale about America's unremitting malice," and had far too often judged historical acts and actors according to the degree they fostered a contemporary agenda. In registering his objection Greenberg pointed as a prime example to the clamorous protest from New Left historians at the 1969 annual meeting of the American Historical Association (AHA). Retroactively choosing sides in that fracas, Greenberg came down heavily on the side of Eugene Genovese, praising him for rejecting "relevant" history, and for denouncing its practitioners—preeminently Jesse Lemisch—as "totalitarians."

Lemisch had promptly replied. And so did Staughton Lynd, who the AHA Radical Caucus in 1969 had nominated as its insurgent candidate for president. Lemisch pointed out that Genovese (who in 1969 was already moving to the right) had in fact delivered "a frothing rant" against Lynd and other radically left historians. ("We must put them down," Genovese had thundered, "put them down hard, once and for all!") Postconvention, a round-robin of letters swiftly followed, including several denunciations of Howard's *A People's History*. Robby Cohen, the future biographer of Mario Savio, made the point in a letter to Staughton Lynd that despite the flaws in Howard's book he'd succeeded in conveying the "excitement of the new social history" with its "bottom up" framework and its critique across time of American racism and imperialism—and in doing so had engaged readers "in a powerful way." Howard's overdue dissection, for instance, of the genocidal policies of long-hailed "heroes" like Columbus and Andrew Jackson had opened eyes and transformed lives.

In the end, my own feeling is that Howard was essentially a moralist, someone who cared deeply about human suffering and scorned those indifferent to it. By several definitions this makes him a patriot. He believed that the country did have unique virtues, but didn't believe—as do traditional "patriots"—that the full story is one of virtue alone. It was Howard's view that where our country did and still does fall short, deviating from its professed principles, it was the historian's core obligation to tell the *full* story. The frequent citation of American "exceptionalism" does not refer to freedom from criminal behavior; it means the insistence on revealing it—on telling the *entire* truth, warts and all. Howard passionately believed that if we continue to ignore our shortcomings and derelictions, we become just another oligarchy, trading in lies, burying our crimes. The claim that we are "a model among nations" can only be justified, as Howard saw it, by full disclosure; revealing only *a portion* of the truth brands us as fabricators, worthy neither of trust nor imitation.

In 1979, the year before Howard completed *A People's History*, Jean Anyon of Rutgers published an essay reporting on her study of seventeen widely used textbooks on American history. All seventeen, Anyon concluded, were grossly subjective, filled with distortions and omissions that parrot the contentions and serve the interests of those in power. (Comparable studies with similar conclusions had earlier been done by Raymond Williams for England and Émile Durkheim for France.) The "liberal" academics who attack *A People's History* with special venom are—in some cases unconsciously—playing a similar role, singling out Howard for failures of objectivity that inescapably characterize the historical profession as a whole.

Going further—and with no concrete evidence at hand—I'd suggest that some of those liberal academics who stridently attack *A People's History* and warn against political involvement as a "contaminant" are revealing something of a guilty conscience for standing apart from the social justice struggles of their own day. The venom directed at Howard may at bottom be a convenient (because unconscious) attempt to justify the academy's refusal to acknowledge its share of responsibility for failing to indict, *vigorously and comprehensively,* our country's episodic cruelty, rapacity, and ruthlessness—for academia's failure to educate the citizenry.

CODA

2013–2022

In the ten years since publishing *Howard Zinn*, I've produced on average a book a year. Obviously, I still *want* to write, though I've at least learned the necessity of television—and naps! I don't fool myself that I'm exactly in demand these days. The New Press, once upon a time my safe house, has published only three of my last ten books: *The Martin Duberman Reader* (2013), *Andrea Dworkin: The Feminist as Revolutionary* (2020), and my young adult book, *No One Can Silence Me: The Life of Legendary Artist and Activist Paul Robeson* (2021). Still in press is a volume of my recent essays, *The Line of Dissent: Gay Outsiders and the Shaping of History.* I know—only a monster of ingratitude would be foolhardy enough to raise even a whisper of complaint.

So I'm a monster—the fact is that getting published hasn't been nearly as easy as before (or as others still assume is true for me). Eli, who pulls no punches, thinks that my writing has gotten better, not worse, in recent years—more effortless and fluid. He ranks five of my ten books of the past decade—*Hold Tight Gently: Michael Callen, Essex Hemphill and the Battlefield of AIDS*; *Jews/Queers/Germans*; *The Rest of It*; *Has the Gay Movement Failed?*; and *Luminous Traitor: The Just and Daring Life of Roger Casement*—as among my best. Some publishers—in particular the University of California Press, Seven Stories Press, and

Duke University Press—have agreed with Eli's estimate. Many more have not, with rejection slips far outnumbering acceptances.

It's confusing, though. Ageism seems to be having an ever-larger impact in deciding who does or does not get published. The many letters of rejection that have greeted my recent work have often included sky-high praise for the manuscripts they then "regretfully"—puzzlingly—turn down. The editor at one mainstream house used the word "sublime" to characterize my prose—just before sighing lamentably over his inability to find a "large enough audience" for it. The book market is in part the culprit: serious-minded books—God forbid they should also be gay themed!—seem to have become ever-tougher to sell. Even the left-wing, "nonprofit" New Press, which had published me for years, "sorrowfully" advised me to turn to the world of university presses. And "the sales force" these days does seem to play a much larger role in making final decisions; idealistic editors are no match for tough-minded sales departments, eyes glued to the bottom line, that seem increasingly to hold sway—everywhere in the country, of course, not simply at publishing houses.

I think there's one more twist, an important one, in accounting for the resistance I've faced in recent years: the actual *content* of the work—innovative in form (*Jews/Queers/Germans*), politically radical (*Andrea Dworkin: The Feminist as Revolutionary*), unapologetically gay (*Luminous Traitor*), and alarmingly confessional (*The Rest of It*). Even in gay circles—and particularly in regard to my admonitory *Has the Gay Movement Failed?*—interest in learning my opinion has noticeably waned. My recent work centers on queering both the contents and the approach to writing history (the insistence that subjectivity is inescapable, even in the purportedly "objective" world of historical works). Not many seem to have noticed or cared. There's been more interest and sympathy abroad than in the United States—particularly for my "novel/histories"—*Haymarket*, *The Luminous Traitor*, and *Jews/Queers/Germans*.

Several of my books have been published in England, Canada, and Australia, and some translations have been done: *Howard Zinn* has been published in French, *Haymarket* in Italian, *Stonewall* in Spanish;

and Turkey (*Turkey?!*—does President Erdogan know?) has gone all out with *Stonewall*, *Haymarket*, and even editions of two of my plays, *Mother Earth* and *Visions of Kerouac*. At home, meanwhile, I've won several "lifetime achievement" awards (when you get past eighty-five, the competition does peter out), topped off with Amherst and Columbia awarding me honorary doctor of letters degrees. So all in all, I've certainly gotten my share of recognition.

Nonagenarians rarely write books, and the few (like me) who have been lucky enough to have preserved their marbles, most of their energy, and above all their tenacity, risk being dismissed as ingrates if anything other than gratitude falls from their lips. And so I simply report the facts: earlier the question had been *which* house to choose from among several eager to publish me. Then, in my eighties, the question switched to "*Who* can I interest in publishing me?" So far, usually after a prolonged search (fortunately I am *tenacious*) I've managed—after surviving eight or ten letters of rejection—to find an editor with enough clout and drive to push through a wall of objections.

As I enter my nineties, I'm trying to cultivate placidity—and maintain a sense of humor. And I do continually remind myself that at least I've *had* a career, and few do; foregrounding gratitude is the only seemly response.

———————

Though it may seem a bit bizarre, I haven't until this past year actually *felt* old, or not *very* old (which, chronologically, I suppose I am). I've had my share of illness—a heart attack, prostate cancer, and in 2013 stomach surgery to remove an "obstruction" that the doctors alternately ascribed to "atypical" Crohn's disease, ileitis, and (their favorite) "scar tissue from my appendectomy at age sixteen"! After ten hellish days in the hospital I had to fake (so I'd like you to believe) an emotional breakdown, complete with the traditional ripping out of the epidural, before I succeeded in persuading the doctors to let me go home. Since then, I've been blessed with good health, give or take the typical litany of aches and pains, along with some considerable loss in stamina. At ninety-two (this book too has taken its time in finding a publisher), I still write (or read) every day, weekends included, and usually for many hours—though ingrate that I am, I resent not being able, as before, to continue into the evening.

Along with a loss of energy, what I've missed most during my late eighties and early nineties is emotional amplitude ("drama"). Over the past dozen years I've had no significant "lows"—a great blessing—though long gone too, which I *do* miss, is any semblance of excess. I would *not* welcome—would possibly not survive—anything like the dramatic collapse I experienced some fifteen years ago. But I *could* use at least a facsimile of the opening night thrill of *In White America*. To miss genuine risk-taking is probably, beyond a certain age, certifiable. What one learns to substitute—with a fair amount of pretense—is gratitude for a long list of blessings; they may not thrill to the core but nor, in this country at this time, are they commonplace. Blessings like having decent health, affordable luxuries like going to a restaurant or theater, and above all the kind of steady, caring companionship with Eli that routs that supreme killer, loneliness.

My days are now mostly quiet, punctuated here and there by a walk, a haircut, an eye doctor appointment. The phone—a landline, of course—rarely rings; when it does it's usually some recorded announcement about the wonders of changing my credit card or expanding my insurance. My e-mails are equally weighty: a moisturizer that *must* be tried, under-eye bags that *must* be removed. I read three or four books simultaneously, interspersed, when I feel deserving, with a long novel. (Ian McEwan is the current favorite.)

I wonder if the essence of getting old is a deepening incapacity to care profoundly about anything. My emotional range, the depth of my reactions, has unquestionably shrunk. I don't cry anymore, don't even choke up, not even when the nightly TV film is on refugee waifs or Bergen-Belsen atrocities. Abstractly horrified, yes. Active tears, no. This is, I suppose, an inescapable part of growing old; to start "closing down" is to start getting ready—if one is lucky enough to have been long lived. Should this, logically, be a source of regret or congratulation? Earlier in my life, I put myself fairly often in extreme situations—and several times got much closer to real danger than I'd bargained for. Nowadays I flee situations that might, even marginally, threaten my equilibrium.

It's true what they say—aging means increased short-term forgetfulness in tandem with some long-term retrieval. Both in dreams and wakefulness, an episode or person reappears that I haven't thought about for decades: Buck, my eighteen-year-old counselor at Camp Idylwold having me (age twelve? thirteen?) give him periodic back massages; the memory definitely has an erotic cast, regrettably truncated . . . the youth hostel bike trip across country in 1948, sleeping outdoors at night in our bedrolls—not even the bear attack on our next day's lunch, wrapped near our heads, waking me—me with the purportedly lifetime "sleep disorder" . . . the outbreak of polio on our youth hostel trip to Mexico and losing Jeff, my closest friend, to the disease . . . another long-lost friend, kicked out of the State Department years before for being gay, ending up in the entourage of an Indian mystic . . . dropping out during the second year of graduate school to return home for one botched surgery after another on a pilonidal spinal cyst, then returning to Harvard anyway and keeping secret from the family the operation I myself arranged that finally "took"—followed by weeks of a visiting nurse coming to my boardinghouse every morning to draw sitz baths on the floor above and to repack the wound . . .

Retrieving memory isn't the same as living in the past. I remain primarily attuned to the present, particularly to political developments. Until very recently, Eli and I would continue to open our apartment for fundraisers—Queers for Economic Justice or CLAGS or the War Resisters League—though more often than not I'd come away feeling that the evening, though necessary, had been mostly an exchange of platitudes. No, I haven't become a curmudgeon; when discomforted, I don't bark (though I do ease away). My social skills—honed in my "nice guy" youth as a barrier against exposing too much—have always been good (when niceness fades, civility takes over). But I do think that parties of more than four people breed superficiality; the swift entrances and exits encourage not communication but chatter, which makes my brain shut down and my legs hurt. As old age descends, so does indifference. Or do I mean equanimity, the wisdom of finally understanding that nothing much matters?

I still sometimes—not often—will venture out to hear a speaker or listen to a panel discussion. They're occasionally a cut above the skin-deep exchanges of a cocktail party, yet now and then a cut below in their boring blandness. A recent case in point: I trundled off one night to hear a German expert give us the latest word on Magnus Hirschfeld. He sat in a chair throughout his talk, his comments directed at his own navel and his voice rarely reaching beyond the first few rows.

During the Q&A that night I brought up what has long seemed to me a basic—and dangerous—contradiction in Hirschfeld's views. On the one hand, I said, he welcomes "diversity" yet on the other insists that same-gender sexual attraction is biological in origin. Does it not then follow, I asked, that same-gender love and lust is felt only by a small minority—is entirely *Other*? In arguing that homosexuality and heterosexuality are discrete phenomena, Hirschfeld seems unwittingly to suggest that heterosexuals *never* experience lustful or loving fantasies toward members of their own gender (and vice versa). Is he not, then, narrowly confining the actual range of impulses in *everyone* in regard to sexual desire (and probably gender expression too), foreclosing a wide range of expansive possibilities? Don't such biological explanations of human behavior in essence deny the legitimacy of what is the common-place capacity for "irregularities" of every kind? (If in doubt, I added, check out the content of your dreams.)

After I sat back down, I thought that perhaps I'd been more contrary than intended. I needn't have worried: no one responded, critically or otherwise. There was a brief pause, and then a rush of canned encomiums magnifying Hirschfeld as the father of gay liberation. Well, yes—I mean, I hadn't said he *wasn't*. He *was* a pioneer, a notable one—but not, after all, the Delphic oracle. I felt like I'd blown the shofar during High Mass. At ninety, one is supposed to sit quietly or, preferably, to doze.

The most notable exception to any shriveled intervention these days is the passion I can still work up over politics—though I rarely have a public platform for expressing it. Where once I debated Andrew Sullivan on *The Charlie Rose Show*, challenging his adherence to the gender binary and his rejection of political solidarity with trans people, I now yell at the TV image of Caitlyn Jenner announcing that she has a "female soul." "What the hell does that mean?" I shout at the TV. "What attributes define a 'female soul'? Do all women have one?—and does every soul have uniform properties? Is Andrew Sullivan wholly devoid of such soulful attributes? Are all men?" Earlier I would have grabbed the mike or dashed off an essay. Today I mumble at the TV about how culture, not genes, determines the *non*biological, nonbinary nature of maleness and femaleness—that is, until Eli asks me to pipe down.

During Barack Obama's two terms as president, I'd heat up only now and then. I was basically an admirer—and thrilled that a Black man had been elected president. Sometimes, though, I wished that his eloquence would culminate more often in actual policy initiatives. I wanted him to break into a sweat. Gay marriage wasn't an issue I cared about—though for tax reasons Eli and I did formally tie the knot—but when Obama in 2012 declared his belated support for gay marriage, I wished he hadn't defended it on the grounds of being "pro-family"—that hothouse for tired stereotypical role-playing.

I also thought he was being cowardly in leaving the issue to the states at a time when thirty-two recent referenda in a row had turned gay marriage down, often by wide margins. Nobody wanted to rain on a parade, but I didn't want to join it either. So I said no when NPR and CBS News invited me (see, I lied: I sometimes do, though not in the past half-dozen years, get asked for an opinion) to tell their audiences about the remarkable progress the LGBTQ+ movement has made since Stonewall, the implication being that we were now, or should be, pleased and grateful. Yes, progress has been real—large-scale progress—in the area of civil liberties. But at the cost of reassuring the country that we're "just folks"—which we aren't.

Similarly, I thought Obama unpersuasive when he supported a pending air strike on Syria. What about the moral implications of "collateral damage"? Why had he decided that Bashar al-Assad's use of chemical weapons would be *the* red line and that crossing it would bring down the wrath of the United States? You can be made just as dead through the use of conventional arms. *Killing* is the crime, not how one is killed. If the "how" is singled out for blame, then how does the United States, singular in its gruesome use of nuclear weaponry, become the appointed guardian of "morality"? Besides, exactly how was our "national security" at stake in Syria? Yes, Assad is a monster, but why wasn't Obama—or Congress or the UN—debating *non*violent ways to depose him? A military strike is just as likely (or more so) to encourage an escalation in the death toll—along with enlisting new recruits for the Taliban and Al Qaeda.

I thought Obama offered a comparably flimsy argument when he announced in 2014 that we had to start bombing Mount Sinjar and Erbil in order to "protect Americans." There *weren't* any Americans on Sinjar, and those in Erbil could easily have been flown out. One downed American plane and cries of "protect our fighting men" rapidly escalates—and back go those boots on the ground. And yet how can a Jew not support the effort to prevent ISIS from exterminating thousands of minority Yazidis? Some effort must be made. Why wasn't the option of a large-scale airlift even considered? Did Sunnis around the globe appreciate our "humanitarian" stance—which boiled down to "we must bomb Iraq in order to save it"? We already know from the civilian toll in Gaza how reliable "precision" bombing is.

When Obama "spoke to the nation" about Syria, his problematic strategy seemed like whistling in the dark. Who were the "coalition" members he referred to? Who among them had actually agreed to join (or replace) American forces? Why were bombs any more likely to crush ISIS than they had the Taliban? If bombing ISIS in Syria wasn't going to strengthen Assad—a prospect Obama failed to address—where were the Syrian "moderates" scheduled to take over on the off chance we did succeed in crushing ISIS? Public opinion, Obama suggested, supported "action," having been "horrified" at ISIS's brutality. Hello? We may not do beheadings, but doesn't anyone remember My Lai, or Hiroshima? Well, at least we were finally going to get bipartisan support on *something*—too bad it had to be killing.

I had other doubts about Obama's presidency (though it was a thing of wonder in comparison to the disastrous Trump reign that lay ahead). I felt particularly unhappy with Obama's heightened use of drones to "take out" our "enemies," and with a two-pronged immigration policy that coupled *increased* levels of deportation with the hope of a DREAM Act that in fact gave preference to the most privileged sectors of the immigrant community (that is, to those with two years of college or comparable military service, thereby casting out the most economically marginalized and desperately needy supplicants). I disagreed, too, with his denunciation of Edward Snowden and other whistleblowers, while leaving homelessness unaddressed, the 1 percent unchallenged, the growth of the war machine unchecked, the prison and police systems unaltered (other than marginally), the disabled still second class, and vets still courting death on waiting lists.

As politics heated up, I started to scribble again in a diary:

June 2013

We opened our apartment for a War Resisters League fundraiser. It drew no more than 30 people, even though Dan Berrigan and Judith Malina served as star attractions. I didn't recognize Berrigan. At 92 he's rail thin and fragile. Barely audible when he spoke, it was nonetheless clear that his mind is intact . . . the few times in the past that I've been with or seen Malina I recoiled from her self-adoration. But when her turn came to speak, she surprised me with her eloquent spunk. Yet the evening overall left me feeling down. Such a tiny group of well-worn pebbles against the surging global tide of militant religious hatred and violence. I felt guiltily apart, far more devoted to churning out the next manuscript, and the next, than to standing futile witness with them.

Summer 2014

We cite "international law" when it supports *our* interests. We ignore it—the invasion of Iraq being one example—when it doesn't. All this at a time when the Supreme Court has further opened the floodgates for the monied class—mostly reactionary—to dominate our political life, and when Republican-controlled state legislatures are busy restricting the right of the poor and minorities to vote. Yes, some hope still resides in the 18–34 age group—but do we have enough time to await its arrival?

Fall 2014

Jeremy Scahill's *Dirty Wars* throws an appalling light on what our country is doing around the world. What possible explanation—let alone justification—can there be for murdering al-Awlaki's gentle 16-year-old son? Can the infuriatingly easy "explanation" of "collateral damage" be given an iota of credence next to images of the bodies of pregnant women in a pit of dirt? JSOC's [Joint Special Operations Command's] escalating savagery makes a mockery of our humanitarian claims. Without the rare Scahills our crimes wouldn't reach even the limited audience they do.

Summer 2015

The standard American attitude toward income inequality is centered on inevitability: "The Poor You Shall Always Have With You." A comfortable, convenient attitude for the "haves." But inequality is no more inevitable than the poverty that accompanies it. Far too many "have-nots" have internalized the belief system that has served the "haves" so well: the poor blame *themselves* for their failure and destitution—their "genetic" inferiority in combination with their character flaws. And they tend to accept the ingrained notion that "nothing can be done." But plenty can be done; what's lacking is the will to do it. A good start would be a progressive income tax plus a guaranteed annual income. As for jobs, how about a long overdue federal works project à la FDR to rebuild our infrastructure? Where's the money to come from?—that's easy: from a swollen defense budget and a grotesque corporate profit structure . . .

In the '80s the AIDS scourge killed millions. Thanks to the release of the protease inhibitors beginning in 1995, the virus has now been contained and these days the topic of AIDS rarely comes up. Yet AIDS remains a deadly reality in much of the world even if our inbred countrymen treat anything global with scant concern. Death, however, can't be *entirely* ignored, not even in the United States. In my own case, like any good American, I don't linger over the subject—not even when cancer and a heart attack descended. Now, entering my nineties, the proliferation of aches and pains makes it difficult to maintain denial. As does the mounting toll of death within my own circle of friends.

During the last decade the loss of two of my political buddies hit me with special force. In 2013, the radical gay journalist Doug Ireland died from a veritable swarm of ailments that included two strokes, diabetes, and kidney failure. Damn the unfairness of it all!—of Doug's poverty, his lousy health, the lack of recognition for his multiple talents and contributions. Two years later came the death from ovarian cancer of Naomi Weisstein, my dear friend of fifty years—the last thirty of which she'd spent in bed with severe chronic fatigue syndrome. Before being cut down in her early forties, Naomi had already forged, against formidable odds, a brilliant scientific career and had become as well an irrepressible figure in second-wave feminism. Like Doug, she'd been a no-holds-barred iconoclast, radically contentious, hilariously funny, audaciously defiant of stale dogma and traditional authority.

Both Doug and Naomi, I strongly felt, deserved some sort of lasting recognition. I decided to gather their fugitive pieces from various magazines, journals, and political rags, some long defunct, into two separate collections, to annotate them fully, and to preface them with ample introductions. I tried to interest various publishers, but even the purportedly left-wing Feminist Press, of all places, turned down the collection of Naomi's work out of hand. Angry, and sharing Doug and Naomi's scorn for ensconced judgments, I went ahead and self-published both collections.

Spring 2016

Bernie appears plausible only because he's never been pressed about his socialism. Astonishingly, I haven't heard a single commentator or broadcaster—or, for that matter, Hillary—put the simple, obvious question: "Bernie: precisely what do you mean by 'socialism'?" Do you mean classic Marxism: government ownership of the means of production and distribution? No, obviously not; he's never once mentioned Marx. OK. So do you mean giving top priority to the needs of the least privileged? (a socialism of ends, not means.) No, not that either. What he wants, or so it seems, is free college, higher corporate taxes, and single payer health insurance. But that's not "socialism"—it's a heightened form of "New Dealism." *If* Bernie harbors a radical leveler vision, and tells us so in a presidential campaign, he'd be buried in a landslide. I'd *love* to bring a "democratic socialist" (of either ends *or* means) to power. But if Bernie really is one, he ain't telling. And if he does tell, the American public—more fundamentally anarchist (though it doesn't know it) than socialist—ain't buying. I'd still vote for him—he's more genuinely a progressive than Hillary—but only if the polls can somehow guarantee that his candidacy won't produce a Republican victory.

Summer 2016

The talking heads are commonly ascribing White male working-class attraction to Trump as a mirror image of their own bluster and swagger. Maybe. But Trump lacks the melancholic tinge that coats their bearing, itself the product of self-blame for failing to "excel." Trump's impenetrable self-regard, largely unearned, puts him at a far distance from the men he claims to represent. Why can't they see it? Because, I suspect, they've thoroughly internalized that ancient and deadly American myth that the path to achievement is wide open to anyone willing to work for it. If you fail, the fault is *yours*—or some hidden, malignant power.

I've been struck, too, by the campaign rhetoric thus far that talks endlessly of the plight of the middle class—but almost never the poor.

*

The two-day CLAGS conference, "After Marriage," was an eye-opener—
a sea of pointedly unscrubbed, wondrously "queer"-looking 20–30-year-
olds. Pre-conference I thought I'd been managing to stay *somewhat*
abreast with my dutiful readings on polyamory and the like. But at the
conference I was astounded time and again at the uncommon wisdom
I heard: homophobia is less durable, less resistant to rebranding than
racism; marriage equality is a *problem*, not a solution, for leading liberatory lives; the Occupy movement (which some of us had hailed) was
dominated by heteronormative White men—and it largely disdained
queer participation; grassroots gay groups like SONG tend to be much
more radical, and much less monied, than the Human Rights Campaign
or Lambda Legal, etc., and they *focus* (unlike HRC, et al.) on issues
like criminal justice, poverty, youth, homelessness. They have different priorities and organizational structures and thereby represent the
only sector of the movement centrally concerned not with "equality"
but with justice and liberation. Joseph [DeFilippis] calls them "a *new*
social movement," one that *deconstructs* identity categories and straddles
borders. It provides wondrous grounds for genuine hope.

I view it as a narcissistic gesture approaching criminality to vote Liber-
tarian or Green in this electoral cycle. *Post*-election I hold out the hope
that the 15 million or so Bernie voters, almost all under 40, will carry
their values forward—in a third-party formation if necessary—with a
needed injection of the insights and platform of the new social movement I glimpsed at the "After Marriage" conference.

Fall 2016

Joseph [DeFilippis] has asked me to read his doctoral thesis on the
new grassroots gay organizations, which he collectively calls the "Queer
Liberation Movement." I've found it fascinating, and learned a lot from
it, even if I come away with more questions than answers. I've sent him
a long critique which I hope will prove helpful. For starters, I think,
he too glibly dismisses what he calls "the equality organizations" (the

Human Rights Campaign, et al.), and their multiple millions, taking as a given that even if their agendas could be broadened to include the issues that motivate QLM (the Queer Liberation movement—SONG, et al.), the "equality" crowd would necessarily botch the job. Why assume that? The question is, of course, ingenuous, since the likelihood of converting the assimilationist mission of the established gay organizations like the Human Rights Campaign (which accurately represents the views of the majority of gay people) is near zero. But would that we could borrow at least some of the funding and managerial skills of the neo-liberal equality movement, along with its multimillion-dollar budgets and its legislative victories.

Nor do I agree with Joseph's view that the neo-liberals succeeded by "silencing" radical queer voices. The radical gay community seems to me to be quite small on the whole (though larger among Millennials); the gay community *as a whole* embraces assimilation, not radical ideology: it supports the neo-liberals. No "silencing" or suppression was needed.

Also, I've been reading the QLM literature and haven't found much detail about what the new movement ultimately aims to achieve. Some of the rhetoric centers on ending capitalism and imperialism (good luck with that!); more plausible would be an agenda that tries to shift the country's priorities so that the needs of the least privileged come first. But even holding out that hope makes the heart sink under the weight of the whole history of the left and its limited accomplishments in this country. But yes, I know, one has to keep trying. . . .

Joseph quotes one of his interviewees making a stab at defining liberation: "having the freedom without penalty to express who we are and to ultimately be ourselves . . . liberated to be those people we are." That strikes me as so generalized as to be nearly meaningless. Who we are keeps changing; even at a given moment, our self-perception is often muddy and contradictory. How do we know when we're expressing "who we *really* are" as opposed to some socialized version which distorts or destroys our "genuine" drives and aptitudes? We would need a philosopher attached to each QLM group . . . maybe a psychoanalyst too.

Joseph's informants from the QLM groups constantly reference "justice" as being in direct opposition to "equality" but *don't* define in any detail what they mean by those gargantuan terms. Do they know? Ditto with the constant appearance of "aiming at larger transformations in the culture." Means *what*? Nobody mentions, for example, transformations in education—meaning in essence, as I've long preached, destructuring the authoritarian classroom in the name of nurturing self-determining citizens.

In regard to the lack of specifics, I was surprised that not one of Joseph's interviewees mentioned a guaranteed annual income as a desirable goal. Since I don't see an anti-capitalist revolution on even the distant horizon, guaranteeing everybody, say, $30,000 a year would at least mean nobody goes without food, shelter, and health care. I strenuously agree with QLM prioritizing the needs of the least fortunate, but am puzzled why they don't highlight a guaranteed income, which would at least achieve the minimal basics NOW. Likewise, QLM seems to consider the unionization movement irrelevant, since they rarely even mention it as one way, potentially, to improve the lot of the least fortunate. Yet historically unions have been *the* agency through which the working class has bettered its condition.

And whatever happened to *sexual* liberation? QLM rightly scorns marriage as an institution (or as a political issue), but no mention is made of the flood of new books deploring monogamy and advocating polyamory; is QLM in agreement with those transformative trumpet blasts? Joseph's interviewees never say—in fact don't seem aware of nonnormative sexual arrangements. Nor, for that matter, does "gender-bending" seem of any interest to QLM; the explicit trans challenge to the male/female binary goes unexplored—not to mention the quite distinct identity emphases within the trans community that range from the surgical to the spiritual. I have similar questions regarding race and class. How are the new liberation groups defining both, and for whom are they claiming to speak? Are they defining class on the basis of job status or educational level or income? Do they speak primarily for those whose income is below the poverty line or do the other components of job status and educational level also contribute to the status of those who are marginalized? No one can satisfyingly answer such cosmic questions, but to leave them wholly unaddressed is to disengage from some central questions emerging in the culture—and to create distrust of the ability of the newest liberation movement to offer competent solutions.

Fall 2016

The election results are in; shockingly, it's Trump. So much for patronizing the liberal Obama/Hillary axis. The nonreflective shoot-from-the-hip bully boy holds the reins—*all* of them, from state houses to Congress to (potentially) the Supreme Court. I'd feel less desolate if I thought he genuinely gave a damn about the working-class suffering and anger that elected him. But he'll stiff them in the same conscience-free spirit in which he's stiffed so many of those who worked to construct his eyesore buildings. My only positive thought: he isn't an ideologue; he'll say and do whatever catches his fancy at the moment. Come to think of it, why is *that* positive? Trump remains a megalomaniac whose narcissism is a bottomless pit. Hillary offered little to the suffering working-class, whereas Trump at least *sounded* concerned with its plight ("I'll make America great again, bring back the coal and steel industries, create job, jobs, jobs!"). With Hillary's limited version of leftism offering no hope to the stalemated and stagnant working-class, they (i.e., its *White* members) turned to someone who could at least mouth the appropriate words. Which means enough of them *might* have voted for Bernie over Trump—perhaps enough to have carried the electoral college.

Trump's cabinet appointments amount to a far-right collection of billionaires and reactionaries. It's appalling—and scary, a gruesome satire. The head of the EPA will be a climate change denier. The attorney general is an old school racist. The labor secretary opposes any raise in the minimum wage. An opponent of the Affordable Care Act will head Health and Human Services. Commerce & Treasury go to billionaire Wall Street insiders. The education department is to be headed by an opponent of public schools. And so on. Opposition to such recklessness resides in local resistance and in entrenched federal employees discharging their duties fitfully. Some opposition!

Winter 2016/2017

I spend more and more time alone, Eli ever busier professionally, me ever less inclined to routine socializing. In consequence, I think of myself increasingly as nonverbal, even monosyllabic—at least as compared to my earlier self. Therefore startled last night when doing a "reading" at General Services bookstore at how easily the words flowed, how readily fluent I became. The capacity is intact; it's the outlets that have shriveled.

I've arranged my life to allow for maximum time—sometimes more than I want—for reading and writing. It's a pattern set in my teen years when, to escape Ma's invasive scrutiny, I'd bury myself in my room to "study." It's proved the perfect arrangement for old age, since it serves as an irrefutable excuse for avoiding both frequent socializing and the avid pursuit of "culture." I do get some pleasure from occasional catch-up dinners, but it seems to me that something close to dailiness is needed for real friendship—regularized, *un*eventful contact that allows for something deeper than a current events report. My craving for an anonymous life is paralleled, yet somehow not contradicted, by the wish for continuing invitations and consistent applause. I doubt if I'm alone in having contradictory impulses. All would change were it not for the comforting, reassuring presence of Eli. If I lived alone, I wouldn't be so caustically smug about isolation.

In reading (belatedly) Stuart Hall for the first time, I feel I'm in the hands of someone I can trust. Theoretical abstraction is deeply foreign to the particularity of my temperament, but what Hall does is emphasize how the specificity of history complicates the truth of any grand design and challenges the determinant view of human behavior. He rescues Marx, on one level, for the humanist tradition of agency (particularly the Marx of *The Eighteenth Brumaire*). Contingency reappears as a (the?) historical force. Hall himself does sometimes theorize at such a high level—like when he tackles Althusser—that I dash for the exit, my brain bucking for air.

Time out to catch up on some novels; needed lubricant for the imagination. The only clear winners are Richard Ford's *Independence Day* and almost anything by Ian McEwan. Otherwise, lots of pleasant reading, but no real grabber. Impressed by the Ferrante quartet, but not as impressed as everyone else seems to be (I prefer her *Abandonment*); gale force passion in the quartet but the central friendship of the two women not persuasive. Several past favorites disappointed on rereading: the boy in McEwan's *The Children* too undeveloped to work as the central narrative device; and neither Tóibín grabbed me (*Nora Webster*, *The Master*). Much more impressed with two "youngsters": Garth Greenwell and Hanya Yanagihara. GG borders now & then on the fey, along with a distanced tone of snotty superiority—but he's superbly in control, supremely sophisticated. Yanagihara is wonderfully prolix, a gush of gorgeous prose; yet at critical junctures the central narrative becomes implausible: Jude's miraculous progress from abused orphan to legal superstar; and Willem's overdone saintliness.

Also tried Dave Eggers again. Still no go; too clever by half. . . . Another whack also at Hollinghurst. Same as before: immensely brilliant, immensely clever, but closer to Firbank than Mantel. His people are brittle one-dimensional stick figures, adroitly nimble and arch. On the descending side, gave up after 20 pages of Ondaatje's *English Patient*—weirdly abstract, like a philosopher had taken to painting. Penelope Lively's *Moon Tiger* had me initially enthusiastic, though the overcondensation required too much work and I gave up. Come to think of it, the real trouble with Hollinghurst is that he can write gorgeously about *anything*—and does, with marvels of descriptive passages about houses and gardens taking priority over the people moving through them.

I rarely read nonfiction these days but in a biography of Kurt Tucholsky, I came across this description of his parents: his father "warm and

gentle," his mother Doris "literal and rigid. Cold and aloof to her children . . . [she] did not understand how to love them." And that's it for
Doris Tucholsky. Not another word, no hint of a moderating corrective.
And so it goes. It's the penalty history regularly enacts on the unanointed.
Doomed to a single reference (most of those who have lived get none),
we'll never know what inner torments may have diminished Doris—some
possibly exacerbated by that "warm and gentle husband" *kindly* telling
her that her wish to write or paint was "inappropriate," "unwomanly"—
thereby stirring up her anger and self-protective "coldness."

Why is Kissinger still alive—and, apparently, in comfort? Isn't that
proof there is no (benign) God?

With Trump's minions savagely threatening to dismember the welfare state,
what's left of the left can no longer afford to dismiss the New Deal's safety
net as merely a deceptive strategy for strengthening—not subverting—
capitalism. Which leaves us—where? Surely not back to collective visions of
utopia that ignore all that we've learned about the *intrinsic* limitations of the
human animal (though I couldn't confidently list them). But where then?
Somewhere along the path that denigrates religiosity and nationalism and
defends anarchism's appreciation for the precious uniqueness of every life.

Spring 2017

My political engagement these days is mostly confined to yelling at the
TV or fuming at headlines, especially two recent ones:

- Gun reform: across-the-board assurances that "recreational shooting" will remain sacrosanct—i.e. killing animals for blood sport.
- Women will be allowed to join combat units—this is being
announced as if it's the latest triumph for feminism. So now
women, like men, can win medals for killing. And here I thought
the point was to stop men.

*

Trump and Charlottesville: the bull is not only rampaging in the china shop but—happily—has brought down the roof on his head. Even the CEOs have started resigning from his Potemkin-like Councils—until he disbanded them to stop the hemorrhaging. All of which would be a source of comfort was not Pence standing in deep shadow in the wings—and the alt-right continuing to flourish. It *isn't* Germany in the '30s; institutional resistance in the media and the judiciary is proving strong, and the groups most under siege (Jews, people of color, queers, feminists) have been quick to sound the alert.

In light of the events in Charlottesville some tough questions have reemerged. I've long regarded myself as something of a First Amendment purist, yet I'm uneasy over defending neo-Nazi hate speech that accompanies the right of assembly; it *does* seem—definitive proof is elusive—to inspire violence against their targets. At which point the right to self-defense enters the picture. The ideal defense is Martin Luther King's nonviolent resistance; yet it's hard not to sympathize with the temptation to curse—or strike—the oppressor. But that *isn't* the equivalent of initiating violent speech and action.

With dozens of athletes kneeling in unexpected protest against racial injustice, it's possible again to hope that Trump's casual brutality doesn't represent, or cancel out, the country's underlying decency.

Fall 2017

I've begun to read and hear talk of limiting the vote to those with demonstrable knowledge of the policy issues at stake—to people capable of rationally weighing the evidence to make choices that do not contradict their own basic interests (like electing a president who all but says, regarding Puerto Rico, "Let 'em eat cake"). But even if restricting the vote to the "educated" was desirable—and no form of mandated inequality is—how could we possibly devise a set of criteria for selection? What does "educated" even mean? Is it best defined by the level of formal education achieved (PhDs ruling the world?), or income (Harvey Weinstein and the Koch brothers dividing the spoils?) or job status (philosopher kings?). Churchill said it long ago: "democracy is the worst possible form of government—except for all the others." We can throw Trump out after one term. Caligula had to be assassinated.

The Ford/Kavanaugh hearings were an abomination, profoundly disturbing. Yet I couldn't look away; canceling plans, I listened throughout the day—and came away enraged, not solely at the belligerent, bombastic Kavanaugh, but also at his Republican handlers—Lindsey Graham being the most shameless—intent on covering for Kavanaugh's self-righteous lies and on preventing a thorough investigation. Yet his ugly, frightening sense of entitlement came through loud and clear—the perfect embodiment of White male power. What a cruel message the hearings conveyed to female survivors of sexual assault: if you dare come forward, we'll grind you to dust. For me personally, the spectacle redoubled my commitment to getting Andrea's story out there [I was currently writing Andrea Dworkin's biography], especially her brave confrontation with male power; she saw clearly, and early on experienced, the horrors inflicted on women who speak out.

Trump has expressed his concern that the Kavanaugh imbroglio would send a "bad" message to young men—namely that a single misjudgment in their youth would haunt their otherwise unblemished lives. Un-huh. He expressed no concern about the message that the denial of Dr. Ford's assault will send young women. As for young men, the really dangerous messages relate to the manly enterprises of football and war—to the brain damage and PTSD that accrue from current definitions of "masculinity." (The one positive aspect of battle is that it makes acceptable the opportunity for heterosexual young men to love one another unconditionally. It's a component of the adrenalin rush that accompanies combat. And a component too of the desperate forlorn-ness so many feel on returning to civilian life.)

August 2018

As the [2020] election—the crucial election—approaches, my doubts about the likelihood of a "blue wave" mount. I don't share the general expectation. The hidden vote for Trump in 2016 remains intact, and the mood in general is ugly: that the Saudis are now our most promising "ally" is a grotesque comment on our country's direction. Perhaps I put too much weight on it, but the Court's Citizens United decision seems in retrospect to have been a decisive turning point, opening the floodgates to corporate interference with elections and launching us into a second robber baron era. The question is whether we're able, eventually, to emerge from it a second time.

The presidential debates begin tonight. The more I learn about the candidates, the more solidly I sit in Elizabeth Warren's corner. I worry about whether her egghead image and schoolmarmish manner will turn off the electorate, but I'll gladly run the risk. I'm not—or not fully—persuaded by all the hype about Biden being the best bet to beat Trump. The more I read and recollect about good old boy Joe's past record, the more turned off I am. Not only did he vote for the war in Iraq and vigorously support the crime bill that stuffed our jails with unfortunates (*not* criminals), but he zealously attacked busing as a plausible tactic for desegregating our schools—and without offering any alternative solution. In my book he's closer to being a hypocrite than a hero.

June 2019

Bernie? If he wins the nomination, then a reluctant yes—over Trump, a *necessary* yes. But aside from his proclaimed rectitude, he isn't nearly radical enough to deal with the *actual* blight of oligarchic capitalism that currently holds sway and rules with the reckless entitlement that turns the stomach—and destroys hope. Bernie's demonstrably in favor of a $15 hourly wage—big fucking deal!—but (so far anyway) hasn't mentioned, let alone pushed for, a guaranteed income which would actually put an end to the multiple miseries of the poor. If that advocacy doesn't leave

Bernie hoarse, he could then—oh sure!—proceed to denounce xenophobic American "patriotism" and the evangelical religiosity that spews forth everywhere with such smug, hate-filled assurance. Bernie, despite those flaring nostrils, is in the long line of incremental reformers. Something bolder is needed—though even to suggest, say, large-scale programs of nationalization would all but guarantee Trump's reelection. Even the disappearing middle class would turn against a broad expansion of social services as the enemy of "motivation"—yeah, the kind that drives single mothers to take on three part-time, dead-end jobs in order to put food on the table. The way things stand, it's hard even for a temperamental optimist like me to conjure up much hopefulness.

The *Times* today reports a broad research study "proving" a significant genetic component to sexual orientation. Garbled and vague, the article makes it difficult to ascertain precisely *what* has been discovered. Though it's clear what will be *claimed*: that genes *dictate* such outcomes as gender identity and sexual orientation; it could therefore follow that gene editing should be made feasible and—in the coming authoritarian state—mandatory, to ensure the disappearance over time of same gender sexual attraction (and culture). It will be a "cure" for homosexuality on a par with the prior efficacy of prefrontal lobotomies. What does this new "discovery" tell us about the current social conditions that made possible so "congenial" a finding? The advance of knowledge must never be impeded—but nor should a headline be mistaken for a text.

Trump has more plainly than ever overtly aligned himself with the world's leading autocrats—Erdogan, Orban, Putin, and Assad. The move was predictable, but the depth of its arrogant stupidity a smidge less so. Most terrifying of all, perhaps, is that Trump's approval rating has barely budged. Erdogan and Trump deserve each other: Turkey still denies the Armenian massacre. Trump, the schmuck, apparently believes that the Kurds should have been part of the Normandy invasion. Hello? The Turks weren't there either. The head spins . . .

And then there's Mayor Pete, the all-American poster boy, the Eagle Scout. If you fill in every mainstream box, as Buttigieg does, the one not checked—sexual orientation—can be ignored as some sort of temporary aberration. Buttigieg doesn't feel your pain. He's had too little of it. That deep-pitched, assured voice belongs in a corporate corridor, and nowhere near the water cooler. A bit prim and proper, too. The priggish boy wonder of the Harvard stacks advocates "reconciliation" as his central goal because he's never felt a wound too deep for easy forgiveness. African Americans have his number; and so do those in the gay community who haven't taken out membership in the Human Rights Campaign. "Family values" and "Faith" mark the outer limits of Buttigieg's formula for "a good society"—which roughly puts us back in the 1950s. Sometimes gay just isn't enough. Shit—he even goes deer hunting!

My harsh view of Buttigieg is probably a stand-in for my general disinterest these days in the tame centrism of the gay movement. Though it hardly matters. Hostility to gay people has given way to indifference (at best), not to understanding—nor a wish to. In urban circles a polite form of homophobia dominates. These days my checks go increasingly to the Rainbow Railroad and the few other gay groups with a mission to serve the poor—like the Griot Circle and the Ali Forney Center—along with scattershot contributions to ground zero mobilizations like Chelsea's Holy Apostles food kitchen. My political hopes and dreams have on the whole shifted back to feminism. Editing Naomi [Weisstein]'s essays and taking on Andrea's biography reflected and served to once again deepen my attraction to radical feminism as among the few avenues to what once was—and will in the future perhaps again be—a central site of transformation.

I think it was the celebration of Stonewall's 50th that pushed me over the line—all that hollow rhetoric about *our* progress, *our* rights. As if no other injustice (poverty, anyone? the grotesque criminal justice system? the ongoing segregation in housing and in our schools?) required—or even deserved—attention. Now that I've managed to raise the NYPL Fellowship in LGBTQ+ to $25,000, I'm done. Henceforth whatever extra money I have will go to rock bottom issues and the activist groups focused on them.

Historians these days do tend to admit that surviving evidence for past events is arbitrary and incomplete. But they don't admit to what follows: that limited evidence necessitates a one-dimensional reconstruction of past events, exiles us from the sort of expansive reporting of experience that might actually speak to our own circumstances. If they do not move *beyond* the strict limitations of the data, then no historian can produce a narrative that resonates for contemporary concerns. Or even a *narrative*.

Most historians patronizingly view "mere" biography as a disreputable stepchild, a trivial, inferior enterprise when compared with their own exalted focus on sociological patterns and causality. They have it exactly backward. They're the true descendants of Toynbee, that master of gaseous overgeneralization, his landscapes devoid of recognizable human beings. Biographers focus on textured lives, including—with luck and some invention—the inner one, that which most closely corresponds to and resonates for later generations, emotion being less susceptible to replacement than empires.

The general disinterest in history reflects presumptuous self-regard, a need to normalize the strangeness of everything that has come before. To acknowledge the idiosyncrasy of past behavior and the "foreignness" of the social conditions that molded it is to face the unintelligible weirdness of our own existence. We are neither duplicates of what came before nor its end product. To assume that it was all the same back then as it is now allows us to turn away with relief from any attempt to understand the past (and ourselves). Since the present purportedly parallels the past or is its culmination, why bother to study what is at base mere redundancy—or some primitive version from which we have evolved?

Winter 2019–2020

Not even Sanders or Warren consistently step outside the "liberal" paradigm. Sanders is smart enough not to say so, but if he's even aware of the current challenge to the gender binary, it would at best puzzle him, at worst terrify. Warren, meantime, persists in identifying herself as a "capitalist." I haven't heard her offer a definition (though she may have) and the system's current rapacity obviously appalls her; yet the words "guaranteed annual income" is unlikely to cross her lips. I'd be thrilled of course if either one got the nomination, though doubtful if either could beat Trump. As for the rest of the bunch, they're all spectacularly preferable to our current neo-fascist. And yet the views of all fall comfortingly within the worn bounds of "liberalism." All seem uniformly to believe—still—in the essential benevolence of our institutions and the authentic superiority of our way of life. Like Obama, they seem oblivious to the need to chart a new course, to move *radically* away from a foreign policy centered on "forever wars," and radically toward a muscular welfare state that doesn't produce record levels of suicide, alienation, and despair. No, finally they're all liberals, convinced of our essential benevolence, and the universal applicability of our purportedly benign values.

COVID-19 has unmasked the structural disadvantages that lower-income people face in this country—from job insecurity to lack of access to decent health care. The crisis once passed, so too, I suspect, will any lasting acknowledgment of the profound depth of our class and racial divisions. The all-American assumption that those on the bottom have only themselves to blame—their shiftless refusal to work hard—will reassert itself and what limited—exceedingly limited—empathy for the plight of the poor will once more recede. . . . With the arrival of COVID we're (rightly) lamenting the horrendous inequities of the rich fleeing to Long Island (or their own island) while the poor suffer job loss and the terror of underfed children. One less obvious casualty is that it's been months since I've read a single news column or heard a single broadcast reference to what might be going on, say, in Syria. When the media underlines for the millionth time the importance of "social distancing" is there even a remote awareness of the sick irony implicit in applying that concept to the millions crowded into refugee camps around the globe?—devoid not only of room to breathe but of basic sanitation, nourishment, and medical services? Suffering in the West is real enough, and deplorable. Yet its sudden proximity secondarily serves as an imaginative blockade to more pronounced suffering elsewhere.

Spring 2020

The pandemic having revealed to blind eyes the country's gross inequities, it may yet produce, inadvertently, a political shift. There are already signs that Biden is moving to the left, absorbing portions of both Bernie's staff and platform—including expanded federal health and child care programs, plus higher corporate taxes and worker wages. All of which, of course, will heighten right-wing resistance, Trump's base, and make for a tight election. Still, it's the best available scenario for the coming campaign. Biden's cozy centrism could earn him votes, but at the cost of destroying any chance of a desperately needed social transformation. . . .

In our cocoon little resonates. The epidemic passes the 100,000 death mark, 40 million people are out of work, and another brutal police killing is setting the cities aflame. We read about it in the newspapers and tsk-tsk over morning coffee, then switch to expressing annoyance that a food delivery is late, complain that the novel we're reading has turned tedious and (the prime indignity) that once again the blueberries are *soft*! WE are the class divide.

The COVID crisis and the deplorable response to it has as a corollary highlighted the inadequacy of "liberal" politics. In place of liberalism a promising coalition has arisen, radical and widespread . . . Black Lives Matter is drawing much larger crowds than Occupy ever did—and is a much more diverse and determined movement. Out of the ashes of these last few years, unexpected hope emerges for a renewed, newly inclusive democracy. It's most likely to falter, as I see it, over the resistance of many left-leaning democrats to tackle two central issues: astronomical police budgets (NYPD's is six billion annually), in conjunction with the wretched fact that African-Americans are incarcerated at more than five times the rate of Whites. Not only are the two linked, but the promising "restorative justice" movement is running into widespread resistance. Biden has made it clear that he won't consider reallocating police funds, and Obama centrists everywhere have long since made it clear that they're against clemency for violent crimes. What we're likely to get are moderate correctives, not structural change. The latter would necessitate sending to jail corporate bigwigs with moral compasses so out of whack that they think raising the minimum wage to $15 an hour attests to their profound generosity!

Trump's latest labeling of protesters as "terrorists" should be read as a trial balloon for declaring an emergency serious enough to warrant the suspension of the normal political process—like reigning in civil liberties and disrupting the national election. I put nothing past his perfervid narcissism and his genetic—it seems that deep-rooted—lack of empathy. Nor is he alone. The Republican Party, with few exceptions, has again demonstrated its cruel disregard for the suffering at stake in pending eviction notices and rising unemployment. There is comfort to be had in Biden's steady move to the left. But he needs to *hurry*.

The mainstream press is in general hailing the Democratic Convention as a triumph of decency and pragmatism. Well yes, in a sense. But also devoid of any sign of a *left* of center agenda. Alexandria Ocasio-Cortez was allotted 90 seconds at the mike, John Kasich close to five minutes—much of it spent on the anodyne "platform," Christian by name, to love our neighbors. Strategically, this may be the shrewdest row to hoe, since AOC progressives are the youngest segment of the voting population and no match in numbers for the Party's mainstream liberals. Biden's stance is designed to appeal to so-called middle-class, mainstream White women—not to progressives, who have nowhere else to go (but might stay home). A more progressive message from the convention—guaranteed lifelines (income and health insurance), controlled policing, greater access to better and higher education—might have won over a portion of poverty-line Whites. Instead, the centrist message, by silent default, has reiterated rather than contradicted the widespread and suspect overestimation of the extent of racism among poor Whites and the *under*estimation of racism among "liberal" centrists.

Here's just the news we needed to complete the year: Melania is thinking of writing a memoir!

Shock after shock, they've been bleeding into each other for weeks: Trump casually dismisses our military dead as "losers" and before we can exhale, Amy Coney Barrett, a plastic Catholic bigot, is on her way to the Supreme Court. Yet the polls show Biden "far ahead"—even as several critical states unaccountably remain "dead heats," with Biden doing *less* well than Hillary did in 2016! As we gaze around for perspective, all we can hear is that the entire planet is one minute to midnight.

Perched on a ledge—like the rest of the country. Feeling vaguely ill, unable to concentrate. As of today, it looks as if Biden *will* squeak through, but probably not with a Democratic-led Senate, and only after Trump exhausts all legal options (unless the lovely Ms. Barrett leads SCOTUS to an *affirmation* of Trump's ascendency). I'm not surprised that Biden failed to inspire the multitude. But I'm shocked at the size of Trump's support. That a brazen, narcissistic bully and liar could hold the allegiance of half the country is a frightening gauge of our (unsalvageable?) decline. The end of daylight saving came at the right symbolic moment. Astonishingly, one exit poll revealed a significant number of *gay* Republicans! "Has The Gay Movement Failed?" Is that still a question?

January 2021

Events of the past week haven't come as a complete surprise—yes of course the police, or a portion of them, treated the nearly all-White rioters with kid gloves—yet every stress symptom I've ever had, from acid reflux to herpes, has reappeared: the body knows. Perhaps the biggest shocker for me was the 150 or so Republican legislators who *after* the

mob had dispersed went right ahead and challenged the legitimacy of
the Pennsylvania electors. Some people don't want their understanding disturbed by facts; the unanswered question is "how many?" For
me, two events cushioned the overall shock: winning both Senate seats
in Georgia; and Biden's surprising backbone, the forcefulness of his
language ("sedition") in denouncing the mob. He rose to the occasion,
showed signs that his seeming frailty and centrism might not be the
sum of his parts.

Yesterday, May 2022

Biden's shift to the left has deepened; we can only hope that his commitment doesn't prove as unsteady as his gait. His ongoing and trite
optimism about "unifying" the country continues to suggest an unre-
coverable past. Still, he's been a major surprise. Our frail-looking,
middle-of-the-road president has initially weighed in with a startlingly
expansive—and notably progressive—agenda. And in the process, he's
helped to unmask the Republicans for what they've long been: devoid
of empathy, defenders of privilege—and seismic haters.

What Biden can't do is prevent a hostile Congress and Supreme
Court from blocking the larger part of his agenda, leaving us with the
mere shards of his original set of proposals, and a legislative stalemate
that more closely resembles the blank Calvin Coolidge than the steam-
rolling FDR. Add in the serious distractions of a stubborn pandemic,
a deepening climate crisis, and the barbaric invasion of Ukraine, and
the odds of any steady progressive advance have substantially decreased,
pushed into a highly problematic future. Ever since Congress awarded
the Pentagon 24 billion *more* than it had requested, it has been difficult
to maintain much hope for Biden's initial agenda. But though we fear
the worst, the chance—no more than that—remains that we may yet
be astonished at a newly invigorated opposition.

> But storytellers aren't seers. Not even at ninety.

ACKNOWLEDGMENTS

I'm deeply indebted to the talented team at Chicago Review Press, who, with artful, painstaking skill, worked with me on preparing the final manuscript for publication. In this regard I want to single out the tireless efforts of CRP's acquisitions editor Jerry Pohlen and its indispensable managing editor, Devon Freeny. My thanks, too, to marketing lead Chelsea Balesh, publicist Connor Deeds, copyeditor Elizabeth Yellen, proofreader Karen Krumpak, indexer Jean Skipp, and cover designer Preston Pisellini.

Finally, I'm profoundly grateful to my life partner, Eli Zal, and to my friend Robert L. Hampel for their astute, indispensable readings of the entire manuscript.

NOTES

Part I: 1930–1986

1. The exchange of letters is in the Duberman Papers, New York Public Library.
2. See, for example, my essay "An Experiment in Education" in Martin Duberman, *Left Out* (Basic Books, 1999), 217–228, and Robert L. Hampel, *Radical Teaching in Turbulent Times: Martin Duberman's Princeton Seminars, 1966–1970* (Palgrave Macmillan, 2021).
3. In regard to "The Abolitionists and Psychology," Howard Zinn wrote me at the time to say how "very happy" he was with the piece and Staughton Lynd proposed that "every word . . . should be mounted in gold on a plaque." No less an eminence than Richard Hofstadter, more liberal than radical, approved my "psychologizing" and found nothing in the piece "that I would care to quarrel with." The letter I most cherished was from the Harvard psychologist Gordon Allport, whose book *Becoming* had been central in formulating my ideas. "I should think that your article on the abolitionists," Allport wrote me, "would result in revolutionizing your profession or else in leading to your exile from it." These scholars felt I'd succeeded in replacing the reigning negative stereotype of the abolitionists and, by implication, all social justice activists with a far more appreciative view. Not everyone, however, was keen on the essay. David Herbert Donald (who'd recommended me to replace him at Princeton), represented the older view. He wrote me to say that "I should be less than candid if I did not say that I dissent from most of your conclusions." All the letters are in the Martin Duberman Papers in the New York Public Library's Manuscript Division.
4. For this paragraph and the section that follows, see the landmark study *Prophets of Protest*, ed. Timothy Patrick McCarthy and John Stauffer (New Press,

2006), as well as Duberman, "memo on 'reformers'" (for the Paul O'Dwyer campaign, September 25, 1968) and Duberman, "Antiwar Statement for the Publishers Group" (May 1970)—both in Duberman Papers, NYPL. Four of my essays on the evolving Black struggle—"'Moderation' Versus Militancy" (1964), "James Meredith" (1966), "Taking Stock" (1967), and "Black Power and the American Radical Tradition" (1968)—which originally appeared, respectively, in *Book Week*, the *Village Voice*, the foreword to *The Civil Rights Reader*, ed. Leon Friedman, and *Partisan Review* (Winter 1968) are reprinted in Martin Duberman, *Left Out: The Politics of Exclusion/Essays 1964–1999* (Basic Books, 1999), 151–187.

5. For a great deal more detail see Robert L. Hampel, *Radical Teaching in Turbulent Times: Martin Duberman's Princeton Seminars, 1966–1970* (Palgrave Macmillan, 2021).

6. Having written elsewhere at length (see especially my books *Cures, Left Out*, and *The Uncompleted Past*) about my nongay political involvements, I decided in this book to keep all of that to a minimum. Yet I now have the feeling, particularly in regard to the war in Vietnam, that I may have unduly condensed the subject, and thus unwittingly trivialized it. Thus, when I came across an unpublished antiwar statement that I wrote in May 1970 and that I thought captured some of the underlying assumptions of those protesting the war, I decided to excerpt it in compensation for the lack of a full-scale treatment:

"War is a necessary evil, they say. It's supposed to have something to do with human nature, to be a natural expression of our innate aggression—what Elder Statesmen mean when mocking the 'romantic optimism' of the protesters and citing what they call 'the overwhelming evidence from human history of our 'depravity' . . . I'm not persuaded that 'aggression' and 'hostility' are equivalents; the former—the healthy insistence of each organism to life—is almost certainly instinctual; the latter, the drive to destroy others, is almost certainly cultural. Human history may indeed be the story of war, pillage and corruption, but it hasn't been proven that such behavior is biological in origin rather than socially derived—not mandated by nature, but acquired through imposed learning (just as we have recently come to understand that almost all the traits we once called 'racial' are in fact ethnic). We have war in Southeast Asia because certain men (not including Yahweh) with large power but limited perspective have made bad decisions—not because men everywhere and always *must* seek aggrandizement through murder. . . . Those who protest the savage war in Vietnam are declared 'naïve optimists,' but I think they're more accurately seen as realists: they point to possibilities of human compassion and affiliation that most people, imprisoned by a Calvinist frame of reference, cannot see. The Death Machine that rules this country not only destroys bodies but also any understanding that potentially what human beings yearn for above all is connection."

7. The letters between Mailer and me that follow are in the Berg Collection, NYPL; those between Mailer and Dick are in the Duberman Papers, NYPL.

8. Dynes to the *Advocate*, March 22, 1978; Duberman to the *Advocate*, April 14, 1978; Dynes to Duberman, May 16, 1978, Duberman Papers, NYPL.

9. For a full account of my experience with bioenergetics, see Martin Duberman, *Midlife Queer* (Scribner, 1996), 141–168.

10. German Lopez, "The Reagan Administration's Unbelievable Response to the HIV/AIDS Epidemic," *Vox*, December 1, 2016, https://www.vox .com/2015/12/1/9828348/ronald-reagan-hiv-aids.

11. The key documents for the narrative that follows about the founding and early years of the Center for Lesbian and Gay Studies (CLAGS) are: Martin Duberman to "Dear Friends," July 10, 1986; Jewelle Gomez to "Marty," July 29, 1986; Duberman to Gomez, August 3, 1986; CLAGS board minutes, September 21, 1986; Joan Nestle to "Martin," September 23, 1986; Duberman to Nestle, September 25, 1986; "Jeb" (Boswell) to "Marty," September 23, 1986; Duberman to Boswell, n.d. [possibly not mailed]; "Marty" to "John" (Boswell), October 3, 1986; "Marty" to "Dear Friends," October 3, 1986; "John" to "Marty," October 6, 1986; Duberman to Ralph Hexter, October 11, 1986; "Marty" to "John," October 17, 1986; Barbara Smith to "Marty," October 29, 1986; "Marty" to "Benno" (Schmidt), November 3, 1986; CLAGS board minutes, December 14, 1986; Adrienne Rich to "Marty," January 2, 1987; Duberman to Proshansky, May 9, August 5, 1987; Jonathan Ned Katz to "Acting Board," May 27, 1987. All are in the Duberman Papers, NYPL.

Part II: 1987–1999

1. For more on the Gay Academic Union, see Martin Duberman, *Cures: A Gay Man's Odyssey*, 10th anniv. ed. (Westview, 2002), 274–279.

2. For a detailed account of my experiments in education, see Robert L. Hampel, *Radical Teaching in Turbulent Times: Martin Duberman's Princeton Seminars, 1966–1970* (Palgrave Macmillan, 2021).

Part III: 2000–2007

1. Paul Robinson, "Becoming a Gay Historian," in *Becoming Historians*, ed. James M. Banner Jr. and John R. Gillis (University of Chicago Press, 2009), 229–258.

INDEX